The Last Days of the Raj

Two years after the Second World War came to an end, on 15 August 1947, India and Pakistan became independent. For the inhabitants of both countries it was, in Pandit Nehru's famous words, 'a tryst with destiny', a new beginning which heralded much promise. But for the British, who had ruled there for over two hundred years, it was the start of a momentous process to discard its world empire. India and Pakistan were declarations: once they had become independent, there could be no going back, and within two decades most of Britain's colonies had gained their freedom from imperial rule.

Fifty years later it is possible to put those stirring events into the context of the times and to understand more fully the political and economic issues which led to the rapid dismantlement of British rule under the last Viceroy, Lord Louis Mountbatten. It is easier, too, to take a more balanced view of the benefits of British rule and to feel a large measure of pride in the achievements and commitment of the British administrators, doctors, missionaries and engineers who served so well. During the war they had combined to fight the threat of Japanese invasion; yet within two years they stood aside to allow the people of India and Pakistan to take control of their own futures.

In the years following the end of empire, British imperial rule was frequently castigated by historians and journalists; but read the memories of those who lived through the period – British and Indian – and the closeness of that connection becomes apparent. It was not always unequal or unfair; neither was it a simple matter of exploitation. Often it was a partnership and, as many in the government and the armed services recall, it was frequently a meeting of true minds.

They are growing old now, those sahibs and memsahibs who remember the last days of the Raj with such affection. I trust that my account of their lives and their service still does justice to one of the most fascinating periods in Britain's post-war history.

Trevor Royle

THE LAST DAYS
OF THE RAJ

JOHN MURRAY
Albemarle Street, London

A catalogue record for this book is available from the British Library

ISBN 0-7195-5686 4

Printed and bound in Great Britain by
The University Press, Cambridge

Contents

List of Illustrations

(between pp. 116 and 117)

1. Gandhi during his visit to London, 1931 (*Popperfoto*)
2. The aftermath of an anti-British riot in Bombay, 1932 (*Topham Picture Library*)
3. Lord Linlithgow (*Topham Picture Library*)
4. Field Marshal Lord Wavell and Field Marshal Sir Claude Auchinleck (*Popperfoto*)
5. Field Marshal Lord Wavell and the Maharajah of Patiala (*Topham Picture Library*)
6. A De Haviland DH86 airliner converted for use against the Japanese during the war (*Douglas Dickins*)
7. Subhas Chandra Bose (*Robert Hunt Library*)
8. Dr Mohammed Ali Jinnah (*Topham Picture Library*)
9. Indian leaders arrive in London to meet Clement Attlee, December 1945 (*Topham Picture Library*)
10. Lord Wavell greets the second Cripps Mission, March 1946 (*Topham Picture Library*)
11. Jawaharlal Nehru and Dr Mohammed Ali Jinnah (*Popperfoto*)
12. The aftermath of Calcutta's 'Day of Action', 15 August 1946 (*Robert Hunt Library*)
13. Nehru and Mountbatten, 1947 (*Popperfoto*)
14. Governor-General Sir John Colville with Chief Minister B.G. Kher, Independence Day, 15 August 1947 (*Brigadier Platt*)
15. Lord and Lady Mountbatten surrounded by jubilant crowds, Independence Day, 15 August 1947 (*Popperfoto*)
16. Presentation of a silver Gateway of India to the Somerset Light Infantry (*Brigadier Platt*)
17. The last regiment to leave passes through the Gateway of India (*Times of India*)

ᘓᘓᘓᘓᘓᘓᘓᘓᘓᘓᘓᘓᘓᘓᘓᘓᘓᘓᘓᘓᘓᘓ

Acknowledgements

My first debt is to my mother to whom this book is dedicated. By having the good sense to be born in India and then to make it her first home she introduced me to the idea of British India: the story of her first experience of the strength of Indian nationalist feeling – as told in the first chapter – provided the spur to write this book.

The book could not have been completed without the ready help of Gillian Wright. She interviewed all the Indian 'witnesses' and in so doing she provided me with many fascinating insights into the country and its people. Well versed in Indian customs and culture, and fluent in Hindi and Urdu, she was a tower of strength throughout the project.

For help and advice in investigating the many different aspects of the British Raj, I would like to thank the following individuals and organisations who gave unstintingly of their time and patience:

Colonel, The Hon. David Arbuthnott, Regimental Secretary, The Black Watch, for help in tracing personnel of the 2nd Battalion Black Watch in Karachi, 1948; John Arnott, Senior Editor, Talks and Features BBC Scotland, for commissioning me to write *Going Home* (1987), a radio documentary about the last days of British India; Pat Barr, author of *The Memsahibs*, for her assistance in tracing witnesses; Dr Richard Bingle, Curator European Manuscripts, India Office Library and Records, for help in locating letters and diaries from the period; Pinak Chakravarty, First Secretary (Press and Information), India High Commission, London, for help in tracing Indian witnesses; Ray Gardner, Features Editor, *Glasgow Herald*, for encouraging me to write an article about the fortieth anniversary of the transfer of power; P.C.F. Gregory-Hood, First Secretary (Information), British High Commission, New Delhi, for help in tracing Indian witnesses; Commander D.J. Hastings, Secretary Royal Indian Navy (1612–1947) Association, for checking the accounts of RIN officers; Dr Rosie Llewellyn-Jones, the British Association for Cemeteries in South Asia (BACSA), for help and encouragement in tracing witnesses; Jeremy Moodey, Second Secretary, British Embassy, Islamabad, for help in tracing Pakistani witnesses; Rev. William G. Murison, Board of World Missions and Unity, the Church of Scotland, for putting me in touch with former missionaries; Raziudain Shaikh, Minister (Information) Pakistan Embassy, London, for help in tracing Pakistani witnesses; Mark Tully, BBC World Service, New Delhi, for help in arranging Indian interviews; G.E.D. Walker, Secretary Indian Police Association, for help in checking the accounts of former police officers; Lieutenant-Colonel R.G. Woodhouse, Regimental Secretary (Somerset), The Light Infantry, for help in tracing personnel of the 1st Battalion Somerset Light Infantry in Bombay, 1948.

I wish to acknowledge my debt to the following who allowed themselves to be interviewed or who provided written accounts. In particular, I should like to thank those who took the trouble to read and comment upon the sections of the book in which they appear, although I hasten to add that all errors of fact or judgement remain my responsibility alone. They all have my thanks.

Britain:
Dr Winifred Bailey, missionary doctor; Tom Berry, RAF; Colonel Neville Blair, 2nd Black Watch; Elizabeth Catto, wife of businessman; the late John Christie, ICS; Sheila Coldwell, wife of businessman; Douglas Dickins, RAF; Alan Flack, ICS; Ron Fraser, jute industry; Major A.F. Frost, 1st Somerset Light Infantry; Commander A.B. Goord, Royal Indian Navy; J.C. Griffiths, ICS; William Hamilton, Indian Police; George Harrison, Indian Police; Mike Hirst, RAF; A.P. Hume, ICS; Alastair MacKeith, Indian Police; Colonel Claud Moir, 2nd Black Watch; Jack Morton, Indian Police; Major Peter Pearson, 1st Somerset Light Infantry; D.J. Penman, RAF; Brigadier John Platt, 1st

Somerset Light Infantry; George Robertson, jute industry; John Rowntree, Indian Forestry Service; Kathleen Beatrice Royle, wife of army officer; Lawrence Russell, Indian Police; Wilfrid Russell, businessman, Killick Nixon and Company; Major Michael Ryall, 1st Somerset Light Infantry; Captain Kenneth Ryden, Royal Bombay Sappers and Miners; Commander E.M. Shaw, Royal Indian Navy; Group Captain Clifton Stephenson, RAF; M.M. Stuart, ICS; Sheila Swabey, wife of oil executive; Dr H. John Taylor, Wilson College Bombay; Stanley Taylor, Indian Police; Major J.D.M. Watson, 11th Sikhs; Feh Williams, wife of army officer; Martin Wynne, Indian Police; Dorothy Younie, doctor; the late John Younie, ICS.

India:
Frank Anthony, barrister and politician; Prem Bhatia, ex-editor, *Tribune*; Nikhil Chakravartty, Indian Communist Party (Marxist); Admiral A.K. Chatterjee, Indian Navy; P.C. Chatterji, Director-General All-India Radio; A.K. Damodaran, Indian Foreign Service; Major-General C. Das, Indian Army; Inder Malhotra, ex-Resident Editor, *Times of India*; Govind Narain, ICS and Indian Administrative Service; Major-General D.K. Palit, Indian Army; Dr Bharat Ram, Chairman of Shri Ram Fibres; Kushwant Singh, novelist and journalist; Badr-ud-Din Tyabji, ICS and Indian Foreign Service.

I acknowledge with thanks permission to include in this volume quotations from the British Association for Cemeteries in South Asia: D.J. Hastings (ed.), *Bombay Buccaneers*; John Christie, *Morning Drum*; Martin Wynne (ed.), *On Honourable Terms*; India Office Library and Records: the papers of John Christie, Sir George Cunningham, Alan Flack, J.C. Griffiths, A.P. Hume, Wilfrid Russell; Indian Police Association: Leslie Robins, *Policing the Raj*; Norman R. Franks, *First in the Indian Skies* (RAF Collection); John Rowntree, *A Chota Sahib* (Tabb House). Every effort has been made to trace the holders of copyright in the quotations included. For any errors of omissions I naturally and formally apologise.

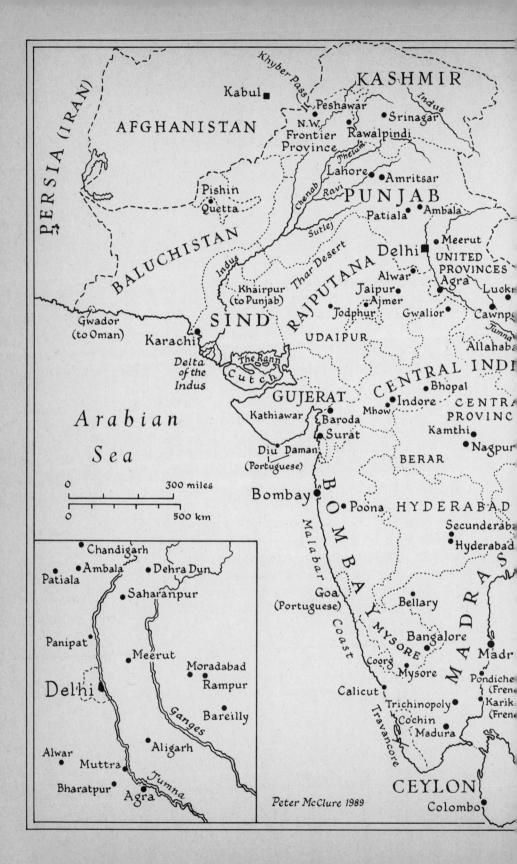

Peter McClure 1989

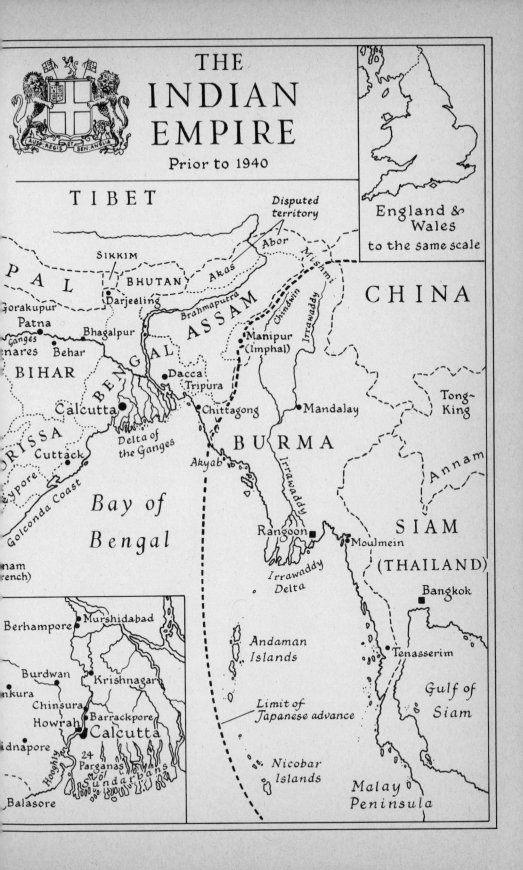

THE INDIAN EMPIRE

Prior to 1940

England & Wales to the same scale

TIBET

SIKKIM

BHUTAN

Disputed territory

Abor

Akas

Mishmi

CHINA

NEPAL

Gorakupur

Patna

Darjeeling

Brahmaputra

ASSAM

Chindwin

Irrawaddy

Ganges

Benares

Behar

Bhagalpur

BENGAL

Manipur (Imphal)

BIHAR

Dacca

Tripura

Tong~King

Calcutta

Chittagong

Mandalay

ORISSA

Delta of the Ganges

BURMA

Annam

Cuttack

Jeypore

Golconda Coast

Akyab

Irrawaddy

SIAM (THAILAND)

Bay of Bengal

Rangoon

Moulmein

nam rench)

Irrawaddy Delta

Bangkok

Andaman Islands

Tenasserim

Limit of Japanese advance

Gulf of Siam

Berhampore

Murshidabad

Nicobar Islands

Burdwan

Krishnagar

nkura

Chinsura

Barrackpore

Malay Peninsula

Howrah

Calcutta

idnapore

24 Parganas

Hooghly

Sundarbans

Balasore

To My Mother

Chapter One

A Time to Keep

It was always the Benares box which drew me back to India. My mother had bought it in Benares – or Varanasi as the Indians now call the city – in 1942 and it had been with her ever since. Substantial and capacious, with a rare smell of seasoned timber, it had a finely carved lid intricately engraved with thin strips of polished brass. Inside was a child's treasure-trove, for it was here that my mother had stored many of the photographs which recorded her family's life in India. Some were rejects, others were copies from the leatherbound albums which could only be inspected under strict adult supervision, many more had been printed as postcards to be sent home to fond relatives: all were sources of wonder.

And what a life they portrayed! Two gentlemen are taking their ease on a long verandah, attended by a white-coated bearer: my grandfather and an uncle at the family home in Ishapore. A group of laughing young men pose in their long shorts and newly acquired topees, beer glasses in hand: my father and friends at his first chummery in Lord Sinha Road, Calcutta. A young woman in shorts drives off from the first tee, her native caddie keeping a respectful distance: my mother playing a shot at Ranchi Golf Club. Another woman wearing a sari stands beside a grave Sikh bearer, babe in arms: me with Mari, my first ayah, in Mysore.

Others recorded the innocent pleasures of a privileged existence: a trip along the Sunderbans in 1937 with high-funnelled Clyde-built river boats in the background; picnics at Bangoan and Mussoorie; the Club's Christmas party, all boiled shirts, black ties and copied Schiaparelli dresses; three wise men and an elephant by the roadside in East Bengal; mysterious rock carvings portraying a

gigantic deity at Sigirya in Ceylon; the snows of the Himalayas
from Darjeeling, the falls at Hindru and, everywhere, Indians –
my mother's servants, my father's soldiers – staring out at me,
loyal, curious, smiling. This was the India that I came to know as
a child.

I was born in India in 1945 in the unlikely surroundings of
Champion Reef Goldmine at Kolar in Mysore. The goldfields
became my place of birth quite by chance as they had the hospital
facilities lacking at the nearby military base where my father was
stationed. My mother's home was India – she had been born in
1916 at Ishapore in Bengal where my grandfather worked in the
Government Rifle factory – but my father was a relative newcomer. He had arrived in Calcutta before the war and had been
commissioned into the Indian Army. A major in the IEME, he
was preparing with his brigade for Operation Zipper, Mountbatten's planned seaborne invasion of Malaya. Some months later
two atom bombs dropped on Hiroshima and Nagasaki scuppered
the operation but the invasion went ahead and my father's unit
was part of the expeditionary force. His photographs tell their
own story: 'Louis takes the Salute', 'Jap officers being told all
about it' before surrendering their swords at Kuala Lumpur
airport.

As it turned out, those were to be my first and last months in
India. Later that year my father resigned his commission and my
mother took me back to England, sailing on the SS *Strathmore*
from Bombay. Like so many others who had gone the same way,
her last view of the country she had known from childhood was
the Gateway of India – the huge triumphal arch erected by the
British to mark the landfall of their King-Emperor in 1911 – and
like them, too, she wondered if she would ever see India again.
For all of us, it was the end of an old song.

Malaya was to be our next home but it was India which cast the
longest shadow over my childhood. Partly, it came from the
Benares box; partly, too, the mood was created by the words we
used at home, long after our return home. A *chota peg* of whisky
might be drunk in the evening, curries were always *garrum*,
children were told to *chup rao* when noise levels became unac-
ceptable and then we might be told that our behaviour was *jungli*.
We knew that tiffin was lunch and laughed delightedly at the
thunder-box in the downstairs lavatory. There were stories about

loose-wallahs and *punkah-wallahs*, about chaps going doolally before they rolled home, about *gharri* rides to church, and we knew that my mother's household consisted of the bearer, the ayah, the *bheesti*, the *mali* and a sweeper. It rarely occurred to me that other people might have lived different kinds of lives.

My parents had decided to leave India because British rule was coming to an end and they realised that there would be no place for them in the new order which would come into being after independence. What had been home for so long had suddenly become alien and fearful. It was time to go. True, a handful of my mother's relations did stay on in the jute business in Bengal and continued their lives much as before, but 'partition' – as we always called it – was the great parting of the ways, just as it was for a whole generation of British people who had chosen to make their lives in India.

Forty years on, it is still one of the great divides in British history. Some will claim that the sorry Suez escapade of 1956 was the true harbinger of Britain's imperial demise but in a very real sense the first blow was struck on Independence Day, 15 August 1947. It was not a matter of throwing away crutches – even by the mid-1950s one-fifth of the atlas of the world was still pillar-box red and as a boy I remember thinking that the privilege of being British was absolute. Rather, the loss of India was a signal that Britain was not prepared to hold on to the empire by force against the threat of Indian hostility and adverse world opinion.

India had been the largest single possession ruled by the British. Indeed, it was almost an empire in its own right, so exotic and various were the land and its peoples. The lives led by the British imperialists – the civil servants, the soldiers, the business-men – had become part of the British outlook, too, exerting a pull on British sentiments in a way that no other colony had ever done. After 1947 the map might still have retained a red hue but, to all intents and purposes, once India, the 'Jewel in the Crown', had gone, the end of the empire was certain.

'As long as we rule India we are the greatest power in the world,' Lord Curzon had boasted in 1901. 'If we lose it we shall drop straightaway to a third-rate power.' Curzon had been one of Britain's great imperial pro-consuls. Ambitious, autocratic, haughty and intelligent, he was Viceroy of India between 1898 and 1905, a period that saw British imperial power at its apogee.

Under his rule the British took their gubernatorial responsibilities seriously and Curzon surrounded himself with a splendid court that seemed to many observers to owe more to the Moguls than to Whitehall. He was the King-Emperor's surrogate and in that guise he regarded British rule in India as his nation's finest achievement; yet forty years after his departure the unthinkable had happened and Britain was on its way – seemingly going downhill. As Curzon had prophesied, all the ports, coaling stations, dockyards, fortresses and protectorates – the 'toll gates and barbicans of empire' – had proved to be an insufficient bulwark against Britain's imperial decline.

Another ruler spiritually bound up with India had made a similar prediction. During the Second World War Mahatma Gandhi had claimed that after India all the other British colonies would follow suit, and so it had proved. By the late 1960s the habit of empire had died, too, and Britain's rule in India, generally known as the British Raj, had become a relic of the irretrievable past. In the minds of some people it had become a shameful thing, all that territory held in thrall against the will of the people; others simply shook it off and forgot about it; a few, mainly those who had spent parts of their lives there or who had family connections with India, lived on with their memories.

Hardly a family in Britain has not been touched in some way by their country's connection with India. After well-nigh three centuries it could hardly be otherwise. It might be the chain of ivory elephants brought back by a distant uncle who was with the King's Royal Rifles in Cawnpore in 1921. Or the Kashmir rug, somewhat moth-eaten now, which was moved into the spare bedroom last year. He always liked his curries extra-hot and embarrassed his family by calling for more lime pickle, *ekdum*, when they ate out at the Star of India. Didn't he have a son who went to India, too – a hippy on the trail of peace and love?

Other memories are enshrined in the many books of memoirs, autobiography and travel diaries that appeared in the wake of independence and which still retain a period fascination. The court pages of London's quality newspapers still announce re-union dinners of such doughty regiments as the Central India Horse, the Royal Bombay Sappers and Miners, the Frontier Force Regiment or the Punjab Regiment, and the obituary pages dutifully record their members' service when they pass on. 'His courage and leadership prevented a massacre,' wrote one of a political officer who saved a trainload of Muslim lives near Ferozepore during the Punjab massacres of 1947.

The lasting memories are obviously felt more keenly by those who had a direct family connection with India and should, therefore, mean little to the generations which have grown up since the Second World War. Yet, perversely, the story of British rule in India refuses to fade into oblivion.

Once upon a time, not so long ago, Rudyard Kipling was reviled as a prophet of empire and critics of his work accused him of pandering to jingoism and vulgarity. Today, his short stories are enjoying a new popularity, not just for their portrayal of the tough and dedicated administrators or the resourceful subalterns but for the delineation of India itself. Kipling's 'great, grey, familiar' India is not the India of the Thomas Cook tourist brochure: it is a big, overwhelming country which crushes and oppresses the empire-builders who try to tame it. Small wonder that they band together in the confines of the club, a beleaguered community which struggles to maintain a sense of identity in an alien land. Small wonder, too, that Kipling poked such fun at their pretensions, at their vulnerability and at their attempts to reconstruct the images of the shires in the plains and hills.

> Everybody was there and there was a general closing up of ranks and taking stock of our losses in dead or disabled that had fallen during the past year. It was a very wet night, and I remember that we sang 'Auld Lang Syne' with our feet in the Polo Championship Cup and our heads among the stars, and swore that we were all very dear friends.

Faced by a hostile environment and by a people with whom they experienced little empathy Kipling's Anglo-Indians attempt to exert their moral authority, usually with unfortunate results. They fail to come to any understanding of India and the Indians and remain completely detached from their surroundings. In that sense India to Kipling was a bizarre conundrum which both attracted and repelled. 'We are only bits of dirt on the hillside,' says Mrs Mallowe in 'The Education of Otis Yeere', 'here one day and blown down with the *khud* the next . . .'

At the height of his popularity and continuing well into the twentieth century Kipling's India, for all its drawbacks, was the

India which most people recognised – or wanted to recognise. It might have been a sombre view but it contained enough surface excitement and glamour to fuel the hopes and ambitions of young men who believed absolutely in the virtues of duty, honour and self-respect. Time and time again Kipling's stories emerge as one of the reasons why so many young men were prepared to look for a life of adventure in far-off India. In his biography of Kipling, Philip Mason summed up his generation's respect for the man and his work:

> No one has had so deep an influence on a whole generation of a certain class as he did. Here was someone who understood the life they were brought up to, their mistrust of politicians and intellectuals, their inarticulate devotion to a cause, the training they had endured, the tenseness that lay beneath the apparently insensitive outer crust, the tenderness they longed to lavish on dogs and children, their nervous respect for those mysterious creatures, women – so fragile compared with themselves, and yet so firmly authoritarian as nurses and mothers.

Mason's career was deeply bound up with India – he joined the Indian Civil Service as a young man and went on to become its principal historian and a shrewd commentator on the twentieth-century period of British India.

Like any other writer who has enjoyed widespread popularity Kipling's reputation suffered a decline shortly after his death. In the period after the Second World War critics were openly hostile to him partly because his style was out of fashion but also because the very idea of empire – other than as an object of attack – was anathema as a literary subject. Instead, they preferred novels like E.M. Forster's *A Passage to India* which was critical of British rule in India.

In the 1970s Paul Scott's *Raj Quartet* was an attempt by the English literary mind to return to the point where it had severed connection with Kipling's India. It is not just the setting of the four novels which remind us of Kipling; it is the subject matter and his examination of the nature of authority and the workings of justice in a big country. His characters, too, represent a sense of duty and responsibility which is very Kiplingesque – although they operate within an ambience that is strictly anti-imperial and anti-ruling class. Above all else, though, it is the gallery of characters and the ramifications of their lives that makes Scott one of the great writers on India. Their interwoven narratives, set in India during the Second World War and the period before the transfer of power, present events from differing points of view and then combine to reveal a complete picture. In the central episode – which is also redolent of Forster's *A Passage to India* – a young British girl, Daphne Manners, is viciously raped by a group of Indians. Her Indian boyfriend Hari Kumar – educated at an English public school – is wrongly accused and cruelly interrogated by the policeman Ronald Merrick, thus providing the novel with a realistic central political metaphor for British India. The repercussions of the Manners rape, and her subsequent death during childbirth, allow Scott to introduce a wide variety of types, all of whom would be instantly recognisable to anyone who lived in British India during that period – Barbie Batchelor, the lonely hapless missionary; Mildred Layton, the hard-drinking memsahib and her two daughters Susan and Sarah; Mohammed Ali Kasim, the Muslim politician with pro-British sympathies and the new man Guy Perron who sees through the façade of life at the tail-end of the raj. Scott knew what he was writing about: he had served in the Indian Army during the Second World War.

When they were made into an impressive television series in 1984 under the title *The Jewel in the Crown*, Scott's novels reached a much wider and similarly enthusiastic audience. Forster's *A Passage to India* enjoyed an equal triumph when it was made into a film during the same period and Richard Attenborough's radical filmed portrait of Gandhi's life supplied a rather different interpretation of the morality of British rule in India. Other writers, like John Masters and Ruth Prawer Jhabvala, have also helped to popularise the subject of British India: Masters with his heroic vision of the Indian Army and Jhabvala with her intimate knowledge of the meeting point between the British and the Indians.

India and the notion of the British Raj suddenly became chic again in the 1980s. Indeed, during the forty years or so that have passed since the transfer of power India has never been far away from the British imagination. In some respects this was merely a reflection of the changing times: the raj offered sepia-tinted nostalgia for a way of life that has passed into the pages of an illustrated history book. The great Delhi Durbar with squadrons of exotically uniformed cavalrymen surrounding the King-Emperor's pachydermal procession might be one, the District Officer sitting in the shade of a banyan tree dispensing wisdom and justice might be another: these images summon up a way of life that seems so recent yet is far removed from the everyday experience of life towards the end of the twentieth century.

Another reason for the continuing and enduring interest in India could be a sign of the times, a characteristic by-product of Margaret Thatcher's neo-Victorian revolution in values. Instead of attacking the idea that Britain once considered its empire to be the strongest and most virtuous institution on earth, people now want to know why that idea persisted and why the privilege of being British had been so absolute. To the pre-war generations – and to a certain extent to those brought up in the immediate post-war period – there seemed to be nothing terribly wrong in the fact that Britain ruled so much of the world, yet in the 1960s and 1970s the idea of empire was met with derision by the younger intellectuals.

The slave trade, economic exploitation of the underdeveloped countries, the wars against unequal native opposition, the reluctance to hand over power, all seemed to be terrible or disgraceful components of the colonial legacy. In the decade of revisionism that followed the sceptical 1960s and 1970s those doubts still prevail but much of the guilt has begun to be sufficiently understood to allow it to disappear. Instead, the benefits of empire – the sound administration, the law and order, the relative prosperity – are being examined again with interest and, let it be said, not a little pride. No other part of the former empire excites such curiosity as India. This is less a simple craving for the artefacts of the past than a desire to know something about the good things which tens of thousands of ordinary British men and women gave in return for their lives in India.

For those who lived there during the last years of British rule, India will always be the memory of a life that will never return, of a job well done, of faces that are slowly blurring with the years. They are a mixed bunch. At their most exalted they might have been the heaven-born of the Indian Civil Service which provided India with its political and legal administration, or they might have been soldiers. For the fortunate few, this meant a commission in the Indian Army where the pay was higher and the expenses lower, an important consideration; or it could mean a tour of duty with a British regiment in which officers led lives of ease while the British Other Ranks put up with the heat and the dust. But for every sublime District Magistrate or major of cavalry, there were many more ordinary people doing everyday jobs: people in service who looked after the forests, built the roads and the railways and tended the public works. There were also those who brought trade and industry to India – the spiritual descendants of the officers of the East India Company – who worked the jute-mills and the tea plantations and in so doing created comfortable lives for themselves and their dependants.

For all that a handful occupied positions of power and responsibility in the government of a huge and exotic country, the majority of the British in India led fairly conventional lives. Social connections were confined to people within the same service or with others of a similar type in the immediate district. The men worked in the early morning and the late afternoon to escape the worst effects of the midday heat. Sports such as tennis, golf, swimming and shooting were played with more enthusiasm than apparent skill and there was a good deal of socialising in the club. If it was a comfortable and privileged existence then sometimes it could also be a dull one. India, with its climate and its wide-open spaces, might have provided a hothouse ambience but the British, as Kipling observed, still tried to exert upon it their own standards of behaviour. A picnic on Observatory Hill in Darjeeling with its majestic views of Kanchenjunga might have been more memorable than a windy afternoon on Box Hill but alter the focus and certain things remain the same. In India servants cleared away the mess but the manners and standards of decorum were, if anything, more exaggeratedly suburban than they ever were in England during the same period.

'It was a very pleasant life,' my mother said of her childhood in India, 'but it wasn't all that different from the way I live now. The only thing was that I had my housework done. It was a very ordinary existence, but it was very nice.'

And yet, for all that it could be a conventional life, especially for younger people, a myth has been created around the role played by the arbiters of taste in India – the memsahibs. According to the usual stereotype the average English mem was a lazy, arrogant creature who was waited upon hand and foot by an army of servants. Her daily life was a round of idle pleasures – bridge and mah-jong by day, drinking and gossiping in the club at night. While her husband sweated away the hot season in the plains she took herself off to a hill station to throw herself into the arms of the first available man. All this she was able to do because her children were either in the care of an ayah or safely packed off to school in Britain. Cruel, narrow-minded and snobbish, she is too bored ever to bother with anything that might disrupt her privileged existence.

So much for caricature. While it is true that those traits – though not all of them and not all at the same time – could be found in any club or hill station, that image of the average mem belongs more to the realm of fiction than to any reality. The women who lived in British India did lead different lives from their menfolk but it was not always a pampered existence. Young wives with no previous experience of India could find themselves up-country living in a primitive bungalow with few basic amenities. There they would be expected to create a home and to subordinate themselves to their husbands' careers – just as older wives had to do further up the ladder. Servants they might have had but this was a matter of prestige and caste: prestige because the British considered themselves to be a ruling class which had to maintain certain standards of behaviour, and caste because social and religious boundaries could not be crossed by the servants themselves. For example, the syce who tended the horse could not cut the grass to feed it and only low-caste servants could carry out the more menial tasks. There was also the question of necessity: life in India could be hard and many hands might be needed to make the workload lighter.

There was a tendency, too, for men in India to idealise European women and to place them on pedestals. This was mainly because there were few marriageable girls and also because there was a certain opposition in the pre-war period to marrying young. In the ICS, the armed forces and the police, older officers would often be bachelors who disapproved of working with married colleagues. 'If you get married too early,' a young police probationer was told by a superior officer, 'you will be unable to mount yourself properly.' As all police officers were supposed to maintain two horses in order to carry out their duties the probationer took the charitable view that the older man was referring to his ability to pay his stabling costs.

And then, if one had to marry, there was the business of finding a suitable partner, one who would fit in. In some regiments it was not unusual for officers to have their intended wives vetted before they went ahead with their matches. If the officer waived this procedure and his wife was thought to be the wrong stuff, he could be asked to transfer, or even to resign. It was a hard system but it was one that had been evolved to preserve the status quo. Ahead could lie some twenty years or more of life in India, living in a society whose manners and social expectations conformed to an unwritten rule that the British in India should never be seen to let the side down in front of an Indian.

All those types were bound together by a common factor: all had chosen to live in India and all felt themselves bound up, in some small measure, with the destiny of the British Raj. Not that they felt themselves to be 'Indian' in any narrow or nationalistic sense. They were British first and foremost and never had any intention of making the country their home. Most would retire at a reasonably early age to live out their lives in the quiet parts of Britain. It was rare indeed for anyone to consider staying on to spend their retirement in India. The climate was too enervating for that and there would have been little in the way of company, for although British India was a compact place most of the people who inhabited it were young. Besides, after a lifetime of service, those who had spent the best years of their lives combating the depredations of the white ant in a hot climate wanted above all to live once more among the green fields of England or the grey hills of Scotland. When the time came they were happy to pack their bags and go home – not forgetting, of course, to throw their solar topees into the blue Mediterranean once the liner had left Port Said.

On balance, most of the things that they accomplished in India were good. A sound administration and a reasonably liberal government brought peace and prosperity to a formerly anarchic part of the globe. Of course, there were times when the rule was bad. All too often Indians were treated as second-class citizens or were simply disregarded, and there was a stultifying suburban snobbery about the lives of the British which appears bewildering, or downright silly, in our more egalitarian times. There was probably a fair degree of economic exploitation, too, and in times of stress people were killed for expressing points of view that did not coincide with those held by the British. Yet there existed an exasperated sense of community between the British and the Indians, a love-hate relationship which survived even the worst of times. The trouble was that it displayed itself in so many different ways that the British and the Indians did not always recognise the hand of friendship – or, more precisely, comradeship – when it was being offered. For that reason they often came to hold rather different views about the period of British rule in India.

There is a tendency, understandable perhaps, for old India hands to talk admiringly about the relationship they enjoyed with the country and its people. To them the Indians were the salt of the earth, racism was non-existent and there was a good level of toleration on both sides. If people tended to lead separate lives then that too was no bad· thing. The religions, customs and culture were all very different and the clash between the two sets could be disastrous. Besides, was it not the case that the collection and codification of most of India's tongues and their literatures had been undertaken by British scholars? Far better, it seemed, to have a business relationship, one based on a frank exchange of views in which sincerity, mutual understanding and respect were more important than intimate friendship. By all means eat with Indian officers in the mess, play polo with them in the field and deal equally with them in the office, but come the end of the day allow each to go to his own kind.

These virtues are very British, based on a belief that a man should keep to himself, never unburden himself except in the privacy of his own home. By long-standing tradition it implied the existence of a pecking order which determined that the man in charge should not mingle too freely with his subordinates. That he should be courteous in his dealings went without saying, but he should never allow himself to become too friendly with the people beneath him. The British understood the morality – and the good sense – of the system; it had been driven into them in the home, at school, in the services, and they accepted it. The trouble was that Indians did not always understand those ground rules. To them the British could appear friendly and open one day, cold and aloof the next, and on each occasion they seemed to be adapting the rules to suit their own needs.

The story of Prem Bhatia's relationship with the British both before the war and during it well illustrates the puzzling point of connection between the two different races. As a young student in Lahore he had thought the British 'a very queer race' whom he always respected but often feared. Part of the problem was their use of the English language. Bhatia had received an excellent education and was considered to be a star pupil, so much so that when a journalistic post became available on the *Civil and Military Gazette* in Lahore in 1934 his principal, Colonel H.L.O. Garratt, put him forward for it. Starting at the bottom Bhatia soon became a news sub-editor and it was then that he came to see the difference between the English he had learned in college and the language spoken by the English themselves.

One day the editor walked into the newsroom carrying the galley of a story which Bhatia had subbed. 'Whose heading is this?' he asked, pointing to an offending headline which read, 'Lady Willingdon Unwell'. Bhatia owned up, only to be told by the editor, 'You can't say that sort of thing about a lady. Don't you know that it means she is having a period?'

Some time later Bhatia was seen to err again when he described an Indian lady politician as 'being in trouble' – she had been arrested by the police. He received another lesson in English usage when his boss reminded him that his article implied that the unfortunate unmarried woman was pregnant.

In spite of these minor linguistic slips Bhatia felt at home in the *Gazette* and he struck up reasonably close links with his British colleagues. He and another Indian graduate were considered to be trail-blazers of a sort because, prior to their appointment, it had always been the custom to use young Englishmen in the newspaper's editorial and journalistic posts. A combination of financial economy – the *Gazette* wanted to save money – and political necessity – it was the time of the Government of India Act – gave Bhatia his chance to turn to journalism as a career. The work also gave him a certain amount of prestige, but as an Indian employed by a British concern he was still having to straddle two very different worlds. And, as he found, he still had much to learn about these strange people, the British.

His colleagues on the *Gazette* might have welcomed him as a keen and articulate young man but the fact that he was an educated Indian working on a British newspaper made him an object of suspicion in the eyes of the local police. The first inkling that he had of the problem was when he was almost knocked off his bicycle by a police car. Inside was the local inspector, a man called Kilburn who was considered to be something of an eccentric. What happened next, though, was far from funny. Bhatia was summoned to the car and given a dressing-down for disorderly behaviour – getting in the way of Kilburn's car. He was then astonished to hear Kilburn say that as he was a *badmash* (unsavoury type) the police would be keeping an eye on him.

The following weeks were a nightmare. At every opportunity Bhatia was harassed by the police and his life was made so miserable that his work began to suffer. Eventually he put his problem to the news editor, Freddy Bustin, who promised to have a word with the inspector at the Gymkhana Club. As good as his word, Bustin spoke to Kilburn that very evening only to be told by the inspector that Bhatia was indeed considered to be a dangerous fellow who was antagonistic to British rule. 'Don't be silly,' retorted Bustin. 'Haven't you seen him play cricket? He's the chap who opens the innings for northern India.' Kilburn was suitably impressed; the following day he removed Bhatia's name from the list of local suspects and the young journalist's life returned to normal. What would have been his fate had he not been a first-class cricketer, he still does not know, but the incident gave him an interesting insight into the power of the British 'Old Boy' network.

In time Bhatia became a committed anglophile who regarded Britain as his second home. When war broke out in 1939 he volunteered for military service immediately and was commissioned into the Indian Army. With their public relations directorate he served under General 'Jumbo' Wilson in Iraq and Persia and it was there that he had an experience which showed him the darker side of the British relationship with India. At the time he was a major, and when he was detailed to travel by train from Baghdad to Basra by troop train he was placed in the same compartment as a British brigadier. While his batman put the luggage in the two-seater coupé compartment Bhatia went off to buy cigarettes. He returned ten minutes later to find that his cases had been thrown on to the platform by a 'tall and beefy' British officer who said very firmly that he preferred to travel alone. Despite all his protestations Bhatia was refused re-entry by his brother officer and told to find a berth elsewhere.

The whole incident was witnessed by the Rail Transport

Officer, an Anglo-Indian captain, who was in charge of the train and who tried to intervene on Bhatia's behalf. Nothing came of his efforts and in an attempt to defuse the situation Bhatia asked to be moved to another part of the train. ('I might drink too much whisky during the night and then murder him,' said Bhatia by way of persuading the young captain.) Reluctantly the RTO agreed to the proposal but so shocked had he been by the brigadier's behaviour that he made an official report which eventually landed on Wilson's desk. Bhatia was summoned to the general's office some days later and although he tried to make light of the matter Wilson insisted that he tell him the truth. As a consequence the brigadier was reduced in rank to colonel and forced to apologise, which he did with bad grace. 'It wasn't very fair of you to complain,' he sneered. 'After all, we're fighting the same war, aren't we?' Bhatia paused before replying, 'I thought we were, until you threw me out of the compartment.'

To Bhatia the incident came to epitomise the love-hate relationship that existed between the Indians and their British colleagues. They could be cool and officious, often to the point of rudeness, as the brigadier had been; then they would make up for their behaviour with a display of justice and fair play. The trouble was that most Indians never knew what type of behaviour to expect. For every news editor or general who treated them fairly and courteously there would be an inspector of police or a brigadier who thought badly of Indians and treated them as second-class citizens or potential enemies.

When the war came to an end in 1945 Bhatia was a lieutenant-colonel in charge of public relations for Eastern Command in Barrackpore near Calcutta. From there he went to work as Director of Information for the Government of Bengal and ahead lay a distinguished career both as a journalist and editor and as a diplomat in India's foreign service. As he was working in an environment which paid great attention to politics he was fully aware of the gathering pace of Britain's desire to get out of India. He was also well placed to judge the British at close quarters. Initially, he was shocked by the calmness with which his British colleagues faced the future. Some seemed to view with equanimity the prospect of transferring power – or, as one fellow officer, a Cambridge graduate, put it, 'of being kicked out' – but then he came across others who held on to straws, dyed-in-the-wool imperialists who continued to believe that the day would never dawn when Britain would leave India.

This was a further conundrum, for even before the war had begun it seemed to many people that Britain could no longer hold on to India, that the claims of the Indians for self-rule were too strong to be denied. Obviously there were those who thought that British rule would go on for ever but, equally, there were also those who never lost sight of the objective of eventual independence. Prem Bhatia only recognised that it would happen in his lifetime once the war had come to an end; for my mother, the discovery had been made somewhat earlier.

She had been brought up in Ishapore where her childhood had been dominated by a sense of ease and privilege. The club had been the focus of the town's social life where she had learned to play golf and tennis, to ride and dance and to get to know everyone in the tightly knit British community. It was the kind of life which she thought would never come to an end: her first inkling that things might be starting to fall apart had come in the late 1930s, shortly before the outbreak of the Second World War. A boyfriend had been bitten by a native dog while breaking up a dog fight and had been taken into hospital in Calcutta for a painful course of rabies injections. The treatment lasted three weeks, so to keep him company she and a party of chums would take him into Calcutta and then go to Firpo's for coffee and ice cream. It was a short enough trip into Calcutta, one that was usually as free from incident as any commuter journey; but one day they ran into trouble. Big trouble. Approaching the Sealdah Bridge, they were stopped by a crowd of angry Indians, all wearing Congress caps and shouting political slogans.

'Don't drive those people,' they told the driver. 'Get out and let them walk! Don't drive them!'

In the best traditions of British pluck, the young man who had been given the course of injections was equal to the task. Fearing a calamity unless he acted quickly, he drew out his pipe and stuck it in the driver's back. 'This is a gun,' he whispered. 'If you don't drive on, I'll blow your head off!' The terrified driver changed down a gear, slipped the clutch and charged the car over the bridge, spinning several of the demonstrators on to the walkway.

For the party it had been an unnerving experience and their first real taste of the strength of Indian nationalist feeling. Yet, as they drove back to Ishapore, they became aware of the paradox that, however raucously the Indians might have been protesting and however frightening the incident might have been, British rule still stood firm in the face of that discontent, that measured tones and a pipe masquerading as a pistol could still uphold the mystique of the British Raj. Within ten years of that moment, though, their dream of imperial perfection was to be shattered, the demonstrators were to have their way, India was to be divided into two separate countries and thousands of British administrators, soldiers, engineers, doctors, businessmen and planters were to take their leave of a country which most of them had come to regard, if not as home, then at least as a place demanding affection, duty and sacrifice.

This is their story and the story of the Indians who watched it all happen.

Chapter Two

The Lives We Always Led

There is a style of writing about life in British India which is so common that it has almost become a subspecies of English letters. Basically, it consists of summoning up familiar images that have lived long in the memory and then racing pell-mell into purple prose. The writer wallows in nostalgia as he recalls his green days in a far-off country: the cool calm of an early-morning ride before the heat of day; the spicy pungent smell of food mingling with the tang of woodsmoke; the lush vegetation, dark and dangerous; the stifling dog-days before the onset of the rains; the sudden darkness on the verandah, ice chinking in long glasses and the steady sound of millions of insects whirring and buzzing in the distant darkness. If he is in a companionable frame of mind there will be kind words about faithful servants – simple natives, part clown, part booby, but always lovable. Those of a literary turn might allude to Kipling with thoughts about the best being like the worst; or they might just observe that India is a country where a man can do as he pleases, but no one asks why. The style is usually heroic, yet curiously pensive, and the adjectives flock in like locusts.

It is all good, entertaining, colourful stuff and there is something in it, too. India is a country which demands superlatives; its very size and strangeness cannot prepare the casual visitor for the powerful sensations which emanate from the subcontinent. For those who chose to live there during the years of British rule, those sentiments were even more deeply ingrained. Small wonder, then, that the memoirs and autobiographies of old India hands are so exuberant and written with such evident gusto! Once experienced, it seems India could never be forgotten; they had tasted the salt of life there and its savour would never leave them.

Yet, paradoxically, the India that one writer described would rarely be the India that another remembered. Of course, there would be similarities and shared experiences – the British in India were a fairly tightly knit community – but India's seemingly limitless horizons prevented the portrayal of a single, instantly recognisable view. The length of British rule and a conservatism which frowned upon change also meant that the description of life in a particular province at one given time might be questioned by a reader from another part of India during a different era. But it was the country's hugeness that really counted: the long distances, the multiplicity of races, creeds and religions, the bewildering babel of tongues and the differing climatic regions. John Rowntree was a Forestry Officer in Assam during the 1930s and he remembered that India was not an easy country to describe, because apart from the colours, it was the smells that claimed you, aromas that differed from one part of India to the next – 'the pungent smell of elephant dung, the scent of burnt grass in the hot weather, pine trees in Shillong, the smell of decay in a forest swamp and the sickly, soporific, often beautiful, sometimes overpowering smell of the vegetation'.

In a very real sense, the geography of the subcontinent determined the British reaction to India. (Here and throughout the chapter I use the word India to mean India under British rule.) Bounded by high snow-capped mountains to the north and by two vast oceans to the east, west and south, India is well protected by natural frontiers. In the days before modern means of communication and travel, the visitor had to approach by sea or through the Himalayan passes from whatever savagery lay beyond them. Once in India, he was more or less isolated from the outside world; even the British, with their railways and telegraphs, sometimes felt that Victorian India was cocooned from reality. This did not mean that India itself was isolated, as China had been for centuries – trade routes with the rest of the world were well established by land and by sea – but it did implant a sense of remoteness and confinement in the minds of the British who lived there. Just as few Indians knew what lay beyond their villages, so too the British often found it difficult to comprehend the physical nature of their adopted country.

In the extreme north are the great mountain ranges of Nepal and Kashmir, with peaks rising to above 28,000 feet. There the air is cool and rarefied and in the mountain valleys are the sources of the three great rivers – the Indus, the Ganges and the Brahmaputra – which determine India's geography. They water the agricultural flatlands which the British called the plains, states which experience extremes of hot and cold at different times of year – United Provinces, Bihar, Bengal, the Punjab, Sind. Moving down the country historic Vijayanager, the last great Hindu empire of the south, embraces the undulating plateau of Mysore and the luxuriant coastal belts of Travancore and Madras. Then there are the cities: teeming Calcutta with its weight of humanity, the eerie Towers of Silence in cosmopolitan Bombay, the historical continuity imposed by Delhi and the open vistas of Madras and Bangalore. And everywhere, the people and the cultures are different. For one country, India has more races, religions, languages and social groups than any other and a man will often say that he is a Sikh, a Tamil, a Bengali, a Brahmin, a Parsee or a Goan Christian before he says that he is an Indian.

From the very outset of the relationship, India had tantalised the British. In the works of Herodotus, Horace and others they had read stories which marvelled at India's wealth and wonders. Here were to be found courts of extravagant grandeur, mighty cities, limitless riches, exotic beasts and a proud people ruled by the mighty Moguls. Even though it was seven thousand miles away from Western Europe, it exerted a powerful fascination and when Portuguese and Dutch adventurers began to establish trading links with India, England wanted to be in on the action. The first English vessel, the *Hector*, paid for by the East India Company and skippered by Captain William Hawkins, arrived off the north-west coast at Surat in 1608. Hawkins was given a cautious welcome in the Mogul court at Agra and even though his visit did not yield immediate wealth – as the Company hoped it would – it had created a precedent. Having sidestepped their Portuguese rivals, English merchants were regular visitors to India throughout the seventeenth century and had soon established a number of factories or trading stations around India's coastline. By 1700, a pattern had emerged and England's interest in India was centred on the three Presidencies of Madras, Bombay and Bengal, each of which enjoyed a degree of self-determination under the overall direction of the East India Company in London.

Commercial profit was the Company's driving force, but it also had to maintain peace, administer justice and exercise diplomacy. The young men it employed had to be masters of several skills: according to their historian Philip Mason, they were 'thrown suddenly into positions where the opportunities for wealth and power were such as have been open to no men since the Roman Emperors asserted their control over the pro-consuls'. Hardly surprisingly, given such scope, competition for jobs was fierce and membership of the Company was much prized among England's professional and commercial families. At the beginning of his career, the aspiring merchant worked as a writer or clerk, five years later he was promoted factor before reaching the heady position of junior merchant within three years. It was a carefully regulated ladder of promotion and the financial rewards could be great. Entry was by patronage, but each successful writer had to covenant himself to the Company's service, promising to be 'sober, industrious and faithful'. Once covenanted, he had joined an élite organisation which was founded on privilege and responsibility – the very ideals which lay behind its successor, the Indian Civil Service.

It might have been an inauspicious beginning for a great imperial undertaking, yet from those pragmatic mercantile origins was born the great tradition of British guardianship in India. Empire-building might not have been in the minds of the early Directors of the East India Company but their servants, living within the confines of a fort or factory leased to them by the local ruler, often found themselves acting as the administrators of the judicial, financial and diplomatic interests of an Indian province ten times the size of Britain. Because travel to India took so long, the Company's servants were more than just tour-of-duty men: they had to put down roots in a country whose climate was hostile to a Western style of living. In the early days the mortality rates for young Englishmen could be wickedly high, especially in Bengal. It was generally reckoned that a man stood a one-in-two chance of surviving in the Company's service in Calcutta, which had been established by Job Charnock in 1690. 'He could not have chosen a more unhealthful place on the whole river,' wrote the Scots-born adventurer Captain Alexander Hamilton – and he was not the only objector to the site. Even a modern admirer and historian of the city like Geoffrey Moorhouse could exclaim with feeling that Calcutta has 'probably the filthiest climate on earth'.

The casualty rate could be equally high in other parts of the country but the handicap failed to dampen the enthusiasm and ambition of young men eager to try their luck in India. The rate of British expansion meant that jobs were regularly available and if the competition was stiff, then the rewards were worth having. Officials could line their own pockets through private trade and profiteering, so that it was virtually certain that anyone who survived his years in India could return home with a small fortune.

But, for many, money was not the only attraction. A goodly number of the Company's servants found that they liked India and the Indians, that they took to Indian life and culture and that there was much to admire in this ancient civilisation. That interest could range from Warren Hastings dabbling in Hindu sacred literature to James Skinner who immersed himself completely in Indian society. The son of Hercules Skinner, a Scot in the service of the East India Company, his mother was a Rajput princess, known to the family as 'Jeannie'. In 1803 he founded a crack cavalry regiment which lives on today under his name – Skinner's Horse. With their yellow tunics and red turbans, Sikander Sahib's Yellow Boys, as they were known, were a striking sight. The life of their founder was no less colourful. Skinner was fluent in Persian, the language in which he wrote his memoirs, and at his death he was rumoured to have had fourteen wives. Nasir-ud-Dowlah Colonel James Skinner Bahadur Ghalib Jang was one of many Company servants who had been encouraged to take an Indian wife – 'Better a Hindu or a Muslim' was the local sentiment – and other military products of mixed parentage in India included Eyre Coote, John Hearsay and Frederick Sleigh Roberts. It was not until 1792 that the Company introduced a colour bar by which 'no person, the son of a native Indian, shall henceforth be appointed by this Court to appointments in the Civil, Military or Marine services of the country.' The increase in the numbers of British women travelling out to India also discouraged liaisons and marriages with Indian girls.

Fortuitously for British ambitions, their rise to power in India at the start of the eighteenth century coincided with the decline of the Moguls. The dynasty had been at its zenith when Hawkins had arrived at Akbar's court but the death of Aurangzeb in 1707 heralded the end of Mogul supremacy. The way was then open for the East India Company to extend its commercial operations in India, in competition with its French rivals, for England – or Britain as we must call her after Aurangzeb's death in the year of the Act of Union – was not the only country in the field. Portuguese opposition to Britain had largely evaporated by the end of the seventeenth century and the Dutch had been encouraged to concentrate on the Indonesian archipelago, but the French remained. They might have been late-comers to India, but they were to prove determined imperialists.

To the Directors of the East India Company, the French presence in India at Pondicherry and Chandernagore was distinctly uncongenial. Not only did the French merchants bring an unwanted rivalry to Indian trade, but they also regarded themselves as colonialists in a way that the British did not. Whenever the Company acquired new territory it was usually as a result of a governor pacifying a frontier; but the French appeared to be working to an organised colonial plan by acquiring new territory through treaty and purchase. They also received considerable financial support from their own government in Paris, a policy of which the Directors of the East India Company thoroughly disapproved.

This state of affairs was brought to an end by the continuing wars which Britain fought with France throughout the eighteenth century. Campaigns were fought not only in Europe and North America but in India as well; gradually by process of victory and treaty India came under the British colonial umbrella. Increasing government interference in Indian affairs also meant that the days of the East India Company were numbered. As early as 1784 a Board of Control had been appointed above the Directors, a move which allowed Parliament to have a say in Indian policy. In 1813 the Company's trade monopoly was abolished and at the same time the introduction of free trade was matched by an equally powerful force, Utilitarianism. In the opinion of men like Jeremy Bentham and James Mill, government could be a potent engine of change and they argued that India was ripe for the implementation of a proper structure of political administration.

More significantly, perhaps, Evangelists also became intrigued by India and shared the philosophy of the Utilitarians that once

Indians received a Western-style, preferably Christian, education the whole fabric of Hindu culture and religion would be changed. In time these Christian gentlemen began to believe that God's providence had brought India into British hands and that it was their duty to redeem the hapless natives. This attitude was in direct contrast to that held by the East India Company whose Directors had always tried to discourage the missionaries from trying their luck in India.

The other factor in the gradual anglicisation of India was Thomas Babington Macaulay's memorandum on education. Asked to adjudicate on two schools of thought, one of which was in favour of Indians being allowed to study their own history and culture and the other which believed in an English-style education, Macaulay came down in favour of the latter, concluding that 'the literature now extant in that [English] language is of far greater value than all the literature which 300 years ago was extant in all the languages of the earth put together.' (To be fair to Macaulay he also introduced, single-handed, a penal code which was clear and humane and which cut sensibly through the intricacies of the Hindu and Muslim systems.)

The Evangelists and their missionaries were to take a considerable interest in India throughout the nineteenth century but their influence was not to be long-lasting; for the truth of the matter was that the Church was not really equipped to enforce a social revolution in the Company's domains. True, customs like *suttee* and *thuggee* were eradicated; and the anglicisation of Indian education did help many an upper-class Indian, but there was no revolution in Indian society as Macaulay hoped there would be. In fact, it could be said that exposure to Western political thought had a contrary effect in that it enabled Indian intellectuals to think of their country in terms of a national unity. If it achieved anything the influence of the Utilitarians and the Evangelists was most keenly felt by the men who ruled India, the British themselves.

Things will have to change if we want them to remain the way they are. Tancredo's advice to the Prince in Lampedusa's *The Leopard* could equally well have been applied to the British in India during the middle years of the nineteenth century. A dominant class will always want to remain in control, yet often refuses to maintain its pre-eminence, believing that power itself is a sufficient bulwark against decay. The East India Company was in that condition – still powerful but its influence steadily eroded by government interference and unwelcome external influences. It needed to be changed for British power to remain the same. The impetus was provided by the Indian Mutiny, or Great Revolt, of 1857: in the aftermath of this sporadic but bloody uprising a status quo was established by which Britain became the dominant power in the Indian subcontinent.

From being a commercial concern, Britain's empire became a bureaucratic machine. The East India Company was abolished a year later in 1858 and its place was taken by the Indian Civil Service headed by a viceroy, while in London a secretary of state for India was appointed with responsibility to Parliament. The Company's army in India was reorganised and in time became an effective fighting force which harnessed the martial instincts of the Indians under British officers. Communications were improved: roads and railways were built and telegraph lines criss-crossed the country. The gradual stabilisation and solidification of British civil and military rule introduced a new and formal life-style to British India. It was distinctly English middle-class in flavour and there was none of the innocent delight which earlier Company servants had taken in their Indian coevals. It did not take long for the British in India to become a separate caste, living in an assured world which was bounded by the cantonment, the club, the cool-weather stations and by 'decent' people. Theirs was a strati-fied society, as rigid as any Indian caste system, and the order of precedence assumed proportions which were faintly ridiculous. At the summit were the upper echelons of the ICS and the Indian Political Service who were followed by their lower ranks; then came the military with all its gradations of rank and regimental standing; business people followed next but, curiously, these descendants of the first merchant adventurers were considered low class and were often contemptuously dismissed as *box-wallahs*. Thereafter followed the British Other Ranks whom Lady Curzon described as being 'less than dust'; and at the very bottom of the system of rank and privilege came the people of no fixed racial abode, those born of mixed marriages. Known variously as Eura-sians, Anglo-Indians or, less agreeably, as *chee-chees* (because of their sing-song speech), they lived in a kind of limbo between the British and the Indians.

For those at the top of the tree life in India was good and it was
said with some truth that the country provided a vast system of
outdoor relaxation for Britain's ruling classes. When he went out
in 1916 to join the Indian Civil Service, John Younie discovered a
new world, one that was very different from the start in life he
had made as the son of a general merchant in Morayshire.

> I waken at 7.30 when my bearer comes and withdraws the
> mosquito curtain. You know those muslin bags in which they wrap
> up meat in summer – well you can imagine what I look like tucked
> away in my byebye entirely surrounded by the diaphanous folds of
> the mosquito net. Immediately on waking I am furnished with
> chota hazri, i.e., little brekker consisting of tea, toast and fruit.
> Then I get up, bath and dress and read the papers etc. Bara hazri,
> or big brekker, consisting of combined lunch (or tiffin) and
> ordinary breakfast comes in about 11 a.m. after which the day's
> work begins and goes on til 5 p.m.

From the very outset of Britain's link with India Scots had made
able servants of the East India Company and later they were to be
stalwarts of the ICS. Walter Scott had described India as 'the corn
chest for Scotland, where we poor gentry must send our younger
sons, as we send our black cattle to the south', and there was
some foundation to his conceit. Less aloof than their English
counterparts and very often from poorer backgrounds, many
Scots saw India as a chance to get ahead in life. In that respect
John Younie was no exception. Level-headed, but with a romantic streak in his outlook on life, he was an authentic lad of parts –
that is, one of the many Scots who rose in life by virtue of his own
abilities and not through any family or political connection. He
paid his own way through Edinburgh University by winning a
bursary and graduated with a first in History in 1915. Thereafter
he was a scholar at Christ Church, Oxford, and a candidate for
the Indian Civil Service in whose examinations he passed out
sixth in 1916. His first appointment was Assistant Magistrate at
Rampur Boalia in the province of Bengal and Assam; he rose
steadily through the service and at the time of his early death in
1942 he was Secretary in the Judicial Department and Remem-
brancer of Legal Affairs in Calcutta. His career, while not
altogether typical of all ICS officers, tells us much about British
India during the ninety years of Crown rule. Not only did the
country offer a first-rate opportunity for advancement and a job

which was often perceived as an obligation rather than a duty, but it provided a life-style which men like young Younie could not have afforded at home. For most of the British expatriates in India after the Mutiny it was a way of living which was singularly agreeable.

Many of them felt that they had experienced India even before they had arrived by reading the work of Rudyard Kipling. The foremost observer of social life in India, Kipling had gained first-hand experience of his subject by working on a provincial newspaper in Lahore where his father was Principal of the Mayo School of Art. Although he only lived there for seven years and emerged as a somewhat awkward young man who was not always popular with the British community, his literary influence was wide-reaching and long-lasting. Not only did his evocation of British India often provide an impetus to many a young man caught dithering about the claims of India as a career, but it helped to delineate the matter of Anglo-Indian society for newcomer and old hand alike.

From his very first encounter with the country, India could seem less strange to the new arrival if he had read Kipling. Cow dung burning in an alleyway could be Amir Nath's Gulley where young Trejago lost his heart to Bisesa; a callow subaltern falling for a bored married woman during the hot season could be recalled as Pluffles of the 'Unmentionables', his saviour Mrs Hauksbee had models who were legion. The story of Dickie Hatt was a dreadful warning about marrying young. Kipling also had things to say about mixed marriages: whether it was the cruel conceit of Georgie-Porgie or the simple silliness of Phil Garron, he believed that the white should go to the white and the black to the black. In Miss Vezzis he drew a suitably comic portrait of the result, a half-caste woman in her 'cotton print gowns and bulgey shoes', and a rotter like Bronckhorst was supposed to have 'country blood' although none could prove it. The stories were published in Wheeler's Railway Library and so popular were they that for many generations Kipling's India was Britain's India.

There were those who did not care for Kipling and who sneered at the pretensions of his Simla set or laughed at his portrayal of British private soldiers in *Soldiers Three*; but the world he created was real enough. He had a journalist's eye for detail and in his detached way he was able to summon up the atmosphere of the bungalow, the club, the officers' mess, the Secretariat and its hierarchy and the ordered calm of Government House. He knew much, too much, perhaps, about the manners and the society of the hill stations where the British took refuge from the summer sun. He understood the rhythms of the bazaar and was interested in the Indians as much as he was fascinated by the British of all classes and ranks – the bored ladies, the vagabond adventurers, the silly subalterns and the wise old soldiers. 'One met men going up and down the ladder in every shape of misery and success,' he wrote in his autobiography, *Something of Myself*. And Kipling knew all about that ladder, too. On many an occasion he had been cut by members of the Punjab Club who suspected him of being not quite a gentleman: Kipling understood that, above all else, the British in India valued a sense of precedence whose rules were sacrosanct.

India had a curious effect on Kipling's generation. Although the British were to bring a commendable dedication to the task of governing the country, they were far too snobbish. In particular they placed an importance on protocol and precedence which was nothing short of ridiculous. James Lunt, a young army officer, recalled that at some formal dinner parties precedence reached 'absurd extremes' as hostesses tried to ensure that the wife of the Jail Superintendent should not be outranked at table by the younger and much prettier wife of the Canals Engineer. So intricate were the rules that the government drew up a Warrant of Precedence which was introduced to ensure that unfortunate mistakes were not made at official functions. Like many others, Lunt believed that women took a keener interest in protocol and were more upset by snubs than were their husbands, but he could also see a good reason for the hierarchical nature of British social life. Because it was a small, clannish society and because everyone knew everyone else – and the level of their salary – some sort of formal order had to be introduced, especially at government receptions and dinners. There is also an argument for suggesting that the British in India unconsciously adopted many of the Indian forms of caste and adapted them for their own use: certainly no Brahmin was ever more disdainful of a sweeper than was the Collector's wife of a British private soldier or a Eurasian ticket clerk.

Even in their private moments, precedence and formality were never far from the daily round. Take the club. This was the social centre of any civil or military station and played an important role in maintaining morale and standards of dress and behaviour. On one level it could be a grand formal place like the Tollygunge in Calcutta which had a six-year waiting list, or the Byculla in Bombay which was founded in 1828 and closed down in 1947 when it was sold to a Muslim merchant for £300,000. Its last admitted member was Wilfrid Russell who worked for the managing agency of Killick Nixon and Company; to his surprise he received £1,000 as his share of the sale. On another level, the one best remembered by most people, it could be a solidly unpretentious establishment offering good sporting and recreational amenities – a social club with its own tennis courts, nine-hole golf course, swimming pool and bowling greens. There was usually a decent dining room and bar – men only was the general rule – and social life revolved round drinks on the verandah after six o'clock in the evening. Formal dress was often worn, especially on club nights when black tie for the men and long dresses for the women were *de rigueur*.

Membership of clubs could be a vexed question in the years before the Second World War. As most clubs had been established as service clubs to meet the needs of the local European community, there was a certain amount of segregation and insistence on precedence. Some clubs in Bengal, for example, were reserved for jute managers and their employees and were not used by the ICS or military; others were out of bounds to those in trade or to those considered to be 'not good enough' for membership. Only rarely were Indians admitted and Eurasians almost never – they were supposed to be happy enough in their own Railway Institutes beyond the pale. Some clubs, though, were happy to admit Indians and made it a matter of policy to do so; in others, Indians would only be admitted as honorary members if they were thought to be sufficiently important in the local community. During the Second World War the rules were relaxed to admit Indians in greater numbers, and, it has to be said, 'less desirable' British members as well – such as clerks in trade and those who held wartime emergency commissions in the army. Until then it was generally agreed that only the British 'of a certain type' could appreciate 'the best kind of club'.

> To the European, a club was a place where he could relax with his
> friends after spending what was often a frustrating day with his
> Indian brothers. The average Britisher looked forward to an
> evening with his own kind and in his own kind of world. He
> wanted to enjoy the atmosphere as near to that of home as
> possible where he did not have to watch his tongue for fear of
> unintentionally giving offence and where, in fact, he could put his
> feet up and let his hair down.

The club at Sibsagar which John Rowntree joined in 1929 was
typical of many up-country clubs. It was the social centre for a
wide area and once a week it held open house for its members,
many of them planters, 'who arrived from far and near to drown
their sorrows, forget the frustrations of the rainy season and
acquire a hangover'. Drinking might have been one object but
the real reason was companionship – to gossip, talk shop and
renew acquaintance with old friends.

If anyone did get outrageously drunk he would be quietly
removed and allowed to sleep it off for although the club was a
place of relaxation it was also ruled by social obligations which
were strictly and decorously observed. It was considered bad
form to be seen drunk in front of the Indian servants, running up
bad debts was a cardinal sin and having an affair with another
member's wife was frowned upon: most rules were introduced to
bolster the prestige and the obligations of British rule, but they
did not preclude high-jinks and fun. Parties, dances, picnics,
fancy dress balls, sporting competitions and amateur threatricals
were all part of the social round and, when the occasion
demanded, the rules too could be bent. After a spell in the Hill
Tracts where he had been the locum for a Collector on leave,
John Christie returned to Chittagong to find that he had acquired
the reputation of a jungle-wallah, or a wild man from the hills.
On his first evening back in the club he felt like Caliban,
unnerved by the presence of so many confident and civilised
people. Two large whiskies corrected the balance and by the
evening's end he found that he could not stop talking – in a merry
company around the piano he 'tore down the curtains, waved
them like a banner, and gave a rendering of the Red Flag'. The
members took it in good part and the following morning Christie
woke to ashes: 'I remembered that I was now the Collector of an
important district, not Maung Pooh Bah in the jungle. For the

rest of my time in Chittagong I hope I conducted myself with decorum and did my duty.'

Christie had entered the ICS in 1928 and his first postings had been in Bengal where he served at Mymensingh, Asansol, Calcutta and Chittagong. Like Eric Blair (George Orwell), his fellow school-mate at St Cyprian's, Eastbourne, he had been born in India and, like him too, he went to Eton and a career in the East. Whereas Blair joined the Indian Imperial Police in Burma after leaving school, Christie went on to Cambridge and in his third year there sat the ICS examinations, was successful and returned to King's College for his probationary year. All successful British candidates to the service had to spend a mandatory probationary year at Cambridge, Oxford or London where they were provided with courses in Indian law, history and an appropriate vernacular language, all of which would stand them in good stead in their first posting. At the year's end they were examined and then had to pass a riding test – an unnerving experience for those wary of horses.

Indian candidates had a two-year probationary period (reduced to one year in 1937), for from its beginnings the ICS recruited Indians, too, by open competition. By 1909 there were 60 Indians in a service which numbered 1,142 members; ten years later, the Government of India Act of 1919 enabled ICS examinations to be held in India and Burma as well as in London, thereby making it easier for Indian candidates, and the process of Indianisation of the service continued apace during the 1920s and 1930s. One of Christie's fellow candidates was Ranjit Gupta who was later to become a Chief Presidency magistrate in Calcutta. For him, as for most Indian candidates, his presence in London was an expensive and hard-won investment, involving not only a large financial outlay but also long hours of study, and for Hindus the possibility of religious pollution in having crossed the ocean to Britain. So worried was Gupta that he might have wrecked his chances in the written examination that he confided to Christie that he would join the French Foreign Legion rather than return home a failure.

(Many other Indian leaders were to enjoy a British education; indeed, it is remarkable how many were sent either to British public schools or to one of the ancient universities. Nehru was a Harrovian, Gandhi enrolled in the Inner Temple and matriculated at London University, the concept of Pakistan was evolved by

Muslim intellectuals at Cambridge and early nationalists like Dadabhai Naoroji, a distinguished Parsee, attempted to foster a sense of Indian national identity amongst Indian intellectuals living in London during the 1860s. The evolution of an educated Indian élite was one of the influential factors on India's road to independence: having savoured the ideals of Bentham and Ruskin they wanted to put them into practice.)

Once through the hurdles of examination and selection, the ICS was an attractive career. Not only were the rates of pay good – a starting salary of around £400 a year rising to a pension of £1,000 a year after twenty-five years – but the ICS had a prestige which money could not buy.

> Never had there been, never perhaps will there be again, such a service. Plato's trained rulers were a philosopher's dream, but the Indian Civil Service was a reality, and our Indian colleagues took, and still take, as much pride in it as ourselves. No wonder that we should be called, by mocking compatriots, the Heaven-born, the White Brahmins, neither Indian, nor civil, nor servants, incorruptible, but unapproachable. The last epithet was not quite fair; for we would be taught the virtue of accessibility, whether on horseback, in camp, in court or in our houses, and it cost some their lives. But the habit of impartiality bred a measure of aloofness, a reluctance to mix too freely, say in the club bar, with those who might be appearing before us in court the following day.

It was an élite service, fully justifying Christie's claims, and many of its members were inclined to make a religion of its high standards and ideals. The majority of its successful recruits were English and Scottish public schoolboys, all had been to Oxford or Cambridge or to one of the four ancient Scottish universities and many had gained firsts. If they were somewhat innocent of the wider world and exalted in such virtues as truth, honour and courtesy, then that, too, was part of the game they had been taught at school. An Englishman's word should be his bond, the individual should subordinate himself to the community, personal striving should only be pursued for the common good and the upholding of tradition should be sacrosanct. Even the separation of boys from parents and the female sex implicit in a public-school education could be useful preparation for a life that could often be lonely and chaste for long periods at a time. As John Rowntree found when he joined the Indian Forestry Service, a public-school education helped to iron out many of the creases in his initial dealings with the Indians but in the long term he found that it had its disadvantages, too: 'Our relationship with the Indians was too much that of prefects with the lower-fourth, one which hardly recommended itself to a people with an older culture than our own.'

Young men chose India for a variety of reasons: family connections, romance, duty or the simple chance to make good in new surroundings. All, though, were bound together by high standards of responsibility, privilege and duty and none were to misplace the trust that had been invested in them. Like their predecessors, the young servants of the East India Company, they were covenanted by contract to serve their new masters, in their case the Secretary of State for India.

After completing his probationary training the ICS cadet went out to India either to the province of his choice or to the province to which he might be best suited – Christie had put down the Punjab as his first choice but fetched up in Bengal; Philip Mason, who passed out first to Christie's second, got his choice of the United Provinces, considered to be a plum posting. They travelled out first class in a P & O steamer, a useful beginning as the line insisted on maintaining the strict standards of behaviour and precedence which were common to Indian society. Passengers had to dress for dinner, for example, and intercourse with the passengers in other classes was frowned upon. Once in India, the cadet returned to the bottom of the pile for a further period of practical probationary training during which he learned the ropes of his first job. Thereafter, a young man could find himself in a district which could be up to five thousand square miles in size; there he administered justice, collected the taxes and saw to the civil administration. One day he might find himself dealing with an obscure ruling over caste matters in a remote village in which he was the only European; another might see him in a hot office coping with the mass of paperwork which governed British rule in India. This was usually the high-water mark of the ICS officer's career in India – the chance to be his own man in areas where he was the ultimate arbiter. In the upper echelons an officer could expect to move upwards into the secretariats of the provincial or national government or he could chose the judiciary which provided the country's legal system. High-fliers could find themselves attached to the

Indian Political Service, an élite diplomatic corps which, amongst other duties, provided Residents or Agents to princely states like Hyderabad or Jaipur.

Entry to the other services such as the medical, forestry and police, was conducted on similar lines. In 1940 the strength of the Indian Police Service was 616, 422 of whom were British, the rest Indian, a small number of specialists to police a population which numbered 380 million – the average police force in any one province was 35,000. Consequently, entry to the IP was exceptionally competitive and when Leslie Robins joined in 1928 there were only eleven vacancies for his intake. Recruits sat the same examination as the army in Burlington Gardens where they were also interviewed. Unlike candidates for the ICS they were not required to possess a university degree, but like them they had to undergo riding instruction at the Royal Military Academy, Woolwich. Indian candidates were examined at provincial capitals in India and were usually expected to possess a degree from an Indian university. The British joined the IP for reasons similar to their colleagues in the civil service – family connections, a sense of adventure or a chance to do something worthwhile. Robins, who went to the United Provinces, admitted that reading Kipling had made a tremendous impression on him and after his brother joined a British regiment in India his mind was made up.

> Where else could you get such a marvellous training, early responsibility and command of men, to deal with crime and riots, ceremonial parades, dacoity, opportunity for riding, pig-sticking, polo, small- and big-game shooting, fishing and sport of all kinds? Nearly all these were otherwise out of the reach of men without private means.

The first indication that they were joining an élite service came – as it had come for their ICS colleagues – on board the liner which took them out to India. Like countless others Robins discovered that he had to measure up to the standards of prestige and service which he would encounter once he arrived.

> The India Office allotted you a first-class passage to India. On board ship you met other young men also on their way out to join the service. You also met officers of the British and Indian armies, returning from home leave, together with members of other Indian services. Among them were the ICS, Forests, Indian Medical Service, Public Works and Railway Engineers. There

was usually a sprinkling of missionaries. In those days, the division between first- and second-class passengers was absolutely rigid. No second-class passenger dared venture on the first-class deck, and attempts by first-class passengers to invite attractive young army wives travelling second class on account of poverty, were discouraged.

Once in India, the cadets were sent to their first training stations as Probationary Assistant Superintendents of Police. Robins went to the Police Training School at Moradabad which had been modelled on the Hendon Metropolitan Police College, the other main centres being Nasik for the Western Ghats, Phillaur for the Punjab, Hazaribagh in Bihar and Orissa, Surdah in Bengal, Vellore in Madras and Mandalay for Burma. Police officers lived in messes like army officers; they were well paid and lived comfortable lives in which they were well-respected members of the British community. Being a policeman, though, did have its drawbacks and it could be a lonely and isolated business, especially during training – Orwell's *Burmese Days* is a grim testimony to his period in Burma where he was thrown in the deep end by unsympathetic superiors and told to fend for himself. The position of responsibility also required IP officers to remain aloof from the rest of the British community and a strict check was kept on their social habits. That sense of separateness meant that many IP officers were regarded in a less favourable light than their ICS or army counterparts – witness Paul Scott's unsympathetic portrayal of Ronald Merrick in *The Raj Quartet* – but Leslie Robins found that in Moradabad at least he was required to live according to standards that would not have been unusual in a crack regiment.

Perhaps my most vivid memory of the Mess is a typical guest night. The table laid out with silver trophies plus a magnificent centre piece presented by the Nawab of Chattari, at one time Home Member in charge of Police. He was a fine-looking man, a Mohammedan and well educated . . . the band played, there was immaculate service by spotlessly turned out servants headed by Maseet, the Mess Abdah. He was the very epitome of handsome dignity through whose hands every Indian Police Officer of the Province from Inspector-General downwards had passed and whom he regarded, with the utmost respect, as his children. The magnificent Mess kit of the Indian Cavalry, the Frontier Force, the

Gurkha Rifles and various Indian Infantry regiments contrasted
with the more restrained dark blue and silver of the Indian police
and the sober tails of the ICS.

At the end of the First World War the Indian Army had emerged
with its prestige unimpaired. Over a million men had fought with
it in all the major theatres of war and they had shown that they
were the equal of any army in the world; in so doing, they had
also suffered heavy casualties especially at the siege of Kut during
the ill-starred Mesopotamian campaign of 1915. During the
inter-war years they returned to their duties as a home defence
force and to a life that James Skinner and his compatriots would
have recognised. Here the horse was pre-eminent, both as a
means of transport and as the companion in such gentlemanly
sports as polo and pig-sticking. There might have been some
trouble up on the frontier, but that too was sport, and life for a
young officer in the Indian Army after the First World War was
much as it had been for Kipling's precocious subalterns.

Officers were still judged by the standards of an earlier
generation: social standing was as important as professional skill
and most Indian Army regiments still expected their officers to
behave with the same courage, devotion to duty and modesty that
had characterised Queen Victoria's army. It went without saying
that successful candidates for Indian regiments were well educated, came from good families and had passed out with high
marks in the Sandhurst examinations. This latter requirement
was rigidly applied and it drove the less-well-off cadets to even
greater efforts, for an Indian Army commission carried with it the
promise of higher pay with lower expenses. While the wealthy
and the well-connected went off to the Guards, Cavalry or Rifle
Brigade, ambitious young men would seek out a career like John
Smyth, who joined the 15th Ludhiana Sikhs, won a VC in France
during the First World War and ended up commanding the 17th
Indian Division in Burma.

So fierce was the competition for places that Indian regiments
could afford to pick and choose. Even after he had been
commissioned into the Indian Army the young subaltern still had
to spend a year with a British regiment in India, a period of
further training during which time his own regiment could make
up their minds about him. The usual procedure was for the
candidate to visit the regiment of his choice and there to be

vetted. If the officers took to him he was accepted; if he made a gaffe, social or professional, he would be told politely to look elsewhere. One of the first things that a candidate would notice on these daunting occasions was that service in an Indian regiment was rather like the ministry of the Catholic Church: being a Frontier Force Rifles subaltern or a cavalryman in Probyn's Horse was not just a profession, it was also a vocation. As John Masters discovered, that sense of obligation was at the forefront of his mind during his first guest night with his regiment, the 2nd Battalion, 4th Prince of Wales's Own Gurkha Rifles.

> They had taken me into this family, and I felt the comradeship of those who had come before me to this table and been received into this home. I saw their graves on the banks of the Euphrates, in the Afghan snows, under the poplars beside the *pavé* to Neuve Chapelle, on the Russian steppes, in the seas and the mountains and the hills – oh, the green hills, the green hills . . .

John Masters had arrived in India in 1934 as a young subaltern fresh out of Sandhurst and had served a year with the 1st Battalion Duke of Cornwall's Light Infantry on the North-West Frontier. In his autobiography, *Bugles and a Tiger*, he described the experience as a bitter-sweet time, mainly because he was in the battalion but not a part of it, and also because he found that British regiments serving in India did not always take kindly to Indian Army officers. During the 1930s there were forty-eight battalions of British infantry in India, four regiments of cavalry and any amount of artillery. This large military presence was a hangover from the aftermath of the Mutiny when it was considered to be necessary for the British to outnumber the Indian troops and British units still marched to church on Sundays with loaded rifles. Most of the British regiments had long records of service to India and a battalion like the 2nd Black Watch, for example, might have been raised in the eighteenth century specifically for Indian service. Because they thought themselves a cut above the Indian Army many of the British battalions carried a sense of *noblesse oblige* to silly extremes. The officers made a point of keeping themselves to themselves, of standing aloof from their men and any Indians; they usually refused to learn any language or dialect and generally tried to maintain home standards in a country which was alien to them. Nevertheless, sentimentally, India was still regarded as the real home of the British Army in that it offered ideal conditions for training the men, the chance for frontier skirmishing and an unparalleled standard of living for the officers.

For the men it was rather different. Cantonments, or barracks, tended to be built as far away from the local towns and villages as was possible and in turn they became somewhat isolated, self-contained communities in which the British Other Rank spent most of his time in India, leaves included. Neville Blair, the last commanding officer of the 2nd Black Watch, found that while his Jocks had little opportunity to meet Indians in general, they did get on well with the camp-followers and regimental contractors. They drank with them and spent their spare time in their company, conversing in a hybrid language whose anglicised Indian phrases soon passed into the everyday vocabulary of the British Army.

With time hanging heavily on their hands soldiers would often turn for company to the Eurasian community who were happy to welcome them both as representatives of the British people and as potential husbands for their daughters. The ordinary British soldier was considered by many families to be the only escape route for their daughters as he occupied much the same social position in India as the Eurasians. 'When the time came for the battalion to leave,' recalls Blair, 'a number of Jocks asked permission to marry Eurasian girls who, I must say, were quite beautiful. There was no point, though, in simply trying to dissuade them not to bring the girls home to a country they didn't know: I could only advise. In the event the WVS stepped in to remind the girls about the problems of living in post-war Britain with its rationing and so on. They also told them about the culture shock of exchanging India for a two-roomed tenement flat in Glasgow.' When the battalion left Karachi in February 1948 it took home with it one Indian wife who had been married to a sergeant for twenty years. None of the relationships with the Eurasian girls survived.

Drafts of troops could spend up to five years at a time in India and it was usually a long and tedious period, punctuated by drill, bull and training. Little was seen of India apart from the countryside viewed from a train or from route marches along the trunk roads, and the pay was too low to allow travel elsewhere

during the annual two weeks' leave. Indian service also provided
the ranker with a precise indication of his position on the social
scale. Respected by the Indians he might have been, and in some
cantonments soldiers were waited upon hand and foot, but as far
as the British community was concerned, he was little better than
an outcast. It seemed that little had changed since Kipling's day.

The civil and military services, though, did not represent the
sum total of the British presence in India. After the First World
War the number of expatriates averaged 160,000, including
women, and of these around 3 per cent were members of the
All-India civil services. Apart from the army the rest were there
in a private capacity, usually in business of one kind or another,
for India had an important economic role to play in the British
Empire. India exported a variety of goods to Britain, cotton,
jute, rice, tea, oilseed and wheat, and in return she was the
largest single market for British imports, especially for cotton
goods and heavy engineering. The economic relationship
between the two countries was underpinned by a massive financial investment in the country – before the Second World War
India was one of the largest single repositories for British capital
investment – only 17 per cent of the capital employed in Calcutta,
for instance, was Indian in origin.

For all these commercial reasons India provided a good career
for the ambitious young businessman intent on bettering himself.
George Robertson was brought up in Dundee and went out to
Bengal in 1934 to join the jute industry: 'That was at the height of
the depression and there wasn't any work, so you just had to go
where you could find it.' Like many other Scots from his native
city he worked in one of the hundred-odd jute-mills in Bengal; as
he admits, it was a hard life but one that held out the promise of a
good salary and a high standard of living. Although the jute
industry had been widely condemned for its appalling conditions
in which Indians laboured ten- or twelve-hour shifts, twenty-four
hours a day, seven days a week while 'Scots managers rubbed
their hands', the satanic mills of the nineteenth century were but
a myth by the 1920s. Legislation had been passed by the Bengal
government to improve the workers' lot and when George
Robertson arrived in India he found modern mills and reasonable
working conditions. 'The Indians looked up to the white management, of course, but there was no question of bitterness between

them at all. They were treated well and they were well looked
after. I found no resentment at all. None whatsoever.'

Just as Dundee made jute and jute made Dundee, so did other
Scots make substantial contributions to other sectors of the
Indian economy. It was said with good reason that if someone
shouted 'Mac!' on the verandah of the Tirhut Club every face
would turn simultaneously. One such Scot was Sir David Yule of
Edinburgh who went out to India as a young man to work for the
family's firm of managing agents in Bengal; in time he took over
control and in an eighteen-year period during which he never
took a holiday he transformed it into the largest single business in
India. Indeed, a glimpse at *Thacker's Indian Directory* suggests
that in many respects Scots were the backbone of India's commercial activity, forming a substantial majority of the British
community, especially in Bengal. This extraordinary publication
gives some idea of the range of experience and expertise which
the British brought to India. Published annually, *Thacker's* listed
the name of every expatriate and the position he occupied –
everyone from the loftiest civil servant in Delhi to the newly
arrived assistant import manager in Planter's Agency in Calcutta.
It also listed those outside that segmented society, such as the
many missionaries representing the Methodist, Baptist, Presbyterian and Anglican Churches. Many found them a stuffy lot who
stood on their dignity even when the conditions suggested
tolerance instead of reliance on their Churches' dogma. When
Dorothy Younie, a member of the Church of Scotland, gave birth
to a daughter in a remote part of Bengal, the only man of the
cloth in the locality was an Oxford Brother. He compromised his
religious doubts by baptising the girl as 'a moribund infant, said
to be the daughter of John and Dorothy Younie'.

The lives led by the British in India during the 1920s and 1930s
were still largely governed by Victorian precepts. Social etiquette
was enforced with a strictness that was gradually being eroded in
Britain and good form was everything. Often there was a good
reason for this. People dressed for dinner as a matter of course,
both to be comfortable at the end of a day's work and also to
remind themselves of their pre-eminence. It was an assured
society, self-satisfied and slightly smug, redeemed by the sense of
service and obligation which the majority brought to their task.
Sadly, though, the self-confidence and the bow ties worn at

dinner could often mask an unmistakable sense of racial superiority. Although there were numerous examples of friendships between British and Indian colleagues, the colour bar was never far from people's minds. There was an unthinking prejudice that Indians were different, separate but not equal, and in many cases that attitude was encouraged by a natural deference amongst the Indians. 'I think Indians gave us a false sense of being in a special position because they were very polite.' Elizabeth Catto was not the only memsahib to discover the barriers that existed between the two communities and that although acquaintanceship was permitted, it was not always possible to develop it further.

Some relationships were encouraged by government decree and this was especially true in the services. Indianisation of the ICS and Indian Army had been put in hand after the Government of India Act of 1919 but it was a slow and ponderous reorganisation which frequently caused disquiet amongst older officers with different perceptions of the Anglo-Indian relationship. They feared that younger British recruits would refuse to serve under Indian colleagues; so strong was this feeling that the army compromised by designating two cavalry regiments and six battalions of infantry as Indian units, that is, units officered by Indians who held the King's Commission. These men suffered a further disadvantage by being educated at Sandhurst in a background they did not always understand and it was not until 1932 that the founding of an Indian Military Academy at Dehra Dun put the Indian officers on a more equal footing with their British colleagues.

When asked about home rule for India, though, most of the British community of the inter-war years would have replied, 'Yes, of course, but not yet perhaps.' When Curzon's old private secretary, the highly respected Sir Walter Roper Lawrence, retired in the 1920s, he argued that it would be difficult for the British to disentangle themselves from India with one easy cut. Likening the relationship to an intricately knotted rope, he pleaded that the two countries take time to untie it rather than rely on 'the clever juggler who throws off the well-knotted cord with one vigorous jerk'. Furthermore, he warned that while it would be easy to cut the knot, such an action would be an act of cowardice and bad faith. Significantly, the preface to his combative study of his years in India, *The India We Served*, was written by none other than Rudyard Kipling.

Some think that the dreamland of Queen Victoria has gone for ever, and that the old relations between the Indians and the Sahibs are fast disappearing into myth and memory: even so, they reflect credit on both and may be recorded. But I believe that for many generations India will have need of the Sahibs and that the young pilgrim, who goes the road I took, will find kindness and welcome if he gives the password and the greetings.

In his prophecy Kipling echoed the thoughts held by many of his compatriots who felt instinctively that it was wrong to give up India, but even by 1927, he was out of kilter with the times. Ever since the end of the First World War Indian nationalism had been growing apace with each succeeding year and for those who had eyes to see and ears to hear it was impossible not to understand that strength of feeling. The British prevaricated by holding conferences, setting up inquiries and yielding authority only gradually, but the truth of the matter was that a sense of impending change was hanging over India. The British might have been loath to realise it, but by 1939 India was ripe for self-rule.

Chapter Three

The Writing on the Wall

If one Indian epitomised the nationalists' aspirations it was Mohandas Karamchand Gandhi. The son of the hereditary chief minister to the ruler of Porbander, a Gujerat state on the coast of the Arabian Sea, he was something of an enigma. Trained as a lawyer in London he had flirted briefly with the idea of settling in Britain before making his way to South Africa to work as the legal adviser to a Muslim business. During the Boer War he served as a medical orderly in the British forces and won a campaign medal, but it was to be politics and not war that was to make his name. He became one of the leaders of the Indian community and discovered among them a strong sense of identity; in their service he developed the concept on which his immediate political doctrine was to be based, *satyagraha*, or non-violent resistance. By 1916, at the age of thirty-seven, he was back in India ready to put that form of defiance into action in his own country. His political growth was rapid and impressive: from an espousal of home rule his growing sense of nationalism turned to a call for complete independence and he ensured that he was associated with everything that was 'Indian'. He started wearing a loincloth, became a vegetarian, practised abstinence and espoused poverty of the body and the soul. Soon his wizened bespectacled features were a source of wonder and inspiration to the Indians and a point of annoyance to the majority of the British population.

'I couldn't stand the sight of him. He was nothing but a poseur and a fake,' was a common enough sentiment echoed in many a gymkhana club; but for every old India hand who only knew Gandhi by reputation there were many others who fell under his spell when they met him. In the early days of Gandhi's *satyagraha* Thomas Sievewright Catto of Yule Catto Ltd reminded him that George Yule, one of the founders of the firm, had been a leading light of the Indian Congress Party and its president in 1888. The great man was delighted: 'Mr Gandhi replied that he was aware of this and that his name was greatly respected in India as one of the pioneers of Indian national development.' Normally dispassionate ICS or IP officers who came into contact with Gandhi also spoke of the man's power and authority – which seems to have been a curious mixture of guile, ambition, shrewdness, honesty and not a little hypocrisy. When Leslie Robins, the policeman, met him in the early 1930s he found to his surprise that although he could not agree with his politics he was fascinated by Gandhi's childlike wiliness.

> In my view the fact that the then Viceroy Irwin gave such importance to Gandhi made many people think that he had to mean something. His gospel was preached pretty well throughout India, and they thought they could get away with it . . . Every sentence he uttered could have three or four meanings. He was very cunning.

A pragmatic civil servant like John Christie recalled that it was Gandhi's ability to dissemble that made him such a worthy political opponent. Even when he was being difficult he still had the power to beguile.

> Once, when Mahatma Gandhi called, Gilbert Laithwaite [the Viceroy's private secretary] who had damaged himself in a fall from his pony a day or two before, was supposed to be in bed. I was about to do duty for him, as the Mahatma arrived, when Gilbert was observed hurrying along the path from his house, his head swathed in bandages. 'Ah, Sir Gilbert,' said the Mahatma, 'what happened to you? Do I see from your appearance that you have been practising some violence?' 'Mr Gandhi, you behold in me a convert to non-violence,' replied Gilbert. 'It is of no use,' said the Mahatma, grinning broadly while his secretary, Mahadev Desai, picked from his shawl marigold petals shed by the garlands of the faithful. 'You have been converted perforce.'

Gandhi's precepts were in fact remarkably simple and found their expression in the truth-force of *satyagraha*, the doctrine which demonstrated to his supporters that India had a moral claim to independence. If all the disparate forces of Indian opposition could be marshalled under a single banner, he argued, then the non-violence of the majority could overcome the strength of the minority British. Rabindranath Tagore called him the Mahatma, the 'great soul', and the title stuck. It was also Tagore who put words into the aspirations of the Indian people after Gandhi had been arrested for the third time in 1931 after the failure of the round-table talks in London to discuss India's future.

> God, again and again through the ages you have sent messengers to this pitiless world:
> They have said, 'Forgive everyone,' they have said, 'Love one another –
> Rid your hearts of evil.'
> They are revered and remembered, yet still in these dark days we turn them away with hollow greetings, from outside the doors of our houses.

Tagore was another unusual and self-contradictory figure whose name was closely linked with the growing call for Indian independence. Born in Bengal in 1861 into a wealthy and sophisticated family, his literary fame outside India rests on his free verse re-creation of the medieval devotional lyrics, *Gitanjili*, which met with the kind of enthusiastic response enjoyed by Macpherson's *Ossian* a century earlier. In 1913 he was awarded the Nobel Prize for Literature and King George V knighted him for his services to literature. Gandhi called him 'The Great Sentinel', or the conscience of India, repaying perhaps the title of Mahatma, and Nehru believed him to be one of the greatest figures of the twentieth century. Yet for all that acclaim, and for all that he put his trust in self-rule, Tagore was frequently critical of Gandhi's policies and believed that independence could only be achieved by cultural and social renewal from within. He had unkind words to say about some of the more extreme solutions adopted by the Mahatma, such as the salt marches and the spinning cult, but on his deathbed in 1941 he was moved to agree with his old friend that the wheels of fate would eventually move the British to give up their empire. 'What a waste of mud and filth they will leave behind!' And it was entirely in keeping both with his firmness of purpose and with the duality of his nature that Tagore should have resigned his knighthood at the time of the Amritsar massacre in 1919 when British-led Gurkha troops opened fire on a group of unsuspecting demonstrators who had gathered in the city for a political meeting on a piece of open ground known as the Jallianwala Bagh.

This disgraceful episode was destined to cast a long shadow over Indian affairs and for many years it soured the relationship between the British and Indian leaders. Most stupidly all, perhaps, it was completely unnecessary. After the First World War there was unrest in many parts of India, particularly in the Punjab which had supplied most of the men for India's war effort. Amritsar, the Sikhs' holy city, had been the centre of much of the agitation and after an English lady missionary doctor had been assaulted by a mob the Governor-General, Sir Michael O'Dwyer, decided to use force. His agent was Brigadier-General Reginald Dyer, a dyspeptic dug-out of the old school who arrived in the city with military reinforcements.

Dyer's first action was to ban all political meetings, a decision that was bound to bring him into confrontation with the local Sikh community. On Sunday 13 April 1919, in defiance of those orders, a large meeting took place on the Jallianwala Bagh and Dyer decided that he had no alternative but to respond with force. Without giving any warning to the crowd his men moved into position and opened fire. The official death toll in the Jallianwala Bagh was put at 379 but was probably higher as the Gurkha riflemen fired 1,650 rounds of ball ammunition in an enclosed space. The following day Dyer introduced a series of demeaning punishments – Indians passing the scene of the assault on the doctor were forced to crawl on all-fours – and then he warned the local merchants that any further resistance would be met with force.

> You people know well that I am a sepoy and soldier. Do you want war or peace? If you wish for war the Government is prepared for it. If you want peace then obey my orders and open all your shops, else I will shoot. For me the battlefields of France or Amritsar are the same . . . Obey orders. I do not wish anything else. I have served in the military for over thirty years. I understand the Indian sepoy and the Sikh people very well. You will have to observe peace; otherwise the shops will be opened by force and by rifles. You must inform me of the *badmashes*. I will shoot them. Obey orders and open shops. Speak up if you want war.

Neither body counts nor bluster could ever heal the sense of bitterness and disillusion created by the massacre. After a good deal of obfuscation London ordered an inquiry and Dyer was retired from the army as a sign of the government's displeasure. At home in Britain, though, some quarters hailed the general as the man who had saved India and a grateful British public, prompted by the *Morning Post*, subscribed a fund of £25,000 for his retirement. In India itself Dyer's action and the half-hearted moves to condemn it came to be regarded as all that was shameful and tyrannical about British rule. Thereafter, Indian political leaders began to believe that independence could only be won through a struggle requiring a display of fortitude and endurance. As for the British, it taught the more enlightened that, unlike the response to the Mutiny, India could not be held by force alone.

Paradoxically, the violence of the Amritsar massacre helped to usher in Gandhi's policy of non-violent opposition to British rule. Although there had been a plethora of home-rule movements in the past and a spate of anti-British outrages, especially in Bengal, Indian opposition to the continuing British presence in their country was disparate and ill-defined. The emergence of Gandhi as a political figurehead changed all that. In a country where violence had been endemic for centuries he replaced the sword with the ploughshare and preached instead the philosophy of non-physical violence. He espoused the cause of the Untouchables, believing all religions, Hindu or Muslim, to be equal, and he developed a policy, somewhat ill-defined, for radical self-rule at village level. Most surprisingly of all, perhaps, he did not pin his faith on the immediate departure of the British as a precondition for home rule, but was more committed to the conversion of his fellow Indians to *swaraj*, or independence.

Such was the missionary zeal of Gandhi's teaching and the power and attraction of his message that he has been elevated in many people's minds to the status of a latter-day saint. Conversely, many doubters hold to the view that Gandhi employed his religious philosophies cynically and unpredictably to further his political cause. While uncritical admiration of the man and his methods ignores careful cultivation of his own legend, there is no denying either the strength of his convictions or his appeal across the subcontinent. 'Truth is not only truthfulness in word,' he said in his autobiography, 'but truthfulness in thought also, and not only the relative truth of our conception, but the Absolute Truth, the Eternal Principle, that is God.' He could have been Jesus preaching his sermon on the mount, and just as Christ's teachings gave strength and comfort to his fellow countrymen in Palestine, so too did Gandhi draw to him his own band of disciples, men like Morarji Desai, a Deputy Collector in the province of Bombay.

> The fact that thousands of people took part in the *satyagraha* against the Government in a country in which the common man had become very weak and fearful showed what a miracle Gandhiji had performed with his unique leadership. He made men from ciphers.

Desai was born in 1896 in a small village in the state of Gujerat and was destined to become prime minister of an independent India eighty years later. As a boy he had shown early signs of the strength of purpose and intellectual precocity that would take him from high school, through Wilson College in Bombay to a post in the provincial civil service. Between 1918 and 1930 his rise through the ranks had been steady, if unspectacular, and he might have gone far as a civil servant had he not listened to Gandhi's message. Like many of his generation who had been educated and were alert to the possibility of home rule, Desai maintained links with the Congress Party but, as he admitted, he was a closet nationalist. It was Gandhi's call for the resignation of titles amongst Indian officials that was to change the course of his life. In 1930 Desai resigned from the civil service to take up nationalist politics and to follow the course which had been prescribed by his spiritual leader. As he told a public meeting in Bombay this was not a sacrificial action but a pragmatic display of his belief in Gandhi's policies.

> If I could not have left the service, my anguish would have been very great. If a man amasses wealth through illegal means and if he ceases to act illegally on the day in which he realises that he has committed a sin by resorting to unlawful means, it cannot be called a sacrifice. People would say that he had realised his mistake and that he had been reformed. So all that can be said in my case was that I was reformed. I could not be said to have made any sacrifice.

Desai's decision to throw in his lot with Gandhi was cemented by the announcement of a so-called 'Independence Day' on 26 January 1930. All over India, Gandhi asked, people should down tools and make a pledge of independence, thereby creating a powerful symbol of India's strength of purpose. His own gesture was to challenge British rule by cocking a snook at a law which forbade the distilling of salt without paying duty. On 5 April, after a lengthy and much publicised march from his *ashram* at Ahmedabad, he arrived at a place called Dandi, then an insignificant village on the coast of the Indian Ocean but soon to become a place of pilgrimage. There he ostentatiously lifted and collected rock salt from the beach. His action was widely reported in the world's press and created a mood of tremendous enthusiasm for his cause. A few days later, Gandhi was arrested and jailed – but he had achieved his purpose by putting India at the centre of the world's political stage. Not only that, but he had brought more people round to his way of thinking, including many of the accompanying press corps who had even allowed him to read their copy before dispatching it, an action almost unprecedented amongst journalists. Glorney Bolton of *The Times of India* had interviewed Gandhi at the start of his march and he was charmed by the man's quiet manners and lack of pretension.

> A sort of great social revolution had started, but it didn't affect the natural chivalry of the Indian. Eventually I came to a house with a large courtyard, I was amazed that a man as old as Gandhi had been able to walk so far in one day. But there he was, quiet and happy with people round him, on the whole very quiet, but now and again you heard Gandhi would break out with that wonderful boyish laughter of his. He didn't know how the march was going to end, he didn't know how the sort of struggle which he had started was going to end, but none the less, there I was, seeing history happen in a strange sort of anti-climax way; something completely un-European and yet very, very moving.

By then few people in India could ignore Gandhi. He had already been imprisoned by the British in 1922 following a period of rioting in Bombay and Calcutta: the sentence was six years but he was released after two and, thereafter, the British did their best to turn a blind eye to his activities, a well-nigh impossible task. He endured well-publicised public fasts to bring together political opponents, and to get his own way, he spent much of his time spinning and weaving and proffering advice and he constantly preached the wisdom of non-violence. People might have disagreed with him – even amongst his followers there were those who doubted some of his economic and political ideas – but few doubted that he had brought about a revolution in Indian politics. 'We became converts out of conviction,' remember his followers in Ahmedabad, 'not as a sort of political stunt or following just for the purposes of winning independence.'

As for the British they were just beginning to comprehend that their days in India were numbered and that the time would soon come when they would have to leave the subcontinent – soon, but not yet. India was still the most profitable part of the British Empire with hundreds of millions of pounds invested there, but it was not just the economic factor that counted. Many people, especially those who had family connections with the place, felt a sentimental attachment to India; son followed father into civil service and army, the managing agencies which serviced India's economy were family affairs and there was, too, an indefinable sense of romance and adventure which persisted, albeit weakly, long after the First World War.

But Britain was changing in the post-war world and outside the India circle there were those who felt that the ties with India had to be loosened. Not many people knew what should be done, but they did know that something had to be: in their heart of hearts they would subscribe to the democratic ideal of self-government for the Indians, but, having done so, they would then ask if the Indians were really capable of ruling themselves. In the best British traditions they prevaricated, compromised, set up committees and boards of inquiry and pondered every move before acting belatedly upon it. It was at this time that Winston Churchill made his infamous and oft-quoted remark about the iniquity of Britain having any truck with Gandhi:

> It is alarming and also nauseating to see Mr Gandhi [he said in the House of Commons], a seditious Middle Temple lawyer, now posing as a fakir of the type well-known in the East, striding half-naked up the steps of the Viceregal palace, while he is still organising and conducting a defiant campaign of civil disobedience, to parley on equal terms with the representative of the King Emperor.

Conservative prejudice notwithstanding, happily there were some politicians who felt that India deserved a degree of self-government, even if that only amounted to dominion status within the empire. This was not the same as independence but it was a step forward and the result was the 'Montford' reforms of 1919, so called because they were pushed through by Edwin Montagu, Secretary of State for India, and the Viceroy, Lord

Chelmsford. Finalised under the Government of India Act 1919, the reforms provided India with a basic model of parliamentary government and the framework for eventual self-rule. A system of dyarchy, or dual control, was established in the provinces, which allowed some topics to be transferred to Indian ministers who were in turn made responsible to the legislature through the electorate. At the same time the franchise was extended, although it continued to consist of a property qualification. Some changes were made to the constitution of the government of India but the greatest reforms were felt in the provinces: the Montford laws eased their links with Delhi, thus giving them greater autonomy, and the theory of dyarchy invited Indians to co-operate with the authorities in the practice of government. In other words, it was a real opportunity for the moderates to work in tandem with the British guardians towards the eventual goal of self-rule.

But just as they took one step forward in India, the British also contrived to take another one backwards. Perturbed by a growing sense of unrest the government passed two Rowlatt Acts in 1919 which permitted judges to try political cases without juries. Neither law was ever put into effect but the frank discussions which surrounded them alarmed many Indians. They were one reason for the uproar in the Punjab which resulted in the tragedy of Amritsar and they encouraged younger Congress supporters like Morarji Desai to take a greater interest in Indian politics. The Acts were later repealed but like the Jallianwala Bagh killings they did great damage to the British cause in India: could the British government be trusted to keep faith with its promises? Gandhi thought not, hence his novel attacks on the authority of British rule and hence, too, the quickening purpose of Indian politics throughout the 1920s and 1930s.

The Congress Party encompassed several different ranges of political opinion yet it remained the main focus for nationalist aspirations. Founded in 1885 as a loose confederation of Indian political opinion Congress was little more than a forum for debate in its early years. During the First World War it had emerged as the only significant body representing All-India opinion, a position it had consolidated with a short-lived alliance with the Muslim League, itself founded in 1906. Other groupings, too, had come into being reflecting India's pluralistic society on the one hand yet besetting Indian politics with communalism and casteism on the other. Of these the Muslim League, representing Muslim nationalist aspirations, was clearly the most important. The Indian Communist Party was founded in 1920 and enjoyed support from Moscow; soon it was able to work hand-in-glove with the All-India Trades Union Congress to organise industrial disruption in Bengal and Bombay. It was a curious time, dominated by long periods of calm, only to be interrupted by riot and bloodshed as Indians demonstrated against British rule or fought against each other, Indian against Indian, Hindu against Muslim.

> It was an exciting and stimulating time for a young man who was ready to burn the candle at both ends. Revolutionary violence was endemic in a small but fanatical minority of a people whose language and culture was different from that of the rest of India; who had an ancient grievance against authority since the days of the Moguls; and who carried the stigma of an unmartial race. It fed on the resurgence of Asian nationalism after the Japanese victories over the Russians at the beginning of the century, was fanned by the discontents flowing from the first partition of Bengal, and later from the liberal and methodical steps towards self-government to which the British rulers were already committed, and which therefore gave the movement the colour of a war of independence.

Bengal, the province to which John Christie had pledged his future as a civil servant, had always been a hotbed of political dissent. There was continuing rivalry between the two main revolutionary parties as well as a series of outrages committed against British rule. These were the days of the Chittagong Armoury raid, the attack on the Writers' Building in Calcutta and on the Railway Institute at Chittagong. Judges were shot dead in court; District Magistrates, British and Indian, were killed, blinded or maimed. A bomb was thrown at Sir Charles Tegart, Commissioner of Police, in Dalhousie Square and this proved to be the signal for further assaults on prominent people. The Governor of Bengal, Sir Stanley Jackson, was attacked by students while addressing the Calcutta University Convocation and his successor, Sir John Anderson, endured a similar shock while attending the races at Lebong near Darjeeling. As John Christie recalled, the vulnerability of the targets was increased by the determination that normal life and business should go on as usual.

Elsewhere in India civil disobedience was carried out on a large scale and Gandhi and his colleagues and adherents had to accustom themselves to a familiar round of arrest, trial, imprisonment and release with re-arrest beginning the whole process again. Unfortunately, the British responded with further own goals. The Simon Commission of 1927, which was established to review the Montford reforms, caused great offence by its inability to include any Indians amongst its number: it was composed entirely of British members of the Houses of Lords and Commons. Not unnaturally perhaps, it prompted an impressive range of Indian opposition with a large number of Congress, Liberal and Muslim League leaders deciding to boycott it.

The British attitude, as summed up by the Simon Commission, also brought into the open some of the divisions that existed within the Congress Party and helped to bring to prominence new leaders like Jawaharlal Nehru who had been educated at Harrow and Cambridge, and Subhas Chandra Bose who enjoyed the support of young student activists and terrorist sympathisers. All of a sudden it seemed that the extremists might win the upper hand: this Gandhi feared because he believed that their activities might sting the British into introducing new repressive laws. It was one of the strengths of his political ability that he was able to dampen the enthusiasm of the extremists and to push their spokesman Bose into a siding where he could do little damage. 'Whenever there were conflicts among ourselves we went to him and he, well, reconciled us or made us accept what his own viewpoint was,' remembered Nehru after Gandhi's death. 'Sometimes, I'm afraid, we accepted it rather rebelliously, but we accepted it all the same.' When he had introduced his first *satyagraha* in 1919 Gandhi had been appalled by the ensuing violence and admitted that he had made a 'Himalayan' mistake; ten years later, he was not prepared to make another.

It was at this time, too, that Gandhi finally lost any remaining faith in the raj and opted for complete independence, strange inner voices apparently telling him in 1930 that this was the right course of action. They led him to his salt march and ultimate imprisonment and by the middle of the following year, 1931, the British had jailed almost 100,000 of his Congress supporters. This time, though, the rulers did not respond with repressive measures: instead of extending the pattern of arrests and declarations of martial law, the Viceroy, Lord Irwin, decided to parley with the nationalist leaders. He had already shown his goodwill in 1929 by declaring for dominion status for India; in January 1931 he ordered Gandhi's release and invited him to come to Delhi to discuss the country's future. In so doing Irwin might have shocked British public opinion and the sensibilities of people like Winston Churchill, but he had powerful allies in Ramsay Mac-Donald's Labour government who also supported the move for India becoming a dominion within the British Commonwealth.

At first the discussions were cautious and polite, no doubt because both Gandhi and Irwin had to find common ground, but because the Viceroy had agreed that the Indian leader should be allowed 'to negotiate and parley on equal terms', they were soon talking man to man. It was fortunate, too, that both men liked each other; indeed, there was a touch of mysticism in Irwin's make-up which struck a chord in Gandhi. The result, after eight meetings, was agreement that Congress would agree to partici-pate in Britain's plans for India's future and Gandhi pledged an end to the civil disobedience campaign. In return Irwin permitted peaceful picketing and gave way on the salt issue. In the longer term, the so-called Irwin–Gandhi Pact achieved little politically, but it did have the profound effect of showing the rest of the world that the British were prepared to treat with the Indians as equals.

One story, more than any other, demonstrates the sense of conviction that each man brought to the discussions. Because Gandhi realised that some Congress leaders would accuse him of betraying their aims, he looked for some form of political concession from the Viceroy. A terrorist, called Bhagat Singh, had been condemned to death; only Irwin could save his life. If he could see his way to pardoning him, argued Gandhi, the decision would have a good effect on the Congress Party meeting in Karachi. If Bhagat Singh were hanged, Congress might turn down the British proposals. It was a tempting offer but Irwin replied that he could neither interfere with the course of justice nor would he use a man's life as a bargaining counter. 'Well, would Your Excellency have any objection to my saying, when I get to Karachi, that I pleaded earnestly with Your Excellency for the young man's life? But that you did not feel able to grant it?' asked Gandhi. None at all, replied Irwin, on the understanding that Gandhi would also tell his followers that the Viceroy had no choice in the matter. This Gandhi did, leaving Irwin with the strong impression that here was a man he could trust. Years later, in a radio broadcast, he admitted that he had 'every reason to have great respect and regard for the name of that very remarkable little man'.

Later that year, 1931, Gandhi was invited to visit London to attend the second session of the Round Table Conference on the framing of a federal constitution for India. (The first session had been held the previous year.) He stayed at Kingsley Hall, Muriel Lester's settlement in the East End, claiming that as he represented the dumb millions of India, he wanted to live amongst the poor and the dispossessed of Britain. That decision impressed London's East Enders who took him to their hearts. The children called him 'Uncle Gandhi' and presented him with a toy woolly lamb, neighbours helped with his laundry and everywhere he went he met with such friendliness and affection that he was moved to tell them that he entertained no animosity towards the British people, only to their rulers who stood in the way of India's progress. He even scored an impressive propaganda coup by being photographed with cheering Lancashire millworkers at a time when their jobs were threatened by an Indian boycott of British cotton goods. And, true to form, throughout his visit he maintained contact with the men who mattered, Irwin, Sir Samuel Hoare (the Secretary of State for India), intellectuals like Gilbert Murray and George Bernard Shaw, and he was granted an interview with King George V who regarded India with a very special interest.

But despite these propaganda triumphs, Gandhi's presence at the second session of the Round Table Conference did not produce any significant contribution to his supporters' cause. Often he felt that he alone was the sole representative of the Indian nation and repeated that claim to Sir Samuel Hoare, but his confident assertion ignored the fact that other Indian leaders were busy putting the case of their own peoples – the Princes, the Untouchables, the Sikhs and the Muslims, who were already pressing for a separate electorate. The outcome was not the great breakthrough envisaged by Irwin and Gandhi but a package of reforms and legislation which appeared later, in 1935, as the labyrinthine Government of India Act, the longest single bill ever produced in the British parliament. Before things got better, though, they were destined to get worse. On his return to India Gandhi was imprisoned once more as a civil disobedience campaign began on a greater scale than before and the gentle, though feckless, Lord Irwin was replaced by the firm hand of Lord Willingdon who had no stomach for man-to-man talks with saintly, ill-clad Indian leaders. Put simply, the British heart was in the right place in that the government wanted to see India free at some future date, but their minds still told them that now was not the time to relinquish imperial power. For their part, the Indian leaders wanted independence but the divisions which appeared amongst them at the Round Table Conference meant that the goal was still a long way off.

The idea of unifying all the factions in a federal India, proposed by the Government of India Act 1935, went a long way to providing the country with a first step towards eventual self-government. Basically, the Act loosened British authority in India, but it did not altogether remove it. Once again, the franchise was enlarged to give the vote to 30 million Indians, the provinces were given virtual autonomy from Delhi and London with Indian ministers being put in charge of all branches of provincial government and a framework was laid down for the princely states to be bound by treaty to the rest of the empire. At the same time the British began to concentrate their power in Delhi, leaving the devolved provinces as the main focus of Indian politics: seen from the vantage point of today these might seem to be a puny set of reforms offering only safeguards, reservations and division of responsibility, but at the time it was considered to be a major experiment in the devolution of power within a British imperial holding. At the subsequent elections the Congress Party dominated the polls in the provinces; recklessly though, they refused to form coalitions or alliances with the Muslim League and in so doing brought forward the time when Jinnah's followers would demand a separate state for Muslims. By then the word 'Pakistan' had come into being: dreamt up by Muslim sympathisers at Cambridge, it envisaged a Muslim homeland in the Punjab, Afghanistan, Kashmir and Sind with the affix of Baluchistan providing the initials of the proposed new state.

Churchill called the Act 'a gigantic quilt of jumbled crochet work' and attacked it at every stage of its progression through

Parliament but, whatever its faults, it did lay down important principles about the decentralisation of power which were later adopted by India after independence. A by-product of the legislation was that it persuaded a younger British generation that India might well become free within the span of their own careers. This was particularly true of the Indian Civil Service. Between 1930 and 1935 only 91 British officers were appointed, as opposed to 130 Indians. That this should have been the case was largely due to the gradual process of Indianisation but the growing shortfall in British appointments was also caused by a realisation amongst the younger officers that they might not see out their service in India. After the passing of the 1935 Act Mike Stuart was surprised to hear a minister in his district (Howrah) tell a political gathering that the only reason for the British presence was that the Indians were not prepared to settle their own differences of opinion. At first he was upset by the remark, but on reflection he could see that it was only the truth: 'There was no reason at all why I should be there permanently.' By that time John Christie had exchanged the relative freedom of the Chittagong Hill Tracts for an administrative post in Delhi with the Government of India. There, and in the hot-weather station of Simla, he still found an air of gaiety, 'but it was the gaiety of the Duchess of Richmond's ball before Waterloo.'

The dance went on elsewhere. Alastair MacKeith joined the Indian Police in 1937, regarding it as an escape from the educational machine of school and university. Before leaving London he was invited to a drinks party given by Lord Zetland, the Secretary of State for India, who informed the newly appointed cadets that independence for India was the ultimate aim of the British government and that they should not necessarily expect to reach full pensionable age in their careers. He was appointed to the North-West Frontier Province where, shortly after his arrival, the strength of educated nationalist feeling was made plain to him by a Pathan officer senior to him. Sitting on the verandah one evening, 'he drinking his orange squash and me with my orange squash laced with gin', MacKeith was politely reminded that the British were regarded in some circles as interlopers who would have to go some day. Like his ICS counterparts, MacKeith is anxious to avoid the impression that this was a universal feeling. On the contrary, during the war, while stationed in Sind he was reprimanded by his subadar for suggesting to the men that Muslims would have to educate themselves if they were not to be dominated by the Hindus when British rule ended. (It was the mention of the possibility of British rule ending that the Indian officer had found so objectionable.) As MacKeith recalls, it was only in the senior echelons of the service that he found any great strength of nationalist feeling. Even then, the dissatisfaction was aimed at the British government as the instrument of foreign rule and not at the British in India as people. The Pathan officer, like other Indians in the service, operated impartially in the public interest and had no inhibitions in serving it.

Other British officers in the government's service have spoken of the left-wing climate of opinion in the universities which made them sympathetic to Indian aspirations. Others found in India a political system which they felt was unjust to Indians and which could only be put to rights by the granting of self-government. At the time of Gandhi's civil disobedience campaign in the early 1930s it was not unknown for groups of young British liberals to drive around Bombay with Congress flags displayed prominently in their cars. They were merely flaunting convention; more realistic were those who joined the Progressive Group of the European Association which had been founded in 1935 by Philip Wade, an executive with Burmah Shell. Originally, the main plank in its platform was the relaxation of the convention that debarred Indians from most European clubs; but later, through its meetings, the group provided a forum for debate with young Indian nationalists. Hardly surprisingly perhaps, the group's activities were not popular with the British community and one of Wade's founder members was soon in hot water with his immediate superiors.

Wilfrid Russell had joined the managing agency of Killick Nixon and Company in 1935 and his first days in Bombay had been a succession of idle pleasures.

> I had come out to India to live the life of an Englishman in his predestined place, mine the bottom of the ladder of commerce and industry, erected by Englishmen for Englishmen . . . the Gymkhana Club in Bombay where I soon found myself captain of the hockey team, of dinner parties on Malabar Hill, riotous Sunday lunches in the bungalow on Pali Hill where we sat down twenty-strong at three o'clock in the afternoon; boating parties at Juhu

beach in the moonlight, English girls of the fishing fleet having the time of their lives; riding, motoring, playing games in the same way we had done in England.

Russell described himself at the time as being a typically upper-middle-class public schoolboy whose rougher edges had been knocked off at Cambridge and by travel in Europe; in India he found that he had to come to terms with his conscience and with his new position in life. Killick Nixon was a successful agency which handled coal, shipping, mining, railway companies and the cement industry. It also provided its young men with well-paid jobs, a career and a position in Bombay society – just what Russell had been seeking before he left England. But exposure to Wade's Progressive Group and to the meetings with young intellectual Indians soon changed his outlook.

The partners of Killick Nixon might have tried to curb his involvement by giving him additional work, and although he feared – needlessly – that his activities might deny him membership of the Bombay Yacht Club, Russell soon became committed to the ideal of Indian self-government. The following year he became a member of the Bombay Legislative Assembly where he was introduced to the hard-line Congress politicians, so very different from the 'gilded Parsee youths' of the Progressive Group. Early on during his stint as a member he was given an instructive lesson by Morarji Desai, then serving as Minister of Agriculture, who had moved that ministerial salaries should be reduced by 90 per cent. When Russell queried his motives he was given a lucid rendering of Congress's hopes and aims for the future.

> You people have been ruling this poor country for nearly two hundred years; you have been ruling it from the point of view of the merchant and the money-maker. You took over the traditions of rule, the pomp and military power of your predecessors, the Moguls. You may have been right from your point of view to live in this way, out of touch with the people. If you were going to live in big houses away from the people, that was your affair, but you can't expect us to do the same; after all, we are the people, and we know what the people think. If we are to rule we must not sever ourselves from them.

Desai's speech also taught Russell the lesson that while the British had encouraged the educated Indians to adopt their ways, they had also alienated them from their own society. Furthermore, they had not really integrated those Indians fully into the British way of life but had tried to keep them apart from British society in India.

One of the difficulties faced by those Europeans who were sympathetic to the various nationalist movements in India was the rich plurality of society and the differences that lay between their various strata. Problems of communalism and casteism had always been central to Indian life: from 1935 until independence and partition in 1947 they became more apparent. The Hindus regarded themselves as next in line of succession to the British; the Muslims demanded their own state, pointing out that they represented 25 per cent of the total population; the Sikhs pressed for a separate Khalistan; the princely states, all 584 of them, wanted to remain within the empire; the Dravidian movement in southern India had ambitions for the creation of a non-Brahmin independent state of Tamil Nadu; Muslim Kashmir had a Hindu prince, Hindu Hyderabad a Muslim: the patchwork of different communities and their disparate aspirations were never easy to grasp, even for an Indian. How much more difficult it was then for the well-intentioned European! In the jockeying for power which followed the implementation of the 1935 Act, each group acted to preserve its own authority within the state assemblies. Gandhi's response was to continue to preach toleration, even at the expense of alienating influential Congress leaders in Bengal and the Punjab through his espousal of Dr Ambedkar's Untouchable Group.

On the surface, here was an entirely honourable course of action: the integration into Indian society of a caste of people who in many instances were literally untouchable. (In southern India, for example, a Brahmin would consider himself to have been polluted were the shadow of an Untouchable to fall upon him.) Gandhi was in favour of absorbing these unfortunate people into the *sudra*, or labouring, caste, an indication of his idealisation of village life; more importantly, perhaps, he also wanted to integrate them into the caste-Hindu Congress Party and it was on this point that he fell out with Ambedkar. Whereas Gandhi wanted to remove the basic disabilities faced by the Untouchables, Ambedkar wanted them to remain a separate political grouping. To his way of thinking, this would preserve their status as an important minority and with the British he negotiated the award of reserved seats through a separate electorate. To Gandhi, the move was not only damaging to his vision of an integrated society, it also left the door open for the Muslims to treat separately with the British. (The Montford reforms had already recognised this need.)

As a result of Ambedkar's obduracy Gandhi decided to fast to death and a compromise was reached in Poona whereby the Untouchables would receive a greater number of members in the Legislative Assemblies in return for a greater flexibility in the general franchise. Ambedkar never forgave Gandhi. Later he was to emerge as India's greatest constitutional lawyer and a statesman of the first order but he entertained a lifelong enmity towards his political opponent of the 1930s. 'He never was a Mahatma,' he said of Gandhi after his death. 'I refuse to call him Mahatma. I never in my life called him Mahatma, he doesn't deserve that title. Not even from the point of view of morality.'

If the inability of the caste-Hindu Congress Party to make peace with the Untouchables was a major irritant, the growing divide with the Muslim League was rapidly turning into a disaster. At the 1937 elections Congress came to power in Madras, Bombay, Central Provinces, United Provinces, Bihar, Orissa and the North-West Frontier Province, and non-Congress administrations were formed in Bengal, Assam, Sind and the Punjab. Many Congress members in all provinces were indeed Muslim but it was noticeable that their vote was high in areas where their co-religionists were concentrated. Jawaharlal Nehru, now President of Congress, took the line that his party spoke for every Indian, Hindu or Muslim but by 1938 his adversary, Dr Jinnah, was not so sure. 'Congress leaders may cry as much as they like that Congress is a national body,' he claimed. 'But I say it is not true. The Congress is nothing but a Hindu body.' His fears were fuelled by further statements from Nehru that the Congress represented nationalism and the British Raj imperialism and that the debate had to take place within that axis. Even the singing of the Congress anthem 'Bande Mataram', with its patriotic Hindu sentiments, was seen as an affront. By 1939 Jinnah was convinced that Nehru and his colleagues were only interested in the creation of a Hindu raj, and he would have none of it. Jinnah had been born in Karachi in 1876 and had trained as a lawyer; originally, he was a moderate member of the Congress Party who advocated political co-operation between the Hindu and Muslim communities, but by the 1920s he had split with Gandhi. Following a period of self-imposed exile in London, he returned to India in 1935 a confirmed separatist: within two years he was claiming that far from being a minority, the Muslims were, in fact, a national majority.

Allied to the Muslims' political disillusionment was a feeling that they were also being disinherited from their culture and their religion. At Legislative Assembly meetings in areas where they formed a minority, members noticed that they were often treated differently and that not only were their clothes out of place but they also could not understand Urdu. Stories abounded of an exaltation of Hindu values and a consequent denigration of Muslim; many of these might have been exaggerated but in some areas rumours of insults could cause the kind of communal violence which disfigured the last days of British rule in India.

As we have seen, Bengal had for long been a cockpit of violence between the two communities. In 1905 the province had been partitioned by Curzon, the eastern sector being predominantly Muslim in character, but the policy was hardly successful. Five years later the policy was rescinded and Bengal re-unified but violence between Hindu and Muslim, largely fomented by terrorists, remained endemic. In the jute industry workers from both communities worked in harmony for most of the time, provided always that work was available and that the managers and foremen were able to keep in check their employees' emotions. Ron Fraser, the manager of the Lansdowne Mill near Dum Dum, recruited most of his workforce from a neighbouring village which was predominantly Muslim. Occasionally, he had to keep the peace between them and the local Hindu population; on a day-to-day level that was easy enough, but feelings could reach a high temperature if a man were found murdered – a common enough occurrence. Whenever that happened, his solution was to conceal the body in his dispensary until the Sub-District Officer could be summoned from Barrackpore. This prevented the workforce from discovering the identity of the victim, but such a ploy was not always possible. Most of the murders took place on the railway line outside the mill, but one day a Muslim was discovered dead in the village itself. In protest the workforce walked out and demanded retribution. Fearing an escalation of the violence, Ron Fraser hurried down to the bazaar to retrieve the body: it was indeed a Muslim but he had been killed by a bomb which had exploded while he was carrying it. 'It blew his side out, and his hands. After we told the workers that it had been his own fault, they all went back to work.' Later, in the violence of 1946 Ron Fraser had to rely on the protection of a British Army unit from Lal Bazaar to guard his workers on their way back to the village. 'I got this crowd formed up in columns of three under the railway bridge and we walked along the main road with them all dropping off into their various *bustis* until we got to the other end. And then everyone said, "Good night, Mr Fraser, we'll see you again tomorrow." They pushed off and I walked back alone.'

Ron Fraser is prepared to admit that despite the ferocity of much of the communal violence he encountered in Bengal, he rarely felt threatened himself. Indeed, after dropping off his workers at their various *bustis* in the village he walked back alone to the mill and never felt himself to be in any danger. Like many other jute managers he was both nonplussed and faintly irritated by the hostility which broke out between the rival political and religious factions amongst his workforce. To him, and to many others, it was a nuisance which had to be tolerated, the general feeling being that it was an Indian problem which had to be dealt with, ultimately, by the Indians themselves. Those who were at the sharp end of the communal violence, the ICS officers, policemen and soldiers, felt rather differently about it. Their job was to keep the peace.

The prime concern of the British was to appear fair and unbiased, whatever the circumstances. How each officer managed to hold such parlous middle ground depended very much on the local conditions, the nature of the disturbance and his own sense of judgement. Sometimes a show of force was called for, especially when the crowd was in an ugly mood; at other times tempers could be soothed by a display of personal authority and officers soon found that a good sense of humour was necessary to keep matters in proportion. Always, the officer had to understand the nature of the difficulty. For example, the Hindu community venerated the cow, while the Muslims regarded it is an object for slaughter. Hindus prized the peepul tree which lined many roads but Muslims regarded it as a nuisance which hindered their processions of *tazias* (emblems in the shape of a tower) during Muhurram; the Hindu harvest of Holi was marked by spraying coloured water but a Muslim would regard a drenching as an insult. Coming on top of the more recent political differences between the communities, these long-established customs could provide a flashpoint for a riot.

In such cases the police would attempt to defuse the danger by the use of batons or *lathis*, long metal-tipped bamboo bludgeons which were effective in breaking up all but the most intransigent crowds. If the officer felt that there might be a danger to life or property he could apply to the magistrates to open fire, provided that a warning had been given to the ringleaders. Indiscriminate fire, or shooting over the heads of the crowd, was not allowed; instead marksmen were ordered to pick off the ringleaders. Most police officers considered that they had blemished their records if they had to resort to firepower, and did their best to avoid it. Each year in Jagatdal, in the subdivision of Barrackpore, the Hindu community would parade a huge idol of Durga, goddess of war, through the streets of the town. In an attempt to keep the procession within limits, Philip Finney, the District Superintendent, had ordered his men to line the streets and had kept an armed force in reserve in case of trouble.

> All went well until the mosque when some devil on the roof threw a hen out towards the idol. I can see that damn thing fluttering down to this day, and sure enough it landed smack in the lap of the idol. This of course was a terrible insult to the whole Hindu community. Seeing this the coolies carrying the idol dropped it straight away, and everybody tried to run, but the constables on either side of the procession prevented this, and the coolies were made to pick up the idol and proceed on their way. Meanwhile there was the beginning of a first-class riot throughout the area.

Finney promptly blew his whistle for the reinforcements and the police went into action. 'After a few bricks had been hurled everybody, sensing that the police were going to take strong action, fled into their houses, dropped the shutters on their shops and hid, and in ten minutes or so every alleyway and lane in the area was cleared and not a soul was to be seen.'

By employing an overwhelming show of force, and after telling the crowd that he would use it, Finney prevented further trouble and avoided the necessity of using weapons. Sometimes, though, force had to be used and there were occasions when use had to be made of troops in aid of the civil power. Such a situation befell Jack Morton in Lahore in 1935 when Sikhs clashed with Muslims over an attempt to desecrate the tomb of a saint. A series of *lathi* charges failed to break up the enraged Muslims, many of whom were armed with swords and knives, leaving Morton with no alternative but to recommend to the District Magistrate that the military be called out. Two squadrons of cavalry arrived on the scene and charged the crowd, using the flats of their sabres. Horses were normally useful in controlling riots but on this occasion they slipped on the cobblestones, unseating their riders. Their failure only served to anger the rioters further; it also meant that Morton had to take the action he had been anxious to avoid. He ordered the crowd to disperse, otherwise his men would open fire. Almost inevitably, they stood their ground, whereupon a platoon of riflemen of the 2nd Battalion Royal Scots opened fire, killing two rioters. 'The crowd panicked and started to run, then rallied and charged only to suffer further casualties. Superior force brought the riot under control.'

With the various nationalist movements gaining strength throughout the inter-war years, it might be suspected that unrest could have breached the ranks of the Indian Army. After all, here was an institution which personified the British Raj, its soldiers were the servants of the King-Emperor and were ordered to act in the interests of his government's policies. To some leaders of the Congress Party, the sepoys and sowars of the Indian Army were little better than mercenaries, traitors who had taken the pay of a foreign power. To the ordinary Indian people of the traditional martial states, though, the army was an honoured institution and soldiering an honourable profession. Sons followed their fathers, grandfathers and uncles into the same regiment, uniforms were handed down from one generation to the next, martial prowess was considered to be a virtue and successful recruits could look forward to a long and secure career in regiments which were more families than military units. For a young man to return rejected from the recruiting station was a black mark both for his family and for his village. It was as important as that.

The army which they joined had its own system of caste checks and balances. At the top of the tree, as in the British Army, were the cavalry regiments; then came a pecking order of infantry regiments with their own system of precedence. Here the so-called Class Regiments ruled supreme, mainly Gurkhas and Sikhs who had retained their individual identities as a result of their loyalty during the Mutiny, but it was government policy to mix up the various groups which made up the bulk of the army – the Punjab Muslims, Garwhals, Jats, Rajputs and Mahrattas. Soldiers from groups like these were placed together in companies according to religion or race but they would serve together in the same regiment. Thus a battalion might contain a company each of Rajputs, Sikhs, Hindus and Punjab Muslims, the whole working together as a single unit, and as in every other army it would develop a fierce sense of *esprit de corps*, based on the concept of individual honour, or *izzat*. That they remained largely untouched by the political events in the outside world says much for their training and for the tact and good sense of their officers. It is noticeable, too, that the authorities preferred to deploy British units or Gurkhas to quell political or communal riots. An officer of the same battalion of the Royal Scots who assisted the police in Lahore during the Sikh–Muslim riots of 1935 was not the only British officer to question this policy. 'We had a perfect illustration of the difficulties which beset the British Government in the discharge of its responsibilities, and the pettiness and narrow-mindedness which can provoke an inflammable crowd to fatal consequences. We may ask, as some of the Indian magistrates and others have openly asked, "What is it going to be like after self-government?"' As he pointed out, his battalion was on good terms with both the Sikhs and the Muslims, yet they were ordered to act violently to keep the peace between the two communities.

Another reason for the relative calm in the Indian Army, as far as politics were concerned, was that it was a society apart and the officers wanted to keep it that way, insulated from external problems. On the face of it, this was an easy task, for the regiments were self-contained units and a strong bond of affection and loyalty – based on the concept of personal honour – existed between the officers and the men. The soldiers, like the men of the British Army, were not encouraged to discuss politics and, in any case, the succession of training seasons, outdoor activities and sport left little free time for deliberation or debate. As one senior officer, Brigadier John Platt, rightly reminds us, serving soldiers often feel uneasy about what happens in the outside world of politics. 'Only the intelligentsia wanted independence,' he claims. 'Most of the ordinary people, the sepoys and the sowars and so on accepted us and were quite content. In the army we were very much of our own community and we lived amongst ourselves. It was the brighter people who wanted independence. And quite rightly.' Platt had been born in India before the First World War and had returned there in 1926 to join the 1st Battalion Somerset Light Infantry: to him, India was an oversize playground in which he could indulge his love of hunting and field sports. In time he was to take command of his battalion which, after independence, was destined to be the last British unit to leave India in 1948.

If the civil servants and the police knew that it was their duty to remain impartial, and if the army wanted to preserve their men's political innocence, one group of Europeans had perforce to meet the Indians head-on, at their own level: the missionaries. Although few of the groups sponsored by the various British, European or American Churches ever succeeded in converting caste Hindus or Muslims, they did play an important role in providing medical and educational services for the ordinary Indian people. Morarji Desai, for example, was educated at Wilson College in Bombay, which was sponsored by the Church of Scotland and as a student his eyes were opened to the liberating influences of European politics and philosophy. The poetry of Shelley and Byron, the works of Hume and Bentham, the ideology of Kant: all these were to play their part in awakening in him a passionate concern for individual liberty which, thereafter, he applied to his own country. 'As terms went on,' he later admitted, 'my sense of patriotism grew stronger and stronger.'

Another Congress leader and alumnus of Wilson College was B.G. Kher, the Chief Minister of Bombay in 1947. So strong were his feelings towards the place that he took time off from the city's Independence Day celebrations to visit the college in order to thank his former teachers for all that they had done for the Indian people. Then, to everybody's surprise, he took himself off to the college hostel to look out his old room. 'This is what it means to me,' he told his hosts. 'My roots are here.' Kher, a middle-class Brahmin, had graduated from Wilson with a degree in Sanskrit in 1906, followed two years later by an LL B and like Desai he had joined the Congress Party in the 1920s.

Many others felt the same way as Kher and Desai for, throughout the 1930s, the lecturers at Wilson had been firm supporters of the move towards self-determination. To them, the constitutional reforms of 1935 were a logical step towards eventual independence and most of them looked forward to the day that India would be free. After all, they reasoned, it was difficult to explain the importance of the Magna Carta as a milestone in British parliamentary history, or the liberalising effect of the French Revolution, while India was still ruled by a foreign power.

Wilson College was not unique in providing a liberal education for a minority of Indians – all church missionary societies had their own schools – but along with the Church of England's Cathedral School, also in Bombay, it was a lively focus for young Indian radical thought. That it should have become so would have suited the ambitions of its founder, John Wilson, a Scottish Missionary Society teacher who had arrived in Bombay in 1829. One of the many remarkable Victorian orientalists, Wilson had two objects in founding the educational establishment which was eventually to bear his name. The first was to carry pupils forward to the higher reaches of European literature, science and Christian theology, and the second was to encourage a lively interest in his Indian pupils' own vernacular tongues. Indeed, no student could enter the college until he had complete mastery of his own language. Indians were attracted to Wilson, said one of his colleagues, 'like steel filings to a magnet; but whatever the motive that brought them to his presence, each went his way warmed and filled with the bread that does not perish in the using.'

Like many other missionary teachers in India, Wilson was a child of the Enlightenment, the period of intellectual growth that saw remarkable innovations in the study of the sciences, medicine and the arts and the growth of a new understanding among intellectuals of the triumph of reason over tradition and faith. Consequently, a strong streak of liberal humanism ran through his work in India and this was reinforced by many of his successors. When Dr H. John Taylor arrived at Wilson in 1927 to teach physics, he found it easy to fall in with his students' ideas and political aspirations. Partly, his enthusiasm was that of a young committed teacher – he was only twenty-one – but partly, too, he believed that independence was the logical outcome to the years of British rule in India. Such a belief might not have found much favour among other members of the British community at the time but many forward-looking missionaries like

Taylor found it easy to accept their unpopularity for the very good reason that they tended in any case to stand apart from the rest of their compatriots.

> We were freer, more independent and less connected with the establishment. I was never very fond of the establishment! I often got into trouble with my friends because I didn't always want to go to Government House parties and that kind of thing. We didn't do the things, at least not all the things, that British officialdom did and I think that we had closer links with Indian people at the ordinary level of common intercourse.

The bulk of British missionary activity was naturally centred on the main cities of Calcutta, Bombay and Madras, but all over the country they were to be found in small and frequently isolated communities working as teachers, doctors and nurses and what would now be known as social workers. The Hon. Mary Scott – known to one and all as 'Auntie Mary' – pioneered the great missionary settlement at Kalimpong, Dr Agnes Henderson opened the so-called 'Sweepers' Dispensary' in Nagpur, Poona became an important centre for introducing specialised treatment for women's illnesses at St Margaret's Hospital. Wherever the missionaries went they established schools, some no more than hastily improvised sessions on the verandah of the mission, others imposing city schools with proud scholastic records like the Madras Christian College, which is now a highly respected university college with its own campus outside Madras.

Those missionaries often led closed and secluded lives which were dominated by the overriding need to serve their communities; as a result they were perhaps more in tune with the aspirations of many ordinary people and, as Dr Taylor discovered, the process of education in which they were involved was having a rather different effect on their pupils than that envisaged by the British establishment. Whereas earlier administrators like Charles Grant and Charles Trevelyan had hoped that educated Indians would become staunch allies of the status quo, they had, in fact, become its hardest critics. True, men like Desai fetched up in the provincial civil service but, as he admitted, his eyes had by then been opened. Instead of being prepared to bolster the system, he found constant fault with it, because the presence of British rule blocked his own and his Congress colleagues' political aspirations. Once the shout of India for the

Indians had been raised, it was a difficult cry for the liberal-
minded, educated young student to ignore.

It has been argued by some moderate Indian leaders that, had
the Second World War not broken out, the constitutional reforms
introduced in 1935–7 would have seen India safely through to
self-government, that experience of government at provincial
level would have worked later on a national scale. On one level, it
is an attractive argument, one of the great 'if onlys' which stalk
through Britain's history, and there is much to the conceit. By
1939 Congress had established itself as an alternative raj. Even
those educated Indians – the majority Hindu – who were not
members saw Congress as the true focus of nationalist aspirations
and voted accordingly. The Congress propaganda output was a
well-oiled machine and stories of party sacrifice in the face of
police brutality and official indifference helped to create a heroic
image; indeed, in some districts a candidate's success at the polls
could depend on his being arrested for an act of civil disobedience. (Smart British police officers soon got wise to this ploy
and refused to co-operate, much to the disgust of many a budding
politician.) Gandhi, too, however much his reputation fluctuated,
was regarded as the guru of the Congress movement and in Nehru
the party had a resourceful and highly respected leader. To Dr
Taylor who met him in Bombay during the 1930s he was 'a man
with a deep philosophical mind, a man of complete integrity and
one couldn't help but admire him'. By the end of the decade
many other Europeans had also come to share that view.

But there was another side to the coin. British relationships
with the minorities and with the princely states remained
muddled and unclear. In 1921 the princely states had formed a
Chamber of Princes to protect their political interests but it was
largely a talking shop; despite promptings from above most regal
families prevaricated, promising the Government of India to
introduce reforms but, in most cases, sweetly doing nothing.
Then there was the continuing problem of the Muslim political
activists who felt themselves disenfranchised from the ever-
growing Hindu raj. There seems to be no one reason why the
communal gulf should have grown so wide and so bitter by 1939.
One cause can be found in the shock that many Muslims felt at
the strength of the Hindu vote in the provincial elections; another
lies in the age-old antagonism felt by the co-religionists at village

and small town level; yet another was Jinnah's persistent call for an independent Pakistan.

Despite his cool and aloof bearing, and despite the fact that he was a convert to Islam, Jinnah was a popular leader who knew how to stir up his co-religionists and to provide them with the leadership that the Muslim activists so craved – during the provincial elections the Muslim League had made a poor showing at the polls, but by 1939 Jinnah had persuaded the Muslim leaders in the Punjab and in Bengal to put their weight behind him on All-India questions. Different from Gandhi, in that he lacked both an outgoing personality and a loving concern for the people he served, Jinnah was, nevertheless, a shrewd politician and a master of *realpolitik*. For example, when the Congress leaders resigned in 1940 in protest at the Viceroy's refusal to consult them before declaring war, Jinnah turned the situation to his own advantage and proclaimed a Day of Thanksgiving.

The declaration of war against Germany brought the constitutional experiment to an end, but, in truth, by then Britain had lost her imperial touch in India. Although her officials had struggled manfully to paper over the cracks in the Government of India Act of 1935 and had tried to make it work, many in senior positions were unable to respond to the growing Indian demands for self-determination. Even many younger officers felt disenchanted, for all too frequently they were overstretched and overworked. Although recruitment had improved during the late 1930s, new officers found that they had to deal with a new set of imponderables, such as having to interpret the emergency regulations imposed by the war, the opposition of Indian nationalist leaders and, in 1943, a disastrous famine in Bengal. 'For those who were serving in India during the last five years of British rule the experience was not unlike that of runners in the last stages of a long-distance race,' remembered John Christie. 'The earlier stages may have been exhilarating, but the last lap, which will end with triumph or disappointment, inevitably has its grim moments.'

During that last lap, others came into the field to share the race with the small British community in India. The armed forces swelled to around two and a half million men, many of them British conscripts with no previous experience of India; of their number a good proportion were to vote in the Labour government of 1945 which would oversee the dismantling of the British Raj. There was also a large American presence, particularly in the north-east where the battle was won to defeat the Japanese in Burma; many of the senior US Army officers and the politicians who visited the front were disposed to smile kindly on the Indian leaders and their aspirations. Together with the unstoppable impetus of the Hindu and Muslim nationalists, they too were to play their part in getting India to the finishing line in 1947.

Chapter Four

Quit India!

For many years it had been a long-held Fenian axiom that 'England's difficulty was Ireland's opportunity'. They dreamed of an outbreak of war in Europe which would involve Britain and thereby provide Ireland with the chance to wrest her freedom from British rule or, at the very least, to win important concessions which would lead to eventual independence. Like all popular sayings it had a ring of truth and in 1914 it was put to a stringent test when Britain declared war on Germany. Here was the ideal moment to cause embarrassment: Britain's attention had been diverted, leaving the back door of Ireland open to mischief and subversion. Yet, at the very time that Ireland could have seized the opportunity, Irishmen from all over the country were answering Kitchener's call to arms and flocking to join Britain's armed forces. Having been on the verge of rebellion early in 1914, Irish relations with her ruling neighbour seemed stronger and more contented than they had been for centuries. That this should have been so was due to the recent passing of an Act of Parliament which would provide Ireland with political devolution, or home rule within the empire, once the war was over. To the young Irish volunteers their services to the British Crown were a means of expressing their patriotism to a new Ireland which would eventually take her place among the small nations of Europe.

Unknown to the authorities, though, another and smaller group of Irishmen was plotting to put the Fenian saying into practice. These conspirators agreed early in the autumn of 1914 to take direct action against Britain while the war was still in progress and to wrest independence from a government whose attention had been diverted elsewhere. The result was the Easter Rising of 1916, a clumsily organised attempt to stage a rebellion in Dublin which was put down smartly and efficiently by the military authorities. In the aftermath many Irishmen condemned the uprising and were pleased to see it fail; but the ensuing executions of the rebel leaders changed all that. As one leader after the other went to the firing squad Irish sympathies turned against the British and in the first general election at the war's end Sinn Fein, the republican party, was swept to power. Three years later, in December 1921, 26 of Ireland's 32 counties had achieved dominion status as the Irish Free State, with Ulster's six counties remaining part of the United Kingdom.

When the Second World War broke out there were several similarities to be drawn between the position in which India found herself and the Irish situation of 1914. Both countries had found themselves, constitutionally at least, on the brink of winning independence at some future date; and in India especially the country's political institutions had put down strong roots within the community. Just as Ireland had been an integral component of Britain's war effort in 1914, so too was India essential to Britain's planning of the Second World War. The Indian Army was central to the strategy being followed in the Middle East and on the whole its officers and men were to remain loyal to their colours. Moreover, India was to become a vital source of men and materials necessary for the war effort and by 1943 she was to be one of the main Allied operational bases for carrying the war into Japanese-held territory. Recruitment to the armed forces was high, largely because of unemployment and also because Sikh and Muslim leaders encouraged their people to volunteer. Not only did they want to keep up their representation in the armed forces but in the early stages at least there was considerable support for the British war effort. The army increased in size from 205,058 in October 1939 to 2,251,050 in July 1945 – all of them volunteers. Britain needed that effort to help win the war just as she had required Irish soldiers and support in the First World War. The big question, in both cases, was, would Britain keep faith in the political promises made before the outbreak of war?

Initially, the Indian political leadership either supported the war wholeheartedly or at the very least remained cool towards it.

Those on the left, like the future novelist Kushwant Singh, had a natural sympathy with the British because they were fighting fascism.

> We believed that the Allies had to win and that was our best bet for getting independence: if the British won we could then twist their arms. But if the Japanese and the Germans won we would have had foreign rule for a much longer time. Not many of us accepted Japan's or Germany's assurances about supporting the Indian independence movement.

Much could have been built on that upsurge of goodwill but at that point the British administration displayed all its old autocratic failings. Linlithgow declared war on India's behalf without consulting the Indian leadership, a move that was bound to be hurtful at such a sensitive time. Although three provincial governments continued to offer their support – Sind and Bengal which were controlled by the Muslim League and the Punjab which combined Sikhs, Muslims and Hindus – eight Congress-dominated governments resigned and refused to co-operate. Even at that late stage, though, not many politicians were willing to voice active opposition to the war and, indeed, Gandhi is said to have wept at the thought of German bombs falling on London. That he should have done so and that his colleagues should have remained uncritical during the early stages of what came to be known as the 'phoney war' was due in no small measure to the principle of democratic benevolent liberalism in which most of the Congress leaders had been educated. It also had much to do with a general dislike of Nazi racism and at this point in the war Britain could have capitalised on that qualified support by winning the goodwill of the Congress leaders. Instead, she put to one side all thoughts of co-operation and set about the task of winning the war. To the Indian leadership this appeared high-handed and seemed to reduce them to the position of onlookers at an event in which they could play no part.

Although it was never stated in so many words, it was Britain's attitude which made Congress believe that her difficulty could be India's opportunity. In fact, Britain managed to add to her own difficulties by refusing to take into account the feelings of the Indian people: not for the first time in her history she gave notice that her attention would not be diverted to other matters while she set about winning a major war. Just as the British government had lost wholehearted Irish support during the First World War, so too did it trample on Indian feelings two decades later.

In October 1939 Linlithgow offered Indian leaders a consultative role in the war effort with the promise of dominion status after victory had been achieved. This offer was repeated at the beginning of 1940 with the result that Congress demanded a new constitution and independence at Ramgarh in March. At the same meeting they also announced a new campaign of non-co-operation and civil disobedience. Linlithgow's response was a reiteration of his earlier offer and a tentative suggestion that a post-war assembly should frame a new constitution. In turn, this was also rejected by Congress and the Muslim League which was by then adamant that a separate state of Pakistan should be formed. Stalemate caused confrontation and the British began arresting Indian leaders: between 1940 and the end of 1943, 91,836 people were to be arrested and imprisoned in varying degrees of comfort.

Most of the British and Indian administrators who served during that period are convinced that the policy of containment was the correct one to follow. In a worldwide conflict Britain was fighting for her life and could not afford to have a large portion of her empire suborned by seditious behaviour. This was especially true after Japan entered the war in 1941, when it seemed to some Indian leaders that the very presence of the British in their country was attracting the attention of a vicious enemy.

Britain's initial setbacks against the Japanese in South-East Asia also helped to undermine her position with the Indian people. Hong Kong had fallen on Christmas Day 1941, Singapore followed two months later on 15 February 1942 and in Burma the Japanese armies were sweeping forward on a tide of conquest from Rangoon to Mandalay. D.K. Palit of the Baluch Regiment was an instructor attached to the army's tactical school in Poona: he was serving with the 6th battalion and was horrified when the news came through that his colleagues in the 2nd battalion had been captured by the Japanese at the fall of Singapore.

> Firstly, it had a tremendous effect on our people – we felt the shame that they had surrendered. Secondly, the fact of the tremendous defeat inflicted on the – till then omnipotent – British had an underlay of feeling that the white races weren't all that

superior. In spite of British propaganda about the poor eyesight of the Japanese and about them not being good fighters their troops swept through Malaya like a knife through butter – and they defeated the British with smaller forces. The news had a tremendous effect on those Indian soldiers who had always felt that the British were supermen.

That feeling was not just confined to the army. Kushwant Singh began to notice that ordinary people were taking great pleasure in the British defeats – a common Urdu joke at the time was that Britain might have been claiming the victories, but the Germans and the Japanese were winning all the territory. Talk of a Japanese victory became commonplace and even Indians who trusted in Britain's supremacy began to wonder if the defeats in Burma could ever be reversed. Prem Bhatia, who was serving in army public relations, was an admirer of the British yet even he found it difficult to believe in the sang-froid of his superior officer. When Rangoon fell he was astonished to hear him remark cheerfully, 'Well, we still have Akyab!' The other side of that stubbornness, though, was a sense of irritation that Congress was refusing to help the war effort. Bhatia recalls that the most commonly voiced reaction was 'What the hell are these so-and-sos up to? Don't they know we're fighting a war?'

Internal security had to be strengthened because if the loyalty of the Indian Army or the Indian Police ever wavered, then the small British community would have been hard put to survive. Ron Fraser speaks for many people who lived through that period when he comments: 'After all, it was largely a matter of bluff that we were able to hold on to the country for so long, because at any time they could have wiped out all the Europeans. No trouble at all. Even though we had guards in the compound, that meant nothing.' It was a concern which was in the minds of many, for although the European presence had grown out of all recognition by the war's end, in 1941 it was still small, scattered and vulnerable.

Had the Indians decided to take advantage of Britain's discomfort in 1940 or 1941 they could have done so without too much difficulty. At the beginning of the war the best Indian troops were in Egypt – they were to become the superb 4th Indian Division which fought with such distinction in the Western Desert and in Abyssinia – and elsewhere in the Middle East theatre of operations Indian units served in Syria, Iraq and Persia in defence of Britain's oil interests. For the ordinary Indian these campaigns were as distant in time and space as the earlier operations had been in Flanders and Gallipoli. Britain might have been fighting for her life in the air war against Germany and in the war at sea, but these were distant matters.

In India itself, life went on much as before. Officers returning from a Britain subjected to rationing and open to air raids found that life in India had not changed dramatically at all. Commander A.B. Goord of the Royal Indian Navy remembers a three-week leave in April 1941 which he was able to take by car, a trip that would have been impossible in Britain.

> At the time Britain was suffering terrible reverses, with neither Russia nor the USA yet engaged, in India there was still no petrol rationing – or, if there was, it must have been pretty liberal. My wife and I drove an ancient Ford V-8 down to the Nilgiris, consuming no less than one gallon every sixteen miles, plus innumerable tyres destroyed by cast bullock-shoes, and relaxed in the old home of the RIN hydrographers.

Others, like John Rowntree in Johat, spoke of the disquiet that they experienced when they compared the ease of their lives in India with the news of disasters at home in Britain.

One reason why Congress – or, indeed, any other Indian politicial group – did not take advantage of the situation was, as we have seen, due to a certain Gladstonian liberalism which pervaded Indian politics. Another was Gandhi's influence and the time-honoured philosophy of non-violence. A more prosaic reason is that the Indians, unlike the Irish republican rebels who organised the Easter Rising of 1916, lacked any cohesive revolutionary force. A terrorist movement operated in northern India under the grandiose title of the Hindustan Socialist Republican Army, in Bengal the Jaguntur Party had carried out the infamous Chittagong Armoury raid of 1930, but apart from these and sporadic assassinations, the security forces had been well able to contain the isolated outbreaks of terrorism. Quite simply, the Indian leadership lacked both the wherewithal and the will to mount a serious armed revolution against the British. The only person who was capable, theoretically, of doing that was the radical Bengali leader Subhas Chandra Bose.

Today, Bose is considered to have been one of the heroes of the independence struggle; his name adorns streets in most

Indian cities, there are statues in his honour, children carry medallions bearing his likeness, but in the first two years of the war his fellow politicians were wary of his extreme points of view. Born in Orissa in 1879 he was educated at Cambridge and would have continued a promising career in the ICS but for the Amritsar massacre of 1919 and Gandhi's dramatic emergence into Indian politics. He resigned his post and in 1921 joined the Congress Party. He was imprisoned between 1924 and 1927, but was then isolated by Gandhi, thus allowing the more moderate Nehru to come to power within the party. Following a period of exile which he spent in Europe – to good effect, immersing himself in the political scene – he returned to India in 1936. There he surrounded himself with a cadre of disaffected politicians who believed that the new provincial ministries had a sound revolutionary potential in that they could use their authority to win over control of the police and the armed forces. It came as no surprise to his enemies when in late 1939 he founded the splinter group, Forward Bloc, and set about trying to convince his fellow countrymen that the war had presented India with a golden opportunity. Bose was sure that Britain would not surive the setbacks of 1940: in speech after speech he promised that the 'empire would melt into nothingness like snow on a summer's day' and that the hour had come to take vigorous action. His proposals were listened to politely but, one after the other, the Indian leaders rejected them: Gandhi and Nehru shunned him and, even though he was prepared to talk to him in Bombay, Jinnah made it perfectly clear that he was interested in collaborating with the British in order to win important concessions later.

Although Bose was considered to be a public menace by the authorities in Bengal and was kept under strict surveillance by the Calcutta Special Branch, the British were at first loath to arrest him. In spite of several promptings from his police officers, the Governor, J.A. Herbert, preferred to keep Bose in the outside world rather than turn him into a political martyr. Indeed, to begin with, Bose was given a freedom that would have been unthinkable in Britain at the same time. In common with the rest of the Indian leadership at the beginning of the war he was allowed freedom of speech, freedom to travel where he wanted and freedom to write what he liked. When he was eventually arrested later in 1940 his address to his followers was published, a clarion call which demanded the ultimate sacrifice.

Forget not that the greatest curse for a man is to remain a slave. Forget not that the greatest crime is to compromise with injustice and wrong. Remember the eternal law: you must give life if you want to get it. And remember the highest virtue is to battle against iniquity, no matter what the cost might be.

Privately, he addressed J.A. Herbert in terms which would have been recognised by Patrick Pearse and his fellow revolutionaries in the Ireland of 1916.

Though there may be no immediate tangible gain – no suffering, no sacrifice is ever futile. It is through suffering and sacrifice alone that a cause can flourish and prosper and in every age and every clime the eternal law prevails – 'the blood of the martyr is the seed of the church'. In this mortal world everything perishes and will perish, but ideas, ideals and dreams do not. One individual may die for an idea but that idea will, after his death, incarnate itself in a thousand lives.

In prison Bose embarked on a hunger strike and was released shortly before Christmas. Fearing that he would be arrested again, and anxious to strike a blow for Indian independence, he escaped from house arrest and travelled to Kabul where he made contact with the German authorities. For a time he was regarded by the Nazis as a potential source of political embarrassment to the British, but even though he was given a diplomatic welcome in Berlin, Hitler had little clear idea what to do with him. Eventually he was transferred to Japan and emerged as the inspiration behind the Indian troops who fought alongside the Japanese army in Burma.

For their part, the British were anxious to show that it was business as usual. The police forces interned German and Italian nationals throughout the country and in Calcutta a thriving local Nazi Party was broken up and its members detained. Amongst their number was the German Consul who was known to be a high-ranking official in the SS: the raid was led by Philip Finney who made his move at 5 o'clock in the morning after war was declared.

The German Consulate General was taken completely by surprise; as soon as I went in and saw the Consul he seized the telephone but I was able to inform him that we had already cut the wires. Our raiding party managed to seize two half-burnt code books which Hildegarde Horton, a resourceful secretary, had started to burn some time earlier in the garden but as it had been raining and they were a bit wet she didn't have much success. The Consul behaved in an extraordinary way, lost his head, became abusive and was most undignified. The Cypher Clerk, Richter, who had previously been careless with his codes, had left three uncoded telegrams by his bedside, which we duly got, together with the code involved.

Earlier, the Calcutta Special Branch had successfully intercepted the German Consulate's postal deliveries by employing an Indian jeweller to forge replica seals. Throughout India similar actions were taken to protect British interests and to display British authority to the Indians. The Calcutta raid was an undoubted success but in Central India Leslie Robins discovered that 'enemy aliens' brought with them additional problems. He was ordered to detain a motley group of seventy enemy nationals, including some German priests, and to place them in an internment camp at Satara in Bombay.

When I got down to Satara it was quite an experience. They were all civilians and were not prisoners-of-war as such. I had never seen such a collection in my life. There were stewardesses taken off Italian ships, there were circus performers, priests and one character pointed out to me, who was a Russian woman arrested with an Afghan spy on the North-West Frontier. She was his mistress and had been sent to this internment camp. A strikingly beautiful woman, she didn't like the camp system of the women being separated from the men. I left them there and some months later I had to go down to that camp again and it really was in a frantic state.

Eventually a review board looked into the problem but not before the police guards had run the gauntlet of resisting the amorous advances of the Italian stewardesses and the Russian woman had spent several days, naked, in a tree in protest at the continuing segregation of the sexes. As for the German priests – who were the only men in the camp – they had been forced to band themselves together to protect themselves from the women.

Other police actions were more symbolic than necessary, such as the decision to open a camp for Italian prisoners-of-war in the Hazaribagh district of Bihar and Orissa. This was situated at Ramgarh where Congress had met to discuss their 1940 campaign of civil disobedience. 'What better way of showing that Britain was not yet down and out,' commented Lawrence Russell who

was in his tenth year of police service. He also remembered that
the Italian prisoners were supplied with ice creams from Calcutta
two hundred miles away, 'until someone decided that perhaps
this was an over-generous interpretation of the Geneva Convention and stopped it.'

Britain's determination to convince Indian public opinion that
she was still in charge did much to defuse the potentially
explosive situation caused by the civil disobedience campaign.
The entry of Japan into the war changed all that. During the early
part of 1942 there were to be many anxious moments when it
seemed all too probable that Gandhi's call for 'open rebellion'
might indeed threaten the stability of British rule in India. It was
also a time when the tenor of life began to change with the
threatened Japanese invasion and subsequent build-up of Allied
forces.

> With the arrival of the army and air force life in Assam became
> very different from what it had been before. The bucolic peace had
> been shattered, the tempo of life had increased and strange faces
> and figures clad in jungle green were visible everywhere. Punjabi,
> Sikh and British troops, gum-chewing GIs and broadly smiling
> East Africans roamed the streets of Johat; the planters' club
> became more of an officers' mess and Americans sprawled in the
> wicker chairs in a manner which formerly would have brought
> down the wrath of the memsahibs on their heads.

As John Rowntree makes clear, there was ample evidence to
suggest that, come the war, things could never be the same again
in India, even in distant Johat. A rapid readjustment of the
Allies' strategic options had led to the reinforcement of Army
Command in eastern India, and the subsequent development of
the country as a war base had turned parts of Assam and Bengal
into huge armed camps. By then, any opportunity of exploiting
Britain's position had disappeared, for not only did the British
have powerful allies in the United States of America and the
Soviet Union but the administration in India had pushed aside
with disdainful ease Gandhi's last attempt to grasp independence
by seizing the moment – the 'Quit India' movement of 1942.

From the very outset Congress's civil disobedience campaign
had been but a token gesture. It lacked the force to shock the
British as it had once done twenty years earlier, and by the end of
1941 attempts to keep the movement in being had run out of

steam. Not only had it proved ineffectual, but the Indians themselves had become bored with it. Moreover, in the provinces where Congress ministries had resigned, the administration had been taken over by the governors employing special powers of authority. If the British were to be moved, something more dramatic was needed. The impetus was provided by a decision taken in London to involve India more deeply in the war effort with the promise of some kind of independence at some future date.

It was known as the Cripps Mission and its instigators were Clement Attlee, the Deputy Prime Minister, and Sir Stafford Cripps, the Lord Privy Seal and Leader of the House of Commons who visited India in the first half of 1942. Ostensibly, the mission had been organised by the British government to get Congress support at a time when Japan was knocking on India's eastern doors, but it was also an attempt to soothe left-wing opinion and to placate Britain's ally, the United States of America. From the official documents which are now available and which have been published in the monumental edition *The Transfer of Power* it is difficult to perceive the full brief that was given to Cripps before he left for India. Indeed, so full of constraints were his terms of reference that the mission was doomed to failure before Cripps began his round of meetings with Linlithgow and the Indian leaders.

Basically, Cripps was empowered to offer in the long term a newly elected constituent assembly which would meet to form a constitution, with the princes participating by nominating their own representatives. This would allow India to remain within the Commonwealth with dominion status, or the right to go for full independence later. In the short term more places would be made available to Indians on the Viceroy's Executive Council. For Britain, the main benefit would be that Congress and the Muslim League would work together for the defence of India and in the longer term India would be provided with the necessary constitutional framework for the transfer of power.

Congress listened to the proposals but gave them short shrift. Cripps found some support from Nehru and Sri Ragagopalachari but the majority found against him and returned his plans with a counter-demand for an immediate and unconditional handover of power and the withdrawal of the British from India. It was at this time that Gandhi compared the British government's offer to a post-dated cheque 'on a bank that is obviously failing'. Cripps also discovered that, in addition to dealing with a recalcitrant Congress Party, he had to cope with obstructive opposition from the Viceroy, Linlithgow, the Secretary for India, Leo Amery and the Prime Minister, Mr Churchill. Whenever it appeared that he was on the point of offering concessions to Congress the trio would go into action to constrain him. Linlithgow, in particular, worked assiduously to block the Cripps Mission: there is no clearer comment on his reasoning than that written by his own hand on 3 April 1942. In the margin of an official telegram from Amery sympathising with his predicament, Linlithgow admitted that he greeted the mission's failure with the words, 'Goodbye, Mr Cripps!'

Quite simply, the British Conservative Party did not want to offer concessions and continued to believe that Britain would have a role to play in India once the war was over. Churchill, for one, was not prepared to let India go: in a speech at the Mansion House in London later that year he told his audience, 'We mean to hold our own. I was not appointed the King's First Minister in order to preside over the liquidation of the British Empire.' His words might have been those of an old-style imperialist uttered with pride by a man who had charged with the lancers at Omdurman in the last years of Victoria's reign, but there was more than bombast to his speech. In the difficult early months of 1942, when Britain was depending more than ever on the plenty of the USA for her continued existence, Churchill was having to fend off increasingly pointed American demands that Britain put her house in order in India and make a promise of complete independence. With their inherent dislike of imperialism and a belief that they were fighting a world war in order to eradicate it – in the shape of German and Japanese territorial ambitions – the Americans took a grave view of Britain's presence in India. When the Cripps Mission did fail there was widespread suspicion in the United States that the talks had been sabotaged at the very moment of a possible solution. Armed with information from his roving envoy in India, Louis Johnson, President Roosevelt warned Churchill that his fellow countrymen had reservations about the continuing British role in India and that the time had come to be magnanimous.

American public opinion cannot understand why, if the British Government is willing to permit the component parts of India to secede from the British Empire after the war, it is not willing to permit them to enjoy what is tantamount to self-government during the war.

Although Churchill recognised that the Cripps Mission could be seen as a sop to American pressure, he was not prepared to bow to pressure from his allies. Like Linlithgow and Amery he had failed to recognise the importance of the Congress electoral victories in the provinces in 1937 and to allow that their success entitled them to a say in the running of a British war two years later. To Roosevelt he replied that it was an ungrateful Congress Party which had been the cause of the breakdown in talks and warned that any hastily conceived offer of independence, made when Britain was at a low ebb, would have to be honoured later. In other words, Britain would have ample time to repent at leisure after the war if she entered into a poorly thought-out agreement with the Indian leaders. In this respect he was assisted somewhat by Cripps's own belief that Gandhi had sabotaged the talks. 'They have come to the very edge of the water, and stripped,' he said, 'but hesitate to make the plunge because the water looks so cold.' Like Attlee and many other sympathetic Labour Members of Parliament he was gravely disappointed that Congress should have rejected the best offer they could have obtained from the British government in 1942.

The failure of the Cripps Mission was a watershed in Britain's relationship with India. One reason why the talks broke down was the 'opting out' clause which would have allowed any Indian principality to have ceded from the new Indian state; another was the deep-seated fear that Britain would not honour her obligations after the war. Both problems, though, could have been overcome at a later date had Congress decided to fall in with the Labour initiative and there is reason to suppose that Indian independence could have been won without sacrificing unity. As it was, the failure of the talks had an immediate effect on Anglo-Indian politics. Congress's decision left them with little or no support in Britain, even amongst their friends, and the general public opinion was that they had behaved disgracefully, if not seditiously, at a time when India was threatened by Japanese

invasion. More importantly for the future course of events,
perhaps, the behaviour of the Congress leaders, and their consequent imprisonment, left the Muslim League with an unreal sense
of its own importance. More than ever before Jinnah became the
Muslim spokesman on All-India matters and by constitutional
process the League managed to capture most of the seats in the
states which would later form Pakistan. By refusing to co-operate
with Cripps and by going into constitutional exile, so to speak,
Congress made certain that future independence could only be
won at the expense of All-India unity.

Yet, for all that it achieved little at the time, the Cripps Mission
did prove one thing: that, *pace* Churchill's imperial tirades, the
British intended to hand over power in India once the war had
been won. It may only have been dimly perceived at the time –
and perhaps not at all by those outside the political swim – but
Cripps's offer of independence within the Commonwealth could
not be withdrawn. There was still much to be discussed and a war
to be won, but many people in India were aware that the
traditional military, commercial and social pillars of Britain's rule
in India had been eroded beyond repair. Of course, it would still
have been possible to control India by force – as France would try
to do in Algeria – but that was a remote and frightening
alternative which most responsible people cared not to think
about. One other thing is certain about the confrontation
between Congress and the British in 1942: it paved the way for
Jinnah to strengthen the Muslim League's claims for the creation
of a separate Pakistan.

The immediate impact of the failure of the Cripps Mission,
though, was to harden attitudes. During the Congress meeting
in Allahabad in April its working committee agreed that as the
Japanese quarrel was with Britain, it should be possible for an
independent India to negotiate a separate peace. Thus was born
the Quit India movement which required Congress to use 'all its
accumulated non-violent strength in a widespread struggle under
the leadership of Mahatma Gandhi'. By August, though, those
non-violent aspects of the Congress campaign had been super-
seded by talk of 'open rebellion'. The working committee might
have made a further call for 'a mass struggle on non-violent lines
on the widest possible scale', but by then rebellion was in the air.
On 8 August Gandhi issued a new slogan – 'Do or Die' – which

seemed to contradict his plea for peaceable non-co-operation, and the following day the Government of India moved to arrest the Congress leaders and the members of the All-India Congress and Provincial Congress Committees. If that had been the ideal moment for Congress to have taken advantage of Britain's extremity then it came too late. The police moved quickly and efficiently to arrest the leaders and, lacking any direction, the Quit India movement was doomed to failure as a political lever to force Britain's hand on independence.

'It was a political mistake. The handling of it showed a surprising lack of understanding of the British character and ethos. So many opportunities were lost to achieve the desire of both parties.' Badr-ud-Din Tyabji, a Muslim ICS officer, was in a good position to judge both sides of the problem. His grandfather had been one of the founder members of Congress, his father was an expert on Indian law and his mother was a prominent social worker in Bombay. Some members of his family were Congress activists whom he respected, yet he also understood the British point of view. He had been educated at Balliol before entering the ICS in 1932 and most of his friends were British. (He also understood British class which he found to be as rigid as the Indian caste system: at Oxford he had been amused to note that men from Eton turned up their noses at fellow undergraduates who had gone to Dulwich.) During August 1942 he felt that he was something of a spectator at an event which was grossly exaggerated in importance both by the Indian politicians and by his British colleagues. 'They thought it was the Mutiny again. They were genuinely frightened.'

Fear is perhaps too strong a word: the British were fighting a war and as Martin Wynne saw it they were not going to be diverted by civil unrest within the empire. It came as no surprise to him as a policeman when the British started arresting the Indian political leadership.

The Congress leaders had hoped and planned for a popular rising against the Government, directed primarily against the Army's and Government's lines of communication and, more generally, against everything connected with the government of the country, including post offices, police stations, treasuries, schools and other government buildings. By stepping in and arresting the leaders immediately after the All-India Committee meeting, the

Government ensured that this carefully planned reaction was over and done with before the Japanese invasion could take place.

By the year's end any hope of a widespread rebellion had come to nought, just as Gandhi's critics had predicted. Amongst those who were glad to see it fail was the Indian Communist Party which fully supported the Allied war effort and refused, therefore, to have anything to do with the Quit India call. Before the war the Communists had been at the forefront of anti-British agitation, but with a war in progress they felt that it would be wrong to impede the Allies in their struggle against fascism. This was, after all, the time of Stalingrad, and the heroic Soviet resistance had been much admired not just by the Communists but also by others on the left. A.K. Damodaran, a student in Kerala and at that time a member of Youth Congress, had been arrested for making a Quit India speech in his home village and while in jail he listened avidly to the radio reports about the battle. 'We used to get the newspapers and watched day after day the movements to and fro of the Stalingrad battle. The fact that we were in a British prison and that the British and the Russians were fighting together in no way lessened our excitement. When the tide turned for Russia we were delighted.'

Another young left-wing student, Nikhil Chakravartty, had joined the Communist Party while reporting the famine in Bengal and at the time he was prepared to accept the party's stance on the call to quit India. Now, though, he is not so sure that it was a good idea. Although the Muslim League profited from the absence of the Congress leaders, in that they were able to win over large numbers of Muslim votes, the Communist Party became isolated from mainstream nationalist politics as a result of its decision.

> Looking at it from the point of the Indian liberation movement, personally I feel that the Communists got themselves de-linked. They were the militant section but once they kept away they earned the hostility of the nationalists – and for that they had to suffer for a long time. Even now, whenever anti-communism is mentioned, they raise the question that the Communists betrayed the movement in 1942 . . . their isolation from the main struggle of that year cost the Communists heavily.

Any split in Indian politics was bound to be of use to the British and there was a generally held belief that anyone, or any group, who supported the war effort should in turn be rewarded. It is hard, for example, to resist the Congress claim that the Muslim League flourished during the war years because its members and leaders aligned themselves with the British. With the Communist Party it was a different matter. Here was a political party which had to be regarded as an ally but its very presence in India was bound to fuel suspicions. Not only did the British administrators believe that help given to the Communists would be used against them when the war was over, but there was also the age-old fear of Russia to the north. If India became independent and voted in the Communists at a future date, then the Soviet Union would acquire an important sphere of influence in the subcontinent. As every British political officer had been trained to believe in the traditional Russian threat to India it was difficult for them to give wholehearted support to the Indian Communist Party. This diffidence not only upset the Communist leadership but it also lent support to the idea that Britain supported the Muslim League because a friendly and strong Pakistan would bolster the North-West Frontier against the threat of Russian encroachment.

Nikhil Chakravartty, like many others on the left, has an ambivalent attitude to the Quit India movement. Ideologically, he was against the call at the time and he can see the damage that it did to his party but he concedes that it did have the virtue of giving a new focus to the concept of Indian independence. The ideas of the Atlantic Charter, in which Roosevelt and Churchill had stressed the essential freedoms, were widely discussed in India at that time and it is not difficult to see that young Indians would have been affected by its terms. 'There was this consciousness of Indian independence being part of the global struggle,' claims Damodaran. 'The fact that the movement had been ignited was more important than its actual existence.'

For him, and for many more young nationalists, the symbol of the jailed leaders was essential to keep that flame burning. Some leaders, like Mrs Aruna Asaf Ali, used the arrests to further their political careers: she was admired by Damodaran as someone who managed to hold out to the very last. That she was able to do so depended on a wide range of friends and sympathisers; even pro-British students like Kushwant Singh were not unmoved by her story.

> One night I was woken up by the *chowkidar* who was sleeping out
> in the open – he said that a lady wanted to see me. It was Mrs Asaf
> Ali who was then underground and being looked for by the police.
> She asked for shelter for the night but I told her that I didn't
> believe in what she was doing. So she left me very angrily. I
> happened to mention it next day at the breakfast table and my
> father was very worried – at that time he was expecting a
> knighthood. My younger brother, though, caught up with her and
> had her stay quietly in the servants' quarters for several days.

Needless to say, the police got to hear about it and the younger
Singh was arrested. His difficulties were exacerbated by the
police's knowledge that Kushwant Singh had allowed Mrs Asaf
Ali to use his father's duplicating machine to print nationalist
propaganda material.

> My poor father was in an absolute dither and didn't know what to
> do. Fortunately the Chief Commissioner, a man called Jenkins
> who was later Governor of the Punjab, was a family friend and he
> realised my father's predicament. He said, 'If this boy tells us all
> he knows we'll do nothing to him.' To my father's credit, he told
> my brother, 'Don't squeal, what you've done is bad enough, but
> don't let your comrades down.'

The story had a happy ending. Because Jenkins had a high regard
for the family he ordered the boy to be released and nothing more
was heard about the matter. Kushwant's father breathed a sigh of
relief and was eventually awarded the knighthood he craved.
Later, Kushwant Singh used the episode in his novel *I Shall Not
Hear the Nightingale*, which is one of the best fictional accounts of
the birth of the new India. As he was to say years after the event,
each side had behaved according to type. The Indians had offered
token resistance to authority in the spirit of the times, whereas
the British had shown a mixture of firmness and fair play.

For all that Gandhi's call to action was nipped in the bud by the
authorities it was punctuated by sporadic violence in Bombay,
Madras, Central Provinces, Bihar and Bengal. The most serious
disturbances took place in eastern India where coal supplies were
prevented from reaching factories involved in the war effort and
the lines taking supplies to the army in Burma were threatened.

For the police it was an anxious time: the lines of communication and government property had to be guarded and large

crowds of Congress demonstrators had to be broken up, usually with tired and overstretched forces. At Kodarma, an important mica-mining area in Bihar, Lawrence Russell and a small troop of policemen were confronted by a mob who threatened to attack the police headquarters, having already burned down the local railway station. Fearing that the violence would escalate unless he acted quickly, Russell arrested twenty-eight ringleaders and gave them ten lashes each with a dog whip before packing them off to jail. No doubt it was an illegal and morally questionable reaction but later Russell argued that not only did it break up the riot but it also prevented further and even greater violence. In many other parts of India troops were often compelled to shoot into the crowd to kill ringleaders and at Kodarma lives were in fact saved by Russell's humiliating punishment.

Bihar was the centre of much of the violence that flared up in the wake of the arrests of the Congress leaders. The Grand Trunk Road and the main East India Railway lines passed through the province and they were both obvious targets for terrorist attacks. Signal boxes in isolated places were burned down with monotonous regularity and telegraph lines destroyed. Fortunately for Britain's war effort – Eastern Army Headquarters was in the province – the military lines of communication were never badly disrupted but confrontations between the police and angry demonstrators often had the habit of spilling over into neighbouring areas. Not only were the people of Bihar more politically motivated but they used their influence in the eastern districts of their neighbour, the United Provinces. Many of the worst incidents took place in the Gorakhpur district which had a long history of terrorism and dacoity, largely because its difficult geographical position allowed outlaws to escape over its northern border into the safety of Nepal. The most violent of the outrages was committed at the Chauri Chaura police station where thirty policemen were overwhelmed by a huge mob, stripped and then burned alive before help could be summoned. At Azamgarh, south of Gorakhpur, a few days afterwards, colleagues of Leslie Robins had a lucky escape when another Bihari-inspired mob tried the same tactics.

The mob surrounded another police station, Madhuban, in which it so happened there was a Magistrate with an escort of an Inspector and some six armed police, in addition to the normal police staff. The mob, which had already overpowered the local police station

in Bihar Province, had elephants with them. They tore up railway
lines, cut telephone wires, destroyed everything they could. They
raided treasuries and then surrounded the police station. Again
they were thousands strong. The Inspector was as brave as a lion.
He organised the police station defence and they held off the
milling mob which got right up to the walls. The only casualty was
a visiting *chowkidar* who happened to be making a routine visit,
who climbed on the wall and was beating off the mob until he fell
over and was beaten to death. This police station succeeded in
holding out the entire day, despite furious attacks, until the mob
became discouraged and dispersed.

Elsewhere, the army had to be called in to restore order or to
lend assistance to the civil power and, inevitably, lives were lost.
When events got out of hand the District Magistrate would be
asked for permission to use armed force, this would be invariably
given and marksmen would fire into the crowd to pick off the
troublemakers after a warning had been read out. It was a duty
which most British officers, police or military, disliked intensely
but it was necessary. Had the Congress-inspired riots been more
widespread, Robins, like many other police officers, believes that
they could have led to open rebellion. With Japan on its eastern
frontier, India was in dire straits and the authorities had to take a
hard line. In Bihar it took six months to put down the troubles,
and to complete the task the police had to be reinforced by two
infantry battalions. Hardly surprisingly, the violence left a bitter
aftertaste. 'This was "Civil Disobedience", and this was "Non-
violence",' says Robins of the notorious Chauri Chaura massacre.
'This incident put an end to that particular civil disobedience
movement of Gandhi's. Even he couldn't dismiss that massacre.'

Later, Congress leaders argued that the ferocity of the people's
reaction in Bihar and elsewhere was instigated by their arrests
and that had they been left alone there would have been no hint
of rebellion. Had the times been normal their argument might
have held good but the wartime conditions made it imperative for
the administration to act quickly and effectively to nip the trouble
in the bud. Altogether 763 Indians lost their lives in 601 violent
incidents in which firepower had to be used to restore order; at
the same time 63 policemen were killed. In other actions 208
police stations were destroyed, there were 664 bomb explosions
and the estimated financial loss to the Government of India was

2,750,000 rupees. These are figures which suggest not all-out rebellion but a thinly spread revolt which was restrained before it became too serious. Although it was not recognised at the time, the troubles also gave a taste of things to come as Britain began to shed her empire: while the politicians talked, it would be left to the police and military authorities to face the consequences of riot and civil unrest.

The troubles also took their toll on the British relationship with the Indian community. For a time Congress and its supporters were in bad odour and the Quit India slogan was thought to be the lowest form of sedition. Memories of the Mutiny of 1857 had been revived by some of the worst incidents in Bihar and Bengal and there was a general feeling that Indians were not wholly to be trusted. Few understood that the Indian leaders were more concerned with constitutional niceties and the need to gain independence than they were with winning the war. Whereas the British needs seemed to be clear-cut – win the war and then talk – the Congress attitude appeared to be treacherous and defeatist. Talk in the clubs and messes tended to dwell on the horrors of the recent revolt. Some were true, such as the brutal murder of two young RAF officers on the Punjab Mail between Calcutta and Delhi. Others were hearsay: the widely believed story of a subdivisional officer being burned alive in Aurangabad was found later to be a rumour. Men kept a watchful eye on the crowds in the bazaar, told their women and children to stay at home and suddenly became wary of Indian society.

Suspicions were also fuelled by fear of a Japanese victory. Burma had fallen and India itself was threatened by invasion. Although most people did not realise it at the time the Japanese had in fact overextended their lines of communication and were not in a position to tackle the mountain barrier between India and Burma during the monsoon season. Nevertheless, there was ample reason for despondency. Indian strategy had been worked out with the western defences in mind; now she had to face eastwards with limited resources. Recruiting was not a problem but the armed forces in India were starved of the arms, munitions, aircraft and ships needed to take the war into Burma. Men, too, had to be trained to fight in the jungle and it was obvious that a great deal of time and patience would have to be expended before the Japanese could be driven from Burma.

American air support was an essential pre-condition but that was dependent on taking the war into North Burma in order to keep China in the war by maintaining the overland supply routes. Churchill agreed to that strategy because he believed that Britain should be seen to recover lost territories by her own military power. Meanwhile, there was a widely held fear that Japan would take advantage of Britain's overstretched resources by threatening shipping in the Bay of Bengal and the eastern Indian Ocean prior to a general invasion. This was the dream of Lieutenant-General Renya Mutaguchi, who saw the possibility of wresting India from the British and bringing down the last vestige of British imperial power in the Far East. Several convoys were in fact attacked and sunk by Japanese warships and aircraft along the Coromandel coast and the British were powerless to retaliate. An air raid on Ceylon had left most of the RAF's planes unserviceable and the Indian air defences were weak and old-fashioned.

The worst scare of this period of the war was the so-called 'flap' when an Indian Air Force Wapiti bi-plane commanded by Squadron Leader David Small sighted a Japanese battle-fleet consisting of a battleship, two carriers, a cruiser, two destroyers and a number of transports steaming towards Madras. Douglas Dickins, a young RAF flying officer, arrived in Vizagapatam – the base which Small commanded – some months later and found that the incident had passed into local folklore.

> Climbing to 8,000 feet, the Wapiti crew shadowed this force for an hour. Below them they saw two Japanese Navy Zeroes flying towards the coast. Had the Japs spotted them, it would have been all over for the Wapiti. But for some reason they were not seen. Normally they would have radioed back to base, but their radio was not working, so they flew low over Andhra University in Waltair, which was Army Headquarters, and dropped a message.
>
> The same crew took off again to check on the latest position, and finally after dark for the third time, determined to have a shot at dropping their two bombs on the enemy. It was indeed a case of David versus Goliath. Perhaps fortunately for this David, they could not find the Japanese fleet and landed at midnight after a total of fifteen flying hours since dawn.

The Westland Wapiti, a large and rugged all-metal bi-plane, was heavy to fly but it was considered to be a reliable machine by the pilots who flew it on anti-terrorist missions in the North-West

Frontier Province throughout the 1930s. As a coastal reconnaissance aircraft, however, it was out of its class. It might have acquitted itself well against the small-arms fire of the Mahsuds and others on the frontier but it was a relic of the First World War and no match for a modern high-speed fighter like the Zero. Small and his Indian pilot must have been aware of the dangers they were facing in attempting to engage the superior Japanese forces and their heroism was representative of the spirit of self-sacrifice that pervaded the British Far East forces in 1942. (Typical of that behaviour, too, was the professionalism and courage shown by three Indian Army battalions – 1st/11th Sikhs, 4th/12th Frontier Force Regiment and 2nd/13th Frontier Rifles – in covering the retreat of the 17th Division out of Burma in May 1942.)

As it was, the Japanese fleet had not been steaming west as Small had originally thought, but northwards into the Bay of Bengal. The Southern Army headquarters was not to know that and the aerial message caused an immediate panic, or 'flap'. Reinforcements were rushed into the area and after Madras and Vizagapatam were bombed plans were laid for the provincial government's departments to be moved inland. Suddenly the war had come to the Indian homeland and in Madras police officers like John Harrison were ordered to co-ordinate the local fire and ambulance brigades into a makeshift air-raid precaution service. Although their task would be to save lives during Japanese bombing raids, they also had to lay plans to withdraw should the invasion ever take place.

> I was also told that I should take with me as much cash as I needed, and visited the office of the Financial Secretary and the Accountant General to obtain a draft for some colossal sum. However, on presenting it at the Treasury, someone seemed to have had second thoughts; I was relieved of the draft and never got my hands on the cash. Another duty imposed on me, should evacuation take place, was to visit the Madras Broadcasting Station next door to my office and hit with a sledgehammer some vital part of the equipment. I was again disappointed and never had this thrilling experience.

Because the Japanese raids were so sudden and terrifying they caused more panic and confusion than actual damage. To Indian nationalists they also provided further proof of Britain's inability

to halt the Japanese advance and the impotence of British air and
naval forces to prevent attacks on the Indian mainland. In
Vizagapatam a population of 75,000 was whittled down temporarily by two-thirds and the municipal power station would have
been shut down but for the single-handed efforts of its European
supervisor, V.E. Lazurus. In Madras, as Harrison discovered,
there were also those Indians who were prepared to take advantage of the situation.

> Slightly less amusing was a call to a cotton mill where rioters were
> setting property on fire. On reaching the gates we were met by a
> hail of road metal, which always seemed conveniently handy at
> times of civil commotion; our driver was knocked out and the fire
> appliance ran into a wall and was later burned out. We all received
> a battering, my topi was damaged beyond repair, but luckily we
> were rescued by the police who were already in the mill.

There is also a strong possibility that Japanese agents in Madras
knew about the raids in advance and were able to use that
information to whip up the inhabitants' fears in the cities along
the coast. As evidence of their operations, Douglas Dickins
points to the fact that a large proportion of the people of
Vizagapatam evacuated the city before the first bombs fell.

Dickins was fairly typical of a new breed of European who had
begun to arrive in droves during the Second World War. His
father had served in the Indian Army but he himself had no direct
experience of the country, other than his childhood memories
and had been posted there after gaining a commission in the
RAF. Left of centre politically, like so many of his generation, he
believed that India would eventually be given self-government
and thought that the offers brought by the first Cripps mission of
1942 were evidence of Britain's good faith.

When he arrived in India his first posting was to Bangalore.
There, the first surprise was the conspicuous consumption of
luxury goods enjoyed by the local white population – a stark
contrast to the privations of wartime Britain. Race meetings were
still held, food was free from rationing and the officers' mess was
situated in a comfortable hotel where five-course dinners were
served, but at a price – 7s 6d, whereas Dickins's daily pay was
only 9s 10d. There was, too, an air of enforced gaiety which
typified much social life in India during the Second World War,
an attempt perhaps to cram as much experience into as short a

time as possible. This was particularly true of his next posting to David Small's coastal defence flight at Vizagapatam at the beginning of 1943. The fear of war had broken down social and racial barriers in a way that would have been impossible ten years earlier.

When work was not too busy we would try to fit in a Saturday visit to Vizag's seaside neighbour, Waltair, for a bathe on the sandy beach or a dance at the club. This was open to officers only but had no colour bar. The local rajah there had a bungalow which was taken over as a residence for WAC (I) officers; many of these girls were very attractive, especially the Anglo-Indians. These attractions, though, had to be weighed against the purgatory of dust and bumps in a fifteen-hundredweight truck for the journey there and back.

I was introduced to a Parsee girl, Miss Chinoy, who invited me to dinner and we made up a foursome with an Indian major and a lady doctor, Miss Naidu, for the club dance. This was almost my first contact with cultured and well-to-do Indians in their own country. Miss Chinoy had been to England where she had studied music and learned to pilot her own plane; she was a remarkable, if untypical, example of young India.

At midnight we moved on to the Railway Institute where there was a gala dance night. This was life with the lid off. Dinner jackets, drinks and demonstrations of dazzling dancing. The Indian railways were the almost exclusive province of the Anglo-Indian community who emphasised their Anglo side, hence dinner jackets were *de rigueur* – strange symbol of the white race! Does it really uplift morale . . .? In Waltair institute it was plainly sustaining the *amour propre* of those earnest youths performing intricate steps with coffee-coloured beauties in pink evening frocks. There is no colour less flattering to an Anglo-Indian than pink and none, alas, more popular.

For the young British serviceman in India during the war, nights like that could be an exhilarating experience and a far cry from the middle-aged stuffiness of the whites-only clubs which demanded more restrained standards of behaviour. During the war most European clubs made special arrangements to allow British officers temporary membership but that arrangement soon presented some of the snootier outfits with a problem. Many officers had been awarded wartime emergency commissions and, thanks to the introduction of new methods of selection, they came from a variety of social backgrounds. Because meritocratic criteria were uppermost in the War Office Selection Boards, class or education did not always count for everything and there was a new feeling in the British armed forces that the officer corps was no longer a snobbish élite. It might have suited the mood of the times but that egalitarian line was not welcomed by every club committee in India who put obstacles in the way of admitting 'officers and temporary gentlemen'. The most common way of fending off unwelcome visitors was to continue the practice of admitting all officers but then to deny them the usual credit facilities or restrict their use of the clubs' facilities. By holding on to the old order the committees no doubt thought that they were maintaining standards: to the impressionable young British officers, their fastidiousness was only a reminder of the hidebound nature of some sections of British society in India.

Similar constraints were often visited on the RAF who were usually outnumbered by army personnel, especially at the beginning of the war. 'There wasn't much love lost between the two Services in those days, though it varied a lot,' recalls Group Captain Clifford Stephenson. 'They tended to regard the Air Force very much an upstart Johnnie-come-lately arrangement. It was understandable, perhaps; some of the old-established Indian Army regiments were almost family affairs.' Stephenson had spent six months as a pilot with 31 Squadron RAF in Lahore before the war and the nature of the relationship between the two services was brought home to him during a routine visit to the mess of the 3rd/11th Sikh Regiment at Drosh in Chitral.

> The CO, after greeting me, handed me over to a very young officer telling him to look after me. Over the mess fireplace was the regimental coat-of-arms, inscribed '11th (Rattray's) Sikhs'. 'Didn't the Colonel call *you* Rattray?' I asked the young officer and pointing to the coat-of-arms. 'Yes,' he replied quite naturally, 'my grandfather!'

31 Squadron was one of six RAF squadrons which had been based in India during the 1930s and they had spent much of their time in the North-West Frontier Province flying Wapitis on army co-operation duties in police actions against the local tribesmen. Their personnel changed every four years and like the men of the

regular British regiments stationed in India they tended to have little direct contact with the local population. The Second World War changed attitudes towards air power when the Indian Air Force (founded in 1933) started to expand from its single regular squadron equipped with Lysanders into a force to be reckoned with. In order to release the regular RAF squadrons for front-line duties Air HQ India initially raised five volunteer reserve Indian squadrons (IAFVR) for coastal defence duties. Most of their personnel were weekend flyers, British businessmen who knew all about flying but who were too old for regular RAF duties. The squadrons, and later their regular counterparts, also contained a growing number of young Indian pilots like Hem Chaudhuri and Drobendra Bhanjdeo, who was killed in 1942 when his Hudson failed to return from a sweep of the Bay of Bengal. They were all trained at Number 1 Flying Training School at Risalpur in the North-West Frontier Province.

Amongst their number was Wilfrid Russell, the Bombay businessman who had been on home leave in 1939. After a short spell with the Ministry of Information in London he returned to India, was commissioned in the IAFVR and then drove the fifteen hundred miles from Bombay to Risalpur. The journey continued a learning process which had begun earlier because it taught him something about the vastness of India and the variety of its different cultures. It was, as he admitted later, the best way to go to war. At Risalpur there was another lesson to be learned. The regular RAF training officers doubted if the Indian volunteers had the ability to make the grade as aircrew. As Russell remembered, their attitude was a mistake: these young pilots were as committed and as professional as their colleagues in the army.

> The leaders among the Indians were not only politically conscious; they were going to fight for their India, not ours – they were aggressive and skilful above the British average.

Throughout the war against the Japanese in Burma Indian Air Force officers and men fought alongside their British comrades with equal determination and courage. One officer, Squadron Leader Mehar Singh from Lyalpur, won the first Indian DFC for landing his Tiger Moth in a jungle clearing to rescue a brother officer, others flew Dakotas over the notorious 'Hump' route into China or flew missions in support of the British defensive position in the Arakan 'Box' in February 1944, and Indian pilots flying Vultee Vengeance aircraft soon became masters of the art of dive-bombing. But there was a conundrum in their war. Hard-line nationalists who supported Congress regarded them as mercenaries, unwitting tools of imperialist aggression; yet those same critics were also irritated if the Indian contribution to the war effort was ignored. Later in the war, while serving with Wavell's inter-service public relations directorate, Russell accompanied Field Marshal Sir Claude Auchinleck, Commander-in-Chief, India, to a preview of the film *Desert Victory* just to make sure that the exploits of the 4th Indian Division had been given full recognition. During the showing of the documentary Auchinleck's worst fears were realised and he had to insist that the final version include more shots of Indian troops in action. This was done at the expense of the New Zealand forces, but then the Field Marshal was an Indian Army man.

Like Douglas Dickins, Russell was struck both by the professionalism and loyalty of the Indian personnel and by the pride they took in their country. Politics might have been barred in the mess but it was plain to him that the pilots and ground crew were fighting the war for India first and Britain second. Like many of the Irishmen who fought in Britain's forces during the Great War they had volunteered in order to give their country an independent voice once the war was over. They had also come into contact with a new and different British service personnel and this, too, had helped them to revise their opinion about the ruling race. Whereas Russell and his class had been charmed by the old-time regulars and 'erks' of 27 and 31 Squadrons with their memories of the frontier and characters like Aircraftman Shaw, the newer recruits were rather different. They had been called up for war service and were prepared to get the job done, but thereafter they only wanted to get home. India was not a land of memory and enchantment but in the eastern states where most of them were stationed it was a country with a vile climate and a hostile environment. Many of them, when asked about Indian independence, would reply that the Indians were welcome to their country. Others, like Flight Sergeant Mike Hirst of 31 Squadron, were more disgusted by the attitudes of those British civilians who still regarded the British Other Rank as an object beneath contempt.

When I joined 31 in 1944 I met many people who had been there for four years or more – 'forgotten' indeed, living rough, almost native and very basic in their isolation, lack of facilities and generally shunned by the white people in India if not of commissioned rank. Believe me, I was a Flight Sergeant, so treated by an aunt's relatives, and the attitude was prevalent particularly in Calcutta.

Not only were these young men often indifferent to the glorious heritage of the raj but many were also friendly to the idea that India should be independent. Kushwant Singh remembered that those wartime commissioned officers were a different breed from the types he had encountered before: instead of spending evenings in the club they would try to meet Indians on equal terms and to discover as much as they could about the customs, languages and culture. 'I remember boys who had been in college with me in England almost going out of their way to be with Indians. Some even attended political meetings, much to the disgust of the pukka sahibs.' To Singh and his friends this new liberalism suggested a change of thinking, a new belief that Britain should get out of India once the war was over. If we are fighting for the rights of nations to be free, argued his British college friends, then that same privilege should be accorded to India. D.K. Palit also found that the wartime commissioned officers brought a breath of fresh air into messes where politics had once been taboo.

Thousands of young Englishmen came out who didn't give a damn what you were. They were friendly and mingled with Indian society if they could. I've seen them eat with their fingers, wear Indian clothes, learn Hindi and something about our music. Before that I don't think I'd known a single British officer who could understand the difference between a *raga* and a pop song.

Another factor in changing Indian attitudes was the presence of the American airmen of the 10th US Air Force who served with 3rd Tactical Air Force on the Burma front. Whenever the RAF or IAF lads came into contact with them they were astonished at the prodigality of equipment and luxury items which the Americans took to war with them. Within hours of setting up camp they had refrigerators and ice-cream machines working, their stores were well stocked and they had vast reserves of equipment and spare parts – all in stark contrast to the hard-pressed British squadrons. The lesson was not lost on the Indians either: the Americans seemed to be better equipped and better off than their British allies. Not only that, but most of them were in favour of Indian independence and had no time for imperial trappings. A British airman in the forward base at Hathazari in Assam was astonished to hear an American pilot telling his Indian ground crew that they had to think in terms of Bunker Hill if they wanted to be free of the British.

Higher up the command level senior American officers also entertained suspicions that the war against the Japanese in Burma was a British imperial campaign and that the British were only using them, the American armed forces, to advance their colonial interests. Their presence in North Burma and Assam, they argued, was for the purpose of bolstering China in her struggle with the Japanese and they were opposed to the liberation of Burma if it was only going to be a stepping stone for Britain to regain her colonial empire in the east. They took a high-principled view of their duties and it was not until the appointment of Admiral Lord Louis Mountbatten as Supreme Commander, or Supremo, of the Allied forces that common ground was reached and the more obvious inter-Allied squabbles settled, but even then many Americans continued to joke, half seriously, that Mountbatten's command, SEAC, was an acronym for Save England's Asian Colonies.

Mountbatten's arrival as Supremo was one of the turning points in the fortunes of war against the Japanese. Not only did he bring a fresh outlook to the strategic situation but from the very beginning he was determined to make a personal impact on the men he commanded. Russell was to fall quickly under his spell.

> The impression we all had was of a man who hated red tape and was determined that because something had never been done before was the best possible reason for doing it now. We could all feel the old fogies folding up their tents and fading into the mist. The infection of his enthusiasm and the magnetism of his personality even caught the most hard-boiled of the newspapermen for a while.

Once established, Mountbatten set up a new and successful command structure which would eventually win the war in Burma. With himself as Supremo he had four outstanding service chiefs in Somerville (Navy), Giffard (Army), Peirse (Air Forces) and Stilwell (Americans and Deputy Supremo). India Command under Auchinleck was made responsible for training as distinct from operations and to complete the team there was a new Viceroy in Wavell who had previously been Commander-in-Chief, India. The arrival of both Mountbatten and Wavell was destined to have a dramatic effect on the course of British Indian politics. Mountbatten's first step was to move his headquarters to Kandy in Ceylon, far from the social distractions of Delhi and Simla; he also insisted on the proper supply, maintenance and care of the armed forces under his command. Over two hundred fully operational airfields were constructed, roads and railways were upgraded and Indian industry was galvanised to construct aircraft, to manufacture weapons and vehicles and to turn out all the paraphernalia of war. The growth and expansion of these essential industries and services was to stand India in good stead in the first years of her existence – from the very outset Mountbatten had made an immediate impact on the future course of Indian history.

Wavell was a different matter. A professional soldier, he had had experience of high command in the Middle East and South-East Asia but by his own admission he had been destined 'to conduct withdrawals and mitigate defeats'. More to the point of his present appointment he was a quiet intellectual – he had written a scholarly biography of Allenby and had lectured on generalship at Cambridge – who seemed to possess all the right paper qualifications to be Viceroy in 1943. He believed in the concept of Indian independence and in private suffered profound embarrassment about Churchill's continuing obfuscation and the unseemly superficiality with which Indian matters were discussed in London. There is little doubt that Wavell genuinely wanted India to be given her freedom from British rule, yet he brought with him to the country one major drawback: Churchill. The British war leader neither trusted him nor did he have a high opinion of him as a soldier – only that summer he had publicly chastised the Field Marshal in front of Roosevelt for the failure of the 14th Indian Division during the Arakan offensive. From the very outset the new Viceroy was aware that not only would he have to deal with an Indian leadership which would regard him as a political adversary but he would also have to cope with enemies behind his back in London. 'I have discovered that the Cabinet is not honest in its expressed desire to make progress in India; and that very few of them have any foresight or moral courage,' he wrote in his diary on 8 October 1943 after proposing – fruitlessly – that he should enter into new negotiations with the Congress leaders.

Churchill, of course, hoped that Wavell would only hold the post fast while the war was in progress so that the day of independence could be pushed forward to some future date. Before the new Viceroy left for India Churchill told him that he had a low opinion of the Indian Army and then rubbed salt into the wound by claiming that, sooner or later, the day would dawn when its soldiers would turn their weapons against the British in order to win their independence. 'He has a curious complex about India,' mused Wavell, 'and is always loth to hear good of it, and apt to believe the worst.'

It has become fashionable in recent years for commentators to mock Wavell and his reign as Viceroy of India. He has been accused of being a defeatist and an unimaginative administrator whose efforts to get agreement between Nehru and Jinnah appear in retrospect to have been heavy-handed or fumbling; yet it was upon the foundation of his efforts that India was eventually to gain her independence. As the editor of his diaries, Sir Penderel Moon, has so adroitly pointed out, two fateful decisions were taken during Wavell's viceregality – the decision to quit India within eighteen months of the war's end and the reluctant adoption of the need for partition. John Christie, by then a Joint Private Secretary on the Viceroy's staff, was a Mountbatten man through and through, but even he admitted that Wavell was 'liked and trusted by all' – British or Indian. That was the way that most of his associates felt about the man who struggled so long and so hard to find a constitutional settlement under which Britain could transfer power to a united India.

Christie was also deeply involved in Wavell's first – and in some respects his finest – service to the people of India. Within days of his arrival in October Wavell was confronted by the aftermath of a disastrous famine which had hit the eastern states, particularly Bengal. India was no stranger to the phenomenon: famine had stalked through the country's history for centuries, bringing with it hardship and death on a large scale. Often it was created by adverse weather conditions such as storm or drought; pestilence was a further cause, man's avarice another, but in Bengal in 1943 the main reason was the war.

Bengal was largely dependent on the import of rice from Burma to make up the deficit of its own harvest but the Japanese had put a stop to all trading; and even in the unoccupied areas there had been a scorched-earth policy. The sudden disappearance of the supply meant that people began to hoard provisions and prices began to rise dramatically. Soon people were paying ridiculous sums of money for the available foodstuffs and they were well able to do so for the war had also brought prosperity to the businessmen and full employment to the peasantry. It was a classic inflationary spiral: money was freely available, food was not, and as a consequence prices rose and the commodity was quickly in short supply. To make matters worse racketeers began controlling the buying and selling of rice and flour, and the poor began to suffer. To this day no one knows the exact number of people who died as a result of the famine – the Government of India at the time estimated the figure to be in the region of one and a half million but it was probably a good deal higher.

The solution to the problem was to introduce rationing and to arrange for the distribution of foodstuffs from provinces with hefty surpluses, but Bengal had a weak administration throughout the period and too little was done too late. By the time Wavell arrived in India refugees had begun to move into Calcutta bringing with them death and disease; on 29 October he visited the worst affected areas and immediately ordered in the army to retrieve the situation.

I found things much as I had expected from what I had read and heard – widespread distress and suffering, not as gruesome as the Congress papers would make out, but grim enough to make official complacency surprising; I don't think anyone really knows the whole situation or what is going on in some of the outlying areas, but obviously we have to get to grips or it may get out of hand altogether. I saw all the Ministers yesterday evening, told them they must get the destitutes out of Calcutta into camps which should have been done long ago, got them to accept a Major-General and staff to help with the transport of supplies and the assistance of the Army generally. (*Diary*, 29 October 1943)

In Delhi Christie was put in charge of grain storage, working with
a Royal Engineers officer, Sir Clarence Bird. Their small department organised a system of controlled procurement and distribution, an efficient transport system was established and sound
storage sheds were built at strategic points where the much-
needed food could be distributed and rationed. As Christie
makes clear, though, it was not an easy task.

> Indians do not take easily to controls which are not a part of their
> own social obligations; and they are more particular about their
> food than most people, mainly on religious grounds. Hindu
> widows in some parts would sooner die than eat milled rice; for
> them it must be hand-pounded. Certain faddists would eat nothing
> but parboiled grain; others must have it polished. Barley excori-
> ated the stomachs of some; millet reduced the social status of
> others. All this complicated the difficulties of food supply.
> Storage was another problem. There were no grain silos, even at
> the ports. Most Indian village households store their grain in straw
> bins, or underground. In innumerable markets great and small,
> there were ramshackle sheds in which sacks of grain lay in
> disorderly heaps, and often they were stacked out of doors.
> Hundreds of thousands of tons of grain were lost every year from
> the depredations of rats, weevils and the damp.

In spite of the difficulties the famine was gradually brought under
control and Christie's next task was to work with the Department
of Agriculture to promote new methods of farming. Various ideas
were tried out – new implements and chemicals were introduced
and irrigation schemes constructed – but there were still age-old
prejudices to be overcome. Farmers allowed cattle and goats to
eat firewood and then burned manure as fuel, new methods might
be abhorrent to religious faith, and even if they were not, they
certainly added to the tax bill. Nevertheless, in spite of all those
drawbacks the Government of India had at least acted quickly
and efficiently to bring assistance to the people of Bengal.
'During the desperate months in which the utmost human effort
seemed only a drop in the ocean of what needed to be done,' said
Christie of his and his colleagues' efforts, 'these varied elements
were fused into an amalgam of skills and experience which was
able to accomplish much of lasting value in the ensuing years.'
 Wavell's intervention, then, was a much-needed initiative and
as men of the British and Indian armies transported food,

distributed it and put their backs into helping the starving and the dispossessed, Britain suddenly became popular again. They were also on the point of turning the tide in Burma, lending strength to Churchill's belief that India could be held for years to come, provided that Britain still had the will to exercise power.

Many Indian politicians in Bengal saw the events in a rather different light. True, the Government of India had come to their aid and, true, Wavell had acted decisively and quickly, but alert Indians could not fail to notice the low priority which had been granted in Britain to the famine. A debate in the House of Commons on Indian food supply had attracted less than 10 per cent of the total parliamentary membership; when questioned on the famine Amery had put it down to 'maldistribution'; Churchill and his Cabinet were more concerned with events in Italy where the Allies had gained a toe-hold in Calabria and Apulia prior to their sweep north; and in India Mountbatten was laying plans for the invasion of Burma and re-conquest of South-East Asia. Quite simply, the British could not spare too much time in 1943 to ponder the reasons for the Bengal famine or its long-term effects; it was enough that aid had been given to the survivors.

But for the itinerant Indian population who had made their way into Calcutta, 1943 was a time of torment and gross affliction. Hardly a day passed between May and October without some new horror story breaking in *The Statesman* or the *Hindustan Standard*. Sleeping beggars, too weak to move, were eaten alive by jackals, starving families sold their children into slavery for pittances, walking skeletons roamed the streets near the Sealdah Bridge and the Lower Circular Road, while relief agencies and hospitals, faced by impossible numbers of the sick and the destitute, were forced to give up the unequal struggle. Wavell might have complained about the exaggerated reporting in some sections of the press, but the truth was horrid enough for those who witnessed it.

Years later, Christie wondered 'how many people remember or have even heard of the Bengal famine of 1943'. It played no apparent part in the move towards Indian independence and as most of the nationalist politicians were imprisoned they could make little political capital out of it. (Gandhi, incarcerated in the comfort of the Aga Khan's summer palace at Poona, asked for permission to visit the worst-hit areas, but this was refused.) Most

British residents were too wrapped up in the war effort to take much notice of it, or if they did, they regarded it as part of the eternal Indian problem of intransigence, inefficiency and over-indulgence in religious scruples.* And yet, for all that the famine appeared to be an unwelcome and disturbing catastrophe, or simply part of the tide of war, it was not insignificant in forming the future of Anglo-Indian politics.

To the British it was another colonial duty, part of their age-old responsibility to the people of India; in other words, it was a mess that had to be cleared up by the calm efficiency of central government. At the beginning of the famine, Bengal's Muslim-League-dominated Provincial Government had made light of the problems and their Food Minister, H.S. Suhrawaddy, had blandly told the outside world that starvation did not exist within Bengal and that help was not required. His incompetence and the lackadaisical attitude of his Prime Minister, Fazlul Huq, exacer-bated the problem and following a brief gubernatorial interven-tion by the sick and dying Governor of Bengal, Sir John Herbert, it was left to a watchful Viceroy and his zealous cohorts in the ICS to bring relief to the beleaguered area. Within weeks of Wavell's decision the ICS and army seemed to have taken control of the situation and the District Officers were able to report that relationships between the British and the Bengalis had never been better. It had all been done in the best traditions of British imperial rule.

For many Indians the famine and its aftermath was but another element in the demolition of Britain's continuing commitment to govern India. Even the most moderate politician could not fail to notice that the famine had been caused by economic factors which could have been controlled and that an early and massive injection of men and money could have done much to relieve the widespread suffering. Moreover, 'at home', seven thousand miles away, the disaster in Bengal was hidden beneath other matters by a government which had more pressing priorities and which was looking forward to peacetime planning. In its own way, then, the famine in Bengal added its weight to a growing belief that Britain would have to quit India, and quit soon.

*At the height of the famine my father ordered his men, mainly Madrassis, to give their rations to the starving Bengalis lining the platforms of the stations through which his troop-train passed. The offer was invariably refused.

Chapter Five

Tryst with Destiny

In his Christmas Day broadcast at the end of 1945, King George VI spoke to the young of his empire about the spirit of sacrifice which had brought about the destruction of their enemies.

> 'You have known the world only as a world of strife and fear,' he told them. 'Bring now all that fine spirit to make it one of joyous adventure, a home where men and women can live in mutual trust and walk together as friends. Do not judge life by what you have seen of it in the grimness and waste of war, nor yet by the confusion of the first years of peace. Have faith in life at its best and bring it your courage, your hopes and your sense of humour.'

He concluded the broadcast with an exhortation which was shared by millions of his subjects: 'Let us face the future with hope.'

After six years of war the people of Britain had emerged weary, battered and drained, but in the midst of the confusion and contradictory expectations of peace, their future was, indeed, not without hope. Germany had been decisively defeated in May, Japan in September following the attacks with atomic bombs on Hiroshima and Nagasaki; slowly but surely – too slowly, as we shall see, for some – the great imperial forces were being disbanded and men and women were looking forward to the brave new world of peace. Henceforth there would be a new style of government in Britain, too, for Labour had won a landslide general election victory, largely with the help of a huge forces' vote, and the machinery was being set in motion for the creation of the post-war welfare state. It had been a long slog and the people of Britain were fed up with war. The armed forces, too, were browned off to a man and wanted to get back to ordinary peacetime life. As they had been told they were fighting for freedom, they now wanted it for themselves and their families.

Above all, they wanted to get home and pick up the strands of life that had been left behind in the world of the 1930s. A fresh start was wanted and for the most part that meant carving out a life in the familiar places of home rather than in the distant corners of empire. Ahead, too, lay the much-heralded benefits of Labour's post-war reconstruction: the nationalisation of the major industries and the radical improvements to education, the health, financial and social services. There might have been continuing rationing and food shortages; economic recession and financial crisis lay ahead on the horizon, the major cities had suffered damage from enemy action and industry was still geared to wartime production, but there was no escaping the general air of optimism which brought 1945 to an end, fully justifying the King's hopes.

For the most part, too, people wanted to stay at home and forget all about imperial adventuring. Later in life, men who had spent time with the forces in India might have waxed sentimental about the days of their service to the British Raj, but at the time few warmed to Churchill's imperial rhetoric. At the first opportunity they had ousted him from office and voted for Attlee's vision of a world based on socialist principles in which the very idea of empire was anathema. Even before the election results were announced Churchill must have been aware that all was not going well for his party or for his chances of holding on to the British leadership. On the very day that the votes were being finally counted he was in Berlin for the Potsdam talks in the company of his political rival. A review of the British troops had been arranged in the Tiergarten and when the two men drove up to the reviewing platform the men broke out into loud cheers. Believing the acclaim to be for him Churchill turned to them with his traditional V-for-victory sign; it was only then that he realised that they were chanting Attlee's name. At seven o'clock that same day Churchill had tendered his resignation to the King in the wake of Attlee's victory at the polls.

In the midst of the expectation there was no little pride and satisfaction, too. Britain had stood firm against a vicious enemy, for two of the six wartime years she had weathered the storm alone and had emerged victorious with her allies of the United

Nations. Churchill had called it a sublime moment and there was good reason for the nation's euphoria. Britain had remained true to herself and to her belief in the benefits of civilisation, fascism had been put down and there was every prospect that the world would live up to Zec's famous cartoon which appeared in the *Daily Mirror* – a war-torn soldier emerges from a tangle of wrecked houses holding the laurels of victory and peace in Europe. 'Here you are,' he is saying, 'don't lose it again.' With the armed forces of the empire at their most magnificent in power and strength that peace seemed to be secure; and with the atlas as red as it had ever been before, from the Mediterranean to the Pacific, British influence still seemed to be at its apogee.

Yet it was mainly illusion. The spirit of global pre-eminence might have lived on in the hearts of the politicians and the diplomats but in reality it was a hollow boast. The war in Europe had been won mainly by the Russians and the Americans, Japan had been defeated in the Pacific by American forces and in most of the operations – bar Italy, North Africa and Burma – Britain had been the junior partner. Moreover, the Americans now held the whip hand financially and politically. They could see no reason why the benefits of their special relationship with Britain should shore up the empire and they were determined to do away with the pre-war imperial tariff systems. This they could well afford to do, for they had emerged from the war as the world's greatest exporter, often backed up by the inducement of generous loans to the purchaser. They also exported a certain type of glamour which hundreds of thousands of cinema-goers recognised immediately, an amalgam of Hollywood, Coca-Cola, chewing gum, be-bop and bourbon. In war-torn Europe it was an irresistible combination and its opulence had more than a passing appeal in countries like India where the US servicemen enjoyed better facilities, superior conditions and uniforms and a more relaxed discipline. This could hardly be missed by their British colleagues and the disparity often caused resentment. When Tom Berry, a young student of architecture from Glasgow, was called up in 1945 he underwent his three months' basic training and was posted immediately to an RAF unit in India where he found the country to be a far cry from the Kipling stories he had enjoyed as a boy. After an uncomfortable flight out in the bomb-bay of a converted Liberator he arrived at the transit camp at RAF Mauripur near Karachi.

The transit billets are great tin sheds [he wrote in his diary] with three tier bunks made up of metal framing with canvas mattress sheets strung between the members. The bunks are pretty high but I am fortunate to have a bottom one. The only snag is that people are climbing over the top of you to get to the upper levels. The place is teeming with bods part Eastbound for indefinite spells like myself and part Blighty bound. Old Sweats from the Burmese jungle. Some of these guys must have slogged the monsoon trail to Mandalay along with Jack [his brother] back home. I spoke to one army bod with a skin like old leather. When I told him I had just arrived yesterday he said, 'I've been out here three and a half bloody years.' How long for me? The old cries of 'Get some in' and 'Get your number dry' have changed now to 'Get your knees brown, mate.'

The old hands Blighty-bound were men who were tired of living where they did not want to be – out East in uncongenial surroundings which were noticeably different from the officers' quarters and the USAF bases near by, with their swimming pools, refrigerators and air conditioning. They had voted in Attlee largely because his party had promised them a new beginning: if one of the planks in his platform was the granting of independence to India, then so be it. If that meant scuttling out of India quickly and precipitately then that, too, might be no bad thing.

The feeling was not just confined to the disgruntled rank and file. Inder Malhotra, then a young student in the Punjab, had been surprised to see British Army officers discussing politics with his professors and talking about such forbidden subjects as Indian politics or the Soviet Union. Many of them had taken the trouble, too, to learn Hindi or Urdu or had interested themselves in Indian culture. To Malhotra and his fellow students they were a different breed from the pukka sahibs of yore and he was not surprised to find that they held different views about the war which had just been fought. To a man they seemed to be Labour supporters and admirers of the Soviet Union and the part it had played in beating Germany and they voiced their disquiet about the use of atom bombs against Japan. Malhotra had first heard about Hiroshima and Nagasaki when a newsboy cycled through the streets with copies of the *Tribune*, shouting, 'A British Tommy has fallen on Japan!' It was only later that he discovered the real nature of this secret military weapon and the damage it had inflicted.

The Labour general election victory had also given fresh hope to the young people of India. Kushwant Singh found himself in a railcar between Simla and Kalka on the night that the news was announced. There had been a breakdown further down the line and in the halted railcar there was a certain amount of tension because it was on that stretch of track that dacoits had murdered six British officers a year or two earlier.

> We sat there waiting for relief to come on this moonlit night in a pine forest and a radio was on. The news that the British Labour Party had won the election came. There were only two Indians and we didn't know each other – the rest were all British. We both got up and started dancing and embraced each other. These poor British sahibs were looking on absolutely disgusted. They knew why we were celebrating – this meant that Britain would relinquish power in India soon.

At a grass-roots level all over India there was a feeling that although Britain had won the war it had lost its military and political authority and that with Labour in power independence suddenly seemed to be within grasp. A.K. Damodaran, the student who had been jailed in 1942, was back at his studies and he remembers that the announcement of Attlee's victory was met with 'absolute delight. The Labour Party was very popular then: at the political level there was now a preparedness for change.'

Within weeks of the war ending in Europe Wavell had been anxious to reopen the Cripps negotiations and to talk to the Indian leadership from a position of strength. Following consultations in London he returned to India, ordered the release of all the Congress leaders and working committees and invited the leading lights to join his Executive Council. Their duties would be to help conduct the war against Japan and to lay plans for the formation of a constituent assembly in India. The conference failed, as did other moves instigated by Wavell, not because of any overt hostility to the British but because the leaders, Congress and Muslim League, were too concerned with bolstering their own political positions.

During the war Cripps had made a substantial offer when he proposed that India should be granted dominion status at the cessation of hostilities, with the chance to go for full independence later. Ironically, that offer, made by British politicians at a low ebb in the war, became the blueprint for the eventual handover of power.

When Attlee ordered an immediate general election in India for the winter of that year it became obvious that the Government of India would have to rely on the newly elected politicians at national and provincial level to co-operate with that transfer of power. It was not a case of 'if' that would happen but 'when', and as Wavell shrewdly pointed out the success of the exercise would have to depend on the support of politicians who were not only antipathetic to each other but also to continuing British rule.

> I feel that it is better to be honest and to say that we are going to hand over power; that it is right that we should do so and leave Indians to govern themselves; that while Congress is not a body one would have chosen as the representatives of the great mass of the Indian people, it is the body that the Indian people have chosen for themselves and we have to do business with the men of their choice. (*Diary*, 12 August 1946)

Unfortunately for Wavell, who gamely attempted to bring together the different Indian political factions, first in 1945 and then again the following year in his interim government, Jinnah and the Congress Party were now poles apart. Hindu Congress regarded itself as the rightful heir to British rule; while the Muslim League, strengthened by its wartime pre-eminence in political affairs, had emerged as an obstinate proponent of an Islamic homeland, namely Pakistan. (Under Jinnah's guidance the League had become the rallying point for the majority of All-India Muslim voters and by 1946 it had considerable political influence both at grass-roots and national levels.) There was also growing concern amongst the Sikhs about the possibility of becoming a minority in an all-Muslim Punjab; the various minorities clamoured to be heard, too, and then there was the continuing difficulty of negotiating with the princely states, many of whose rulers believed that Britain's promise of independence would evaporate with the war's end and an Allied victory. The Indian general election only served to solidify the stalemate. Predictably, the Congress Party swept the board in the Hindu states while the Muslim League emerged as the mouthpiece of Muslim India, winning the majority of the seats reserved for them.

In an attempt to reach agreement on independence for a united India – if that were possible – Cripps was again dispatched to India, but his latest mission met with little success. Basically the British negotiators – Cripps was accompanied by Lord Pethick-Lawrence and A.V. Alexander – offered India a three-tiered union or federal structure which on paper at least appeared to give Congress and the Muslim League the greater part of their demands. The union envisaged the provincial governments on one level, followed by provincial groupings with a union at the centre which would deal with All-India matters. At the same time both parties were invited to form an interim government based on an expanded Viceroy's Executive Council. Predictably, neither party was in any hurry to move towards agreement and although the plan was accepted with some reservations it failed to work in practice. Yet another initiative had failed, not because the parties were hostile to Attlee's government but because they were opposed to each other. Just as predictably perhaps, conservatives in the British community in India felt that neither the government in faraway London nor its mission in Delhi really understood the problem of India. Sheila Coldwell, the wife of a successful Calcutta businessman, speaks for many with her belief that British post-war policies towards India were without aim or purpose.

> The British in charge didn't understand what was likely to happen. They didn't really know India and people like Attlee and Cripps had no idea about what was going to happen as a result of their talks. I think that they believed that it was all going to be done peacefully. Only Wavell really knew what the outcome would be – but, of course, he *knew* India.

This was a commonly held view and although it was unfair – both Attlee and Cripps had a thorough grounding in Indian politics – it did carry a grain of truth. Britain was not prepared to make a quixotic last stand to keep India within the empire: political opinion at home, a fast-deteriorating financial situation and adverse international opinion had seen to that, but, clearly too, her administrators and politicians had lost the imperial touch. India was fast becoming ungovernable and gone were the days when a decree from Delhi or the tact and good sense of the District Officer could solve every communal problem. In an oblique way, the intellectually gifted Wavell, by borrowing Lewis Carroll's 'Jabberwocky', made his own comment on the post-war situation:

> Twas grillig; and the Congreelites
> Did harge and shobble in the swope,
> All jinsy were the Pakistanites,
> And the spruft Sikhs outscrope.

Another reason for London's pressing desire to get the British out of India promptly was the continuing political pressure from America which had already built up a head of steam during the war. Although Roosevelt had not pushed Churchill overhard on the matter of Indian self-rule, he had made it clear that the US forces in India should not be used as agents of British imperialism and that after the war he expected British troops to be removed from their garrisons in the subcontinent. The financial crisis of the post-war years put Britain further into American debt and the negotiation of a £3,750 million loan imposed restrictions on the British economy, including the removal of imperial trade preferences. This need to placate adverse, or even hostile, American opinion was a constant theme in governmental circles in India; some leaders, like the Australian Governor of Bengal, R.G. Casey, believed that good Anglo-American relations were of paramount importance in the post-war years and that the British would be mad to squander them.

> If we are obliged to remain in India [he minuted on 17 August 1944] ill-disposed Americans will use this as a very heavy stick to beat us with – and this will poison Anglo-American relations – which is the most important matter in prospect in the post-war world. Personally, I would rather get out of India tomorrow than risk the damage to Anglo-American relations that would inevitably be entailed by any long drawn out negotiations for a settlement of the Indian problem.

Gradually a pattern was beginning to emerge, one that might not have been discernible to the Indian in his village or to the British planter in his club, but one that was clear enough to the politician and the administrator. There was no doubt that Britain wanted to leave but the stumbling block remained the discovery of a method that would suit all parties. It was all a bit of a muddle, really, just as Wavell had said. Men like Tom Berry were still being sent out to replace the demobbed war servicemen, British businessmen like Wilfrid Russell were still looking forward to a profitable future, the Indian Army still hoped to retain 50 per cent of its British officers and plans were afoot for

1. According to Churchill, he was 'a seditious Middle Temple lawyer posing as a fakir'. Gandhi faces the cameras during his visit to London, 1931.

2. The results of non-violence. Stones and rubbish litter the streets of Bombay after an anti-British riot in 1932.

3. He declared war without consulting the Indian leaders. Lord Linlithgow, Viceroy of India, 1936–1943.

5. He understood India but was misunderstc by his political masters in London. Field Marshal Lord Wavell, Viceroy of India, 1943–1947, with the Maharajah of Patiala

4. The Old Guard. Field Marshal Lord Wavell inspects troops of the Indian Army. Behind him stands Field Marshal Sir Claude Auchinleck.

6. A De Haviland DH86 airliner was converted to carry two 250lb bombs, and was stationed at Cochin when the Japanese threatened India in 1942.

7. Comrades-in-arms. Subhas Chandra Bose with new-found Japanese friends, 1944.

8. Dr Mohammed Ali Jinnah presses the claims of an independent Pakistan in Delhi. 'We shall not submit to any scheme of government prepared without our consent.'

9. A last attempt to settle differences. Indian leaders arrive in London to meet Clement Attlee, December 1945. Lord Wavell, the Viceroy, stands beside Jinnah, Baldev Singh and Lord Pethwick-Lawrence.

10. Lord Wavell greets the second Cripps Mission in March
1946. Standing left to right are A.V. Alexander, Lord
Pethwick-Lawrence, Wavell and Sir Stafford Cripps.

11. So near yet so far apart. Jawaharlal Nehru
and Dr Mohammed Ali Jinnah.

12. The aftermath of Calcutta's 'Day of Action', 15 August 1946.
It will never be known how many people were killed.

13. The best of friends. Nehru confides in Mountbatten, 1947.

14. Independence Day, Bombay, 15 August 1947. The Governor-General,
Sir John Colville, and the Chief Minister, B.G. Kher, take the salute.

15. Jubilant crowds break cordons to shake hands with Lord and Lady Mountbatten
on India's first day of independence.

16. The last parade. John Platt, commanding the Somerset Light Infantry, accepts a silver Gateway of India from General Bateman.

17. 'Should auld acquaintance be forgot . . .' The Colour Party of the Somerset Light Infantry passes through the Gateway of India, 28 February 1948.

recommencing the recruitment of British ICS officers. Many people in India were blissfully unaware of the events that had been set in train. In the epilogue to the diary he kept between 1946 and 1948 Tom Berry admitted, 'I never saw a drop of blood spilt or heard a shot fired in anger during my stay in India. I was surrounded by monumental political changes and sickening slaughter, none of which touched my life.'

Winifred Bailey, an Edinburgh medical graduate, arrived in Poona in 1946 to work as a medical missionary. Although she was 'fully aware' that India was going to get independence, and welcomed it, the actual political facts remained blurred. 'Strangely, one knew relatively little about it which, looking back on it, appals me. I was in Poona which was a long way from the seat of government and we didn't know all that much about politics. But I personally felt that it [independence] was long overdue and was happy about it.'

Even those nearer the seat of government could not always understand what was happening behind the closed doors of the Viceroy's House in Delhi or Viceregal Lodge in the hot-season retreat of Simla. Elizabeth Catto was in Simla in 1945 – her husband, a Calcutta businessman with Yule Catto, was a wartime staff officer – and she felt that the release of the Congress politicians and their subsequent talks with Wavell were unremarkable at the time and had to be related to more pressing problems in the rest of the world. 'Far worse things were happening elsewhere, in Britain and in Europe. People were still in prisoner-of-war camps under the Japanese in the Far East. We felt relatively protected and safe in India.' When Nehru and his colleagues arrived in Simla, though, they stayed in the house opposite, and then it seemed natural enough to treat them as celebrities.

> I was in the house with my mother, and my half-brothers went over to get Nehru's autograph. They were frightfully chuffed when he agreed; the thing was, you see, that the Indians themselves never bore any personal grudges against the British.

Pleased they might have been, but Elizabeth Catto admits that at the time she failed to recognise that independence was going to come so quickly. Like many other people who had long regarded India as their second home, she could not really believe – or chose not to believe – that Britain would surrender her authority in India so soon after the conclusion of the war. Three events, all of which were related and all of which occurred around the time of the Cripps Mission, changed that and made it clear that Britain's days in India would have to be numbered if further bloodshed were to be avoided: the trial of three INA officers in Delhi, the Royal Indian Navy mutinies in Bombay and Karachi and the Muslim Day of Action in Calcutta which resulted in the massacre of thousands of Hindu innocents.

During the Second World War the manpower of the Indian Army had expanded dramatically to include recruits who did not come from the officially recognised 'martial races' – Sikhs, Marathas, Dogras, Garwhalis and so on. This did not make it less efficient as a fighting force; far from it, for the new men brought to the army new specialist skills in transport, engineering and ordnance, but it did threaten the regimental and communal loyalties of the older regulars. Men were less inclined to take so seriously the customs and traditions which bound the regular to his unit, ties honoured by time which made the regiment as much a family as a fighting formation. Many were politically aware, too, and had listened to the arguments put forward by the Congress and Communist parties; they might have been prepared to fight against the Japanese and Germans because these were the enemies of India, but they preferred not to be described as mercenaries by their fellow countrymen. Other facts of military life also disconcerted them. They had lower pay and fewer privileges than their British counterparts and those who had served in Malaya before 1941 had been subjected to crude racism and petty snobbishness by the ruling planter caste – just weeks before the fall of Singapore there had been an outcry in the European clubs because Indian officers had been given permission to use the swimming pools.*

They had also been shocked by the speed and ease of the Japanese victories and by the pathetic and half-hearted defence put up by the British armies. The fall of Singapore and the victories in Malaya and Burma were as clear examples as any of the military superiority of an Asian race over the supposedly invincible sahibs.

*This is not to say that the Indian Army ever lost sight of its professionalism and fighting ability. It served with distinction in North Africa, Italy and Burma. 'My Indian divisions after 1943 were among the best in the world,' claimed General Slim. 'They would go anywhere, do anything, go on doing it and do it on very little.'

When they were captured they were easy prey for the Japanese call of 'Asia for the Asians' and the blandishments of better treatment if they changed sides. They listened, too, to the arguments put forward by Indian propagandists who told them that the British were finished and that they would be given the chance to fight for a free India. Separated from their officers many of them had difficulty in reconciling what they had been told with the reality of their soldiers' oath. To their eternal credit large numbers of soldiers refused to pay any heed to the promises – these were mainly cavalrymen and Gurkhas – and went on to face a harsh regime in Japanese prisoner-of-war camps. Many more, sometimes whole battalions, threw in their lot with the enemy. By the end of August 1942, 40,000 Indian Army officers and men in Japanese captivity had joined the newly formed Indian National Army which was led by a Sikh officer, Captain Mohan Singh, who was also a perfervid nationalist. He held out the offer of better treatment and the chance to strike a blow for Indian freedom now that Britain was on the point of collapse. It was a compelling argument, one that gained its strength from the lack of information that was available to the prisoners-of-war and from the example of the loss of morale and physical degeneration of their fellow British prisoners.

Singh hoped that the INA would eventually grow into a force half a million strong which would then fight alongside the Japanese army for the liberation of India. When he discovered the unpalatable truth that the Japanese had no intention of treating him as an equal and that they had a low regard for his army because it was made up of despised surrendered men, Singh had second thoughts and tried to disband the INA. He was also dismayed by the Japanese refusal to commit themselves to the ideal of an independent India; eventually he was arrested and spent the rest of the war on a remote island off the Johore Straits. 'When the Japanese failed in their attempts to brainwash a person,' he admitted later, 'they seldom hesitated to smash his brains!'

There the matter might have ended but for the arrival of Subhas Chandra Bose. Here was a new voice, one which spoke with authority and one which the Japanese trusted. In October 1943 he proclaimed himself *Netaji*, or leader, of *Azad Hind*, or Free Government of India, and set about resuscitating the INA.

While in Germany he had enjoyed limited success in raising a *Frei Hind* force made up of Indian prisoners-of-war; but they had never been used in battle. In the Far East it was a different matter. Before the war was over he had raised a force some 20,000 strong, made up of men who believed that they belonged to an army of liberation which would march on Delhi and be greeted as saviours by their fellow countrymen. Small matter that the Allies were now on the offensive and that the Axis powers were no longer interested in, or capable of, invading India: the *Netaji* had told them that they would not halt until they were inside Delhi's Red Fort.

Bose could see the political advantage to be gained from the sight of the INA fighting together as a single unit. Against their better judgement – they would have preferred to have used them attached to their own formations – the Japanese armed and equipped Bose's force, but the INA proved to be a mixed blessing to the fortunes of their new masters. From his home in Delhi, Kushwant Singh noted that the INA soldiers had been just as quick to surrender to the British as they had been to cross over to the Japanese in the prison camps.

> I felt embarrassed because I knew that the INA was not the right thing to have done. I don't think that they covered themselves with glory . . . their performance in the field of battle was so miserable and their standing with the Indian populations in the areas they occupied in Burma and Malaya was also not very glorious. They were always collecting money for one thing or another and when it came to fighting they didn't put up much of a fight . . . I think they're an extremely second-rate lot, the INA.

At Imphal in 1944, 6,000 INA men fought on the Japanese side but their losses were appalling: 700 deserted, 800 surrendered, 400 were killed and a further 1,500 died in hospital from wounds or disease. By that time the extent of the INA problem was known to the Indian Army but it was decided to conceal the matter until the war's end. In Burma the official policy was to accept the surrender of INA units and to treat the men as prisoners-of-war; but in many instances the time-honoured remark, 'too late, chum', was used by enraged sepoys who regarded their fellow countrymen not as liberators but as traitors. The evidence of Japanese atrocities and the maltreatment handed out to loyal Indian Army soldiers filtered back to India and it was impossible to keep the matter under wraps. Large numbers had been taken prisoner at Pegu, north of Rangoon, when the IVth Indian Corps drove out the 28th Japanese Army and they had to be transported back to India where their presence created a good deal of public consternation. At first, Indian opinion was ranged against the INA because of the dishonour they had brought upon their fellow countrymen who had remained loyal to the Indian Army; but in the first days of peace attitudes began to change. When senior British officers, like Lieutenant-General Sir Francis Tuker (GOC, IVth Indian Corps), began talking in terms of sending the INA soldiers back to Japan as prisoners-of-war, or of using 'the wall and the firing squad', unease began to creep through the ranks of Indian politicians. Had not the British Empire fought the war to defeat tyranny and to uphold the dignity and freedom of the common man? Yet here was talk of revenge and executions.

As the authorities began to ponder the best solution to the problem of the INA, Congress leaders began to think about turning the situation to their own advantage. Soon a different gloss was being put on the INA: instead of being regarded as mutinous traitors they were transmogrified into freedom fighters who had devoted themselves to Mother India. Evidence of maltreatment of other Indian prisoners in Japanese prisoner-of-war camps was conveniently forgotten as was the INA's lamentable record in action, and the imprisoned leaders awaiting trial suddenly became national heroes. Nehru, who had publicly reviled the INA during the war, now decided to take up their cause and he spoke for many of his colleagues when he claimed that any punishment meted out to the men would 'in effect be a punishment on all India and all Indians'.

The British had in fact already started punishing other mutineers who had tried to subvert British authority in the war against Japan. Seven Indian gunners who had mutinied and surrendered to the enemy on Christmas Island in 1942 were tracked down, tried and sentenced to death, but their sentences were later commuted to life imprisonment. In Colombo three bombardiers of the Ceylon Coastal Artillery had been hanged in 1942 for attempting an armed uprising on the strategic RAF bases in the Cocos-Keeling Islands, and there had been a potentially serious occurrence in the Central India Horse who had mutinied in

Bombay in 1940 while under orders to serve in the Middle East. Their Sikh squadron had been influenced by the radical Kirti Lehar movement – a Communist-inspired nationalist group – and their tempers had not been improved by being forced to wait thirty-six hours in a railway siding prior to embarkation. Nothing could persuade them to obey their officers; the ringleaders had been tried and sentenced to penal servitude in the Andaman Islands where they later became prisoners of the Japanese. One body of opinion, shared by many Indian Army and Indian Police officers, was that the INA men should be treated in much the same way.

> If, at the end of the war against Japan, the INA ringleaders had been court-martialled in Burma and sentenced to the firing squad or imprisonment there would have been no reaction. The general Indian Army opinion would have been that they had got their just deserts. Indians have very strong views on being 'true to the salt'.

Leslie Robins's solution could only have been implemented had the war still been in progress and tempers hot, but at the end of 1945 it would have caused an outcry amongst the Allies, especially the Americans. The most sensible option would have been to court-martial the ringleaders and then to dismiss them with ignominy from the Indian Army, but that was rejected in favour of a show trial of the leading INA officers. No doubt the authorities felt that this would satisfy the honour of the officers and men of the Indian Army who had remained loyal, but the decision to charge the men with treason under the Indian Penal Code turned out to be a serious error.

Peace had softened men's hearts and many British officers doubted the wisdom of punishing men who would soon be the responsibility of an independent India. There was also the risk that the men – Captain Shah Nawaz (Muslim), Lieutenant Dhillon (Sikh) and P.K. Sahgal (Hindu) – who all came from influential backgrounds, would become folk-heroes or martyrs in the cause of Indian independence. To compound the basic error it was agreed to hold the trial in the Red Fort in Delhi, the symbolic centre of Mogul power, which had a deep political significance for all Indian nationalists. The proceedings, therefore, provided all the political parties with a unique opportunity to challenge the British Raj by espousing the ideals of the INA: soon, those

Indian leaders who had attacked it in wartime began to champion the leaders in peace and to vie with each other to come to their assistance. Nehru, who had not practised law for years, helped with the defence, an action which outraged many British people but one which Jack Morton could understand.

> His argument was that the British had always maintained that the Indian Army was a volunteer army fighting the Axis Powers for the independence of India, which had been promised as the prize of victory. The Indian Congress on the other hand had insisted that the army was a conscript, or mercenary force. However, taking the British case, how did the British behave when they were routed by the Japanese in the jungle? They abandoned their gallant Indians to the enemy and made haste to save their own white skins. The Japanese then promised their prisoners independence for India if they fought on their side to defeat Britain. To whom were the renegade Indians disloyal? Certainly not to Mother India.

Britain, by trying to compromise, he argued, had satisfied no one.

First of all, though, some 11,300 INA prisoners had to be interrogated at the main centres of Calcutta, Jingaragacha and Nilganji. According to the level of their involvement they were classified as whites, greys or blacks. The whites, those who had not been disloyal but merely misguided, were transferred to other units; the greys, those who had been committed to the INA cause but had not been involved in atrocities, were discharged. The most serious offenders were the blacks, mainly officers, those who had been guilty of treachery in serving the Japanese army. They were ordered to be sent for trial, in the same way that civilian collaborators were also rounded up for punishment.

It took some time for the police and military authorities to work their way through the flotsam and jetsam of the INA prisoners and eventually it became a tedious task which took up time and manpower. In Madras William Hamilton hit on the novel expedient of returning all Madrassi INA soldiers to their villages in civilian clothes, with only a rail warrant and a modest 10 rupees to their name. 'The Madrassi villager was no fool and when an ex-JIF [Japanese India Forces] arrived in the village destitute, if he boasted of his exploits with the Japanese, the villagers would ask him what he had got out of it. The Madras government agreed and Madras absorbed all its JIFs with little or no disruption to village life.'

Hamilton's ruse worked in Madras, but other police officers were not as lucky as he had been. In volatile United Provinces, Bengal and Bihar and Orissa the show trial in Delhi had created a wave of anti-British feeling and emotions were running high. It would have been understandable had Wavell decided not to proceed with the Red Fort trial but he was a soldier and knew that officers who had broken their oaths of allegiance had to be punished. After lengthy and frequently heated proceedings the three men were found guilty, cashiered and sentenced to transportation for life. The announcement of the findings caused an uproar and new riots broke out in the major cities; once again it seemed that Britain had taken the wrong option by trying to punish men who had turned their backs on an allegiance which Britain was on the point of surrendering. Fortunately, Auchinleck decided to quash the transportation sentences and to release the men, both because he feared fresh trouble and also because he wanted to display magnanimity. It was a defeat of a kind, though, and when the men made a triumphal procession around the country they were greeted everywhere by rapturous crowds. To Jack Morton, now a senior officer in Lahore, their arrival in his city and the inability of the police authorities to control the demonstration was the clearest sign yet that Britain was no longer able to maintain the status quo. An order was in force preventing the assembly of five or more persons in one place, but when the ex-INA officers arrived by train all he and his men could do was to keep 'a low profile'.

> The incident had a deeper significance in that it accentuated the divisive post-war influence affecting the loyalty and cohesion of the Army. From a police point of view, I feared that we could no longer expect to be able to call upon military forces of unquestioned integrity to support us in containing and suppressing internal communal strife.

This was the same Jack Morton who had called in the military in Lahore in 1935 to help him deal with a potentially serious riot between Sikhs and Muslims.

There were similar incidents elsewhere. At Lucknow's Indian Military Hospital discharged INA patients were spreading disaffection amongst the local garrison and the police were powerless to interfere. The arrival of Shah Nawaz exacerbated the situation and when he announced his intention of inspecting the men the brigadier in charge feared that there might be a riot. If he forbade his men to line Shah Nawaz's route – as they had threatened to do – they could mutiny; if he allowed it, there would be a serious breach of military discipline. Leslie Robins knew that there was little his policemen could do to help as they were outnumbered; instead of meeting the threat head-on, he decided to make use of his local contacts.

> This was where police influence and power really counted. By putting pressure on to the political leaders who were Shah Nawaz's hosts, we had him bundled into a car and driven out to the airport before dawn. He was decanted into an aeroplane and out of the District before the INA patients were out of bed. Later, some of them saw his empty car being driven away from the aerodrome and saluted it, but there was no general disobedience of the Brigadier's order. So a very sticky situation was sorted out – for mutiny at Lucknow would have spread like wildfire.

Although Robins's plan had worked his ruse had succeeded at some cost to British prestige. The news of Shah Nawaz's precipitate departure soon leaked out and in the cold light of day it seemed that British fears had been exaggerated. To those who supported the INA leaders it appeared that the will of the people had triumphed over the will of those who held power.

Bose, too, became a national hero and even the news of his death in a plane crash while attempting to flee to the Soviet Union – where, presumably, he hoped to enlist Stalin's support – failed to dampen public enthusiasm for his wartime exploits. No obstacle had seemed to be too great for him to overcome and there were those who continued to believe for years afterwards that he was not dead but would return like King Arthur to save his country in her greatest need. Bose had believed quite genuinely that it was possible to create a social and political revolution in India which would have overthrown the British: ironically, what he had not been able to achieve during the war was accomplished by his INA during the first weeks of peace when, for a few weeks, rebellion was in the air. Ironically, too, it was as prisoners that his men eventually came to Delhi's Red Fort.

When the furore died down it was possible to put the INA into a more reasoned perspective. To regular officers like K.P. Candeth and D.K. Palit its formation was an aberration of the traditions which held together the Indian Army. The 2nd battalion of Palit's Baluch Regiment had been captured at Singapore, yet it

had remained loyal and it was not until 1944 that he was able to comprehend the full extent of the INA's activities. Today he believes
that the Japanese atrocities in the prison camps must have unhinged
many a soldier who saw in the INA the opportunity to escape from
impossible conditions – a point that is shared by Candeth who later
rose to the rank of lieutenant-general in the Indian Army.

> A lot of them did it because of duress, because the conditions
> under which they were living were so grim that they thought nearly
> anything would be better. And there were others who really did
> feel that the Japanese would help them to make a free India.

On the other hand Candeth was not in favour of the INA men
rejoining the Indian Army after independence. Such a move, he
argued, would have been an affront to the many thousands of
Indian soldiers who had remained loyal in spite of the blandishments of the INA and the cruelty of the Japanese. There was
a feeling, too, that the men had been duped by Bose during the
war and that they were being exploited by the Indian political
leadership in the first year of peace.

> The INA is one of the great hoaxes of Indian history [claims
> Kushwant Singh]. They were lionised by Nehru when he was quite
> sure that Bose was dead – because he was the main rival. The
> whole country rose in great fervour for the INA at the time and
> that was the main reason why Congress swept the polls soon after.
> But I don't think that any thinking man had any illusions that the
> INA were traitors to both the British and the Japanese.

Singh's protestations notwithstanding, Wavell was so unsettled by
the disturbances that he told London that it would no longer be in
British interests to test further the loyalty of the army and the
police 'in the suppression of their own people'. India had been
united by the trial of the three INA officers and the political
parties had temporarily laid aside their mutual antagonisms to
lend support and sympathy to the accused men. What had started
as a matter of honour to the British had quickly turned into a
powerful manifestation of Indian nationhood and the officers and
men of the Indian security forces would not have been human had
they remained untouched by it. Within weeks of the ending of the
INA uproar their loyalty was once more put to the test.

The trouble occurred where it was least expected: within the
ranks of the Royal Indian Navy which, like the Royal Indian Air

Force, had gone through a period of rapid growth during the Second World War. Its ships might have been on the elderly side and confined to escort duties, but by 1946 it had 28,000 officers and men, most of whom had seen wartime service. The navy's principal base was at Bombay which housed both a large naval dockyard and the combined Royal Navy and Royal Indian Navy Far Eastern Signal Training School, HMIS *Talwar*. It was there that the first rumblings of unrest were heard at the beginning of February 1946.

At the time the establishment was under the command of Commander F.W. King RIN, an experienced naval officer who, nevertheless, was given to using uncouth language in front of his men. Several of his brother officers had noticed that he would address the ratings as 'black buggers', 'coolie bastards' or 'jungli Indians' – but he was not alone in the custom. Many of the officers in Bombay were reservists who retained what they called old-fashioned planter attitudes towards Indians, but in the highly charged political atmosphere of 1945–6 the habit naturally caused great offence. The flashpoint came on the morning of 8 February when King dressed down a group of ratings who had been wolf-whistling a parade of WRINs. Ordered to stand up, the men refused to obey and it took the intervention of the Executive Officer, Lieutenant-Commander E.M. Shaw, to defuse the situation. 'I made enquiries,' he wrote in his diary, 'and six V/S ratings were brought before me as having been in the barracks at the time stated by Commander King. I said I expected my ratings to set an example in *Talwar* and that I did not want to hear of any more reports like the one I had just received.'

However, that was not the end of the matter. The response to Shaw's talk was a request by the ratings to be allowed to complain to the Commander about his use of insulting language, a request they were entitled to make. This was granted, but when King met the men on Saturday 16 February, Saturday being the normal time for 'Requestmen', he told them that their allegations were 'untrue' and gave them twenty-four hours to reconsider the matter. The fuse had now been lit and it burned slowly over the weekend. On the Monday the ratings in *Talwar* refused to eat their breakfasts, ostensibly because they said the food was bad and they wanted improved rations, but in reality to start a mutiny. Their chants quickly changed to anti-British slogans and

the officers, British and Indian, were forced to beat a hasty
retreat, leaving the men in charge of the signals equipment. Soon
the news was being flashed from establishment to establishment
and from ship to ship – a similar strike took place later that day on
HMIS *Hooghly* in Calcutta. Left without their own signal equipment the senior officers were forced to use the private transmitter
of the Cable and Wireless Company and as a precaution Shaw put
through an immediate phone call to the Duty Signal Officer in
Whitehall warning him that all codes and ciphers on board RIN
ships could have been compromised.

The following day saw the mutiny spread to Fort Barracks and
Castle Barracks and to some of the naval vessels in the harbour,
including HMIS *Hindustan* and HMIS *Narbarda*. The white
ensign was hauled down and replaced by Congress and Muslim
League flags; the Communist Party mobilised its members in the
dockyards and a mass meeting was held. By the day's end on 19
February the whole naval dockyard area in Bombay was in a state
of ferment with police unable to control the flag-waving, slogan-
chanting demonstrators.

At first, the British thought it best to treat the disturbances as a
'strike'. Shaw, faced by the problem of coping with large numbers
of men who were still on duty, confronted Admiral Rattray, the
Flag Officer Commanding, Bombay, and asked what he should do.

> He said, 'Well, you will have to tell them the truth – tell them what
> has happened.' To this I replied, 'Tell them that *Talwar* has
> mutinied, sir?' To which Admiral Rattray replied, 'Good God, no,
> Shaw – what a dreadful thing to say – no, tell them that the ratings
> in *Talwar* refused duty.'

By the following day it was impossible to minimise the serious-
ness of the situation. There had been armed clashes between
naval ratings and men of the Mahratta Light Infantry at the
Castle Barracks and lives had already been lost – during the two
days' fighting some two hundred Indians were killed and many
more injured. The worst incident occurred on board the corvette
Hindustan where sailors opened fire with oerlikon guns on troops
and trained the ship's main guns on the city. *Narbarda* followed
suit: Wilfrid Russell was in the Yacht Club at the time and had
the disconcerting experience of seeing the ship's four-inch guns
being trained in the direction of the club's verandah while he was
having drinks before lunch. 'A very black day in Bombay's

history,' he recorded, 'perhaps the blackest . . . of course the temperature throughout the city went up by leaps and bounds and one had the feeling that anything might happen . . . what a tragedy that this should ever happen and that it should start in the RIN of all things.'

The leaders of the mutiny had five demands: better standards of food, parity of pay and conditions with Royal Navy personnel, a gratuity on release, all underpinned by the need to take disciplinary action against Commander King. Rattray was prepared to listen to them and to promise that action would be taken once the men had returned to their posts but he could not ignore the fact that the men had taken part in the serious crime of mutiny. Negotiations broke down on the question of clemency for the ringleaders and in Delhi Wavell and Auchinleck decided that the insurrection had to be put down with a show of force. British troops were rushed into the area and the Indian Army was also ordered to take part in the peacekeeping operation. Part of the force included a British armoured regiment which, had it been used, would have taken part in the first ever major tank-versus-ship battle. Happily, its services were not required, although *Hindustan* had to be bombarded into submission by mortar and artillery fire: six RIN ratings were killed and twenty-five wounded. Other British precautions included the arrival of a Royal Navy squadron with the light cruiser HMS *Glasgow* and the deployment of RAF Mosquito fighter-bombers which buzzed the ships held by the mutineers. By nightfall on Saturday 23 February black flags were flying from all the ships and shore establishments to indicate surrender and the mutiny was at an end.

Throughout the mutiny the loyalties of the Indian Army troops in Bombay had been strained to breaking point. Naval ratings hooted and jeered at the men of the Mahratta Light Infantry who opposed them and although there were suggestions at the time that the sepoys had provided the mutineers with small arms, there is no evidence to prove that anything untoward happened. The Mahrattas stood firm and arrested the ringleaders at the Torpedo School, HMIS *Valsura*, for instance, and their example was copied elsewhere, not only in Bombay but also in Karachi and Calcutta. Once again in the history of the raj the authorities had shown that they were prepared to use force to maintain the authority of their power, but it was, in truth, a final fling. They

were fortunate that the mutiny had been such an impulsive occurrence and that the ringleaders had not been able to mobilise other
servicemen – a strike in sympathy with the sailors in RIAF Bombay
had been quickly settled – or to engage the support of the mainly
Communist dockers. Had they done so, the riots in Bombay, serious enough, would have been more widespread and the attacks on
British authority would have been more serious than the assaults
on Indians wearing Western dress witnessed by Russell.

The mutiny had started, as so many others had done in the
past, for obvious reasons – lack of firm leadership, the inefficiency and inexperience of the officers and petty officers, and a
strong local grievance. Another cause might have been the
example set by RAF strikers at the tail-end of January. Twelve
hundred men below the rank of sergeant had gone on strike at
RAF Dum Dum near Calcutta and had refused all orders to
return to their posts. Their grievance was the slow rate of
demobilisation; having completed their wartime service they
wanted to get home quickly, but inequalities in the dates of
release meant that men in RAF trades were given later demob
dates, whereas soldiers and sailors were released in groups
according to their age and service group.

By 28 January the strikes had spread to Cawnpore, Mauripur,
Karachi, Poona, Vizagapatam and Allahabad. Rumours also
began to spread that the men were being kept on to provide
transport facilities for the British forces in Java where the Dutch
colonial government was being given assistance in regaining
political control. (This was disputed when the matter was aired in
the House of Commons on 29 January but the RAF did have a
strong transport command presence in India and one of its
transport units, 31 Squadron, was involved in the Indonesia
operations.) There had also been demonstrations in American
bases with US servicemen threatening to go on strike if they were
not given immediate demobilisation, and their action had brought
results. As General Tuker pointed out at the time the RAF
personnel and the US servicemen had set a bad example to the
local population and their strikes were bound to cause unrest
within the Indian services themselves.

Unlike those strikes, the RIN mutiny quickly became a Quit-
India-type revolt, but it was doomed to failure because the men
had not developed any firm political ideas and found themselves

being used by outside agitators. A vital factor in restoring law and order was the attitude of the Congress Party and Muslim League leaders who had been thoroughly alarmed by the mutiny and the violence it had unleashed. They also felt that the Communist Party was using the mutiny to its own advantage by encouraging a general strike among the civilian workers in the city. With memories of the so-called '1942 betrayal' still strong they were determined to prevent the political initiative passing to the Communists. Not only would their opposition to the strike preserve their own positions but as Nikhil Chakravartty observed, it would also add to their standing with the British: 'That was just at the time that the Congress leaders were negotiating with the British. First round. So the working committee decided there should be no strike because they would show them that they could run the country without rowdyism.'

Nehru then turned the situation to Congress's advantage. 'India has no need for violence in her struggle for freedom,' he said when he arrived in Bombay to inspect the situation. 'If I am satisfied that violence is needed, I shall be the first to give that call.' Gandhi was even more forthright in his condemnation. 'They are setting a bad and unbecoming example to India,' he said of the mutineers' behaviour. Having refused to support the RIN ratings the political leaders then backed up the naval authorities and approved the appointment of Commander S.G. Karmarkar RINR in place of King.

Not unnaturally, perhaps, the mutineers felt let down by that lack of political support and by the public condemnation of their actions. They could hardly have expected anything else; by mid-February it was known that the Cripps Mission was coming to India and at that crucial juncture neither the Congress Party nor the Muslim League wanted to rock the boat. It had been one thing to support the INA leaders but the resulting riots and bloodshed had unnerved the politicians, partly because they espoused a policy of non-violence but mainly because they were scared of starting an armed revolution when independence was so near. It is also worth noting that neither the naval mutiny nor the behaviour of the INA soldiers boded well for the future: if officers and men could change sides once, they might do so again and it would always be difficult to trust ratings who had refused to obey orders. Besides, both the Indian leadership and the regular officers of the armed forces were already looking forward to the future. India would require a navy after independence and it would have to be served by responsible officers and men. 'You must keep on serving,' Sardar Patel told Lieutenant A.K. Chatterjee RIN. 'One day we will be independent and you guys will come in handy.'

Chatterjee had joined the navy in 1932 and during the Second World War had served on Atlantic convoy duty; by the war's end he was the RIN's senior anti-submarine officer. At the time of the mutiny he was at the naval radar school in Karachi; when the signal came through from *Talwar* he called his men together and told them its contents. Then he offered this advice:

> I said, 'Don't do that because eventually you will get punished badly, being mutineers. For heaven's sake, if you don't want to work for four days, I'll give you four days' leave.' Headquarters wouldn't have it, though, and sure enough, eventually the Black Watch surrounded the camp with machine guns and ordered the men into their classrooms. I told the men, 'Does it feel nice now?'

The men had remained loyal to Chatterjee, however, and the naval radar school was spared a mutiny. Today Chatterjee is inclined to believe that the mutiny in Bombay had no political roots but was largely a matter of bad conditions, poor leadership and a slow rate of demobilisation. Like other senior Indian officers – he later became an admiral – he has little time for the mutineers or for the INA soldiers. 'I could never support the INA. How could you support anyone who had been disloyal to their oath?' he claims. 'We lead by tradition: you must be loyal to the colours which pay you or command you.' As a Bengali Chatterjee always had a soft spot for Bose as a man but he disagreed strongly with his political policies.

Significantly, no INA leader was ever given high rank in the armies of India or Pakistan – in India INA soldiers had to wait until 1974 before they were awarded pensions – and when the imprisoned sailors were released after independence they were disappointed by the complete lack of official recognition of their efforts.

After the inquiries had come to an end and the ringleaders punished, Commander Goord noticed that a subtle change had taken place among the men he commanded.

> The mutiny and its political results brought to an end the hitherto rising tide of anti-British feeling. With independence in the offing, the focus turned to communal problems. So it was that, when the time came, British officers were able to take their leave from the

Service in an atmosphere of goodwill, in a subcontinent seething with strife.

Wilfrid Russell, too, felt that the naval mutiny had been a last gesture against British authority and that the difficulties in the months to come would be to keep Hindu apart from Muslim. Jinnah's intransigence over Pakistan and the reluctant British admission that its creation was inevitable had put him in a gloomy mood. On the day that the mutiny ended he wrote in his diary that most people he knew in Bombay wanted to shift responsibility on to Congress shoulders, even if that meant ignoring Jinnah.

> The Congress will undoubtedly have to ask our help in maintaining law and order. We shall have to impose a stiff price: constitutional rule and firm handling of trouble-makers, including Muslims and Communists, with no anti-British mud-slinging. As soon as that starts to happen, out we go. They know now what a turmoil they will be faced with. These riots have at least had that effect.

It was a policy of despair, one that Britain could not possibly adopt, but its origins can be seen in the events of the mutiny. At the beginning, Muslim, Sikh and Hindu ratings had stood shoulder to shoulder but even after three days their solidarity had begun to crumble. Muslim sailors started by protesting about the presence of Congress peacemakers like Sardar Patel who addressed the men and undertook to prevent excessive reprisals; yet these same men had only been equalled by the Sikhs in the vehemence of their hostility to Britain. Now their voices were raised in support of the Muslim League and Pakistan and against the domination of a Hindu raj once the British had left India.

With the ending of the naval mutiny and the settling of the INA trials, it was obvious to many that India was fast becoming ungovernable. ICS officers reported that Indian politicians in the provinces were more interested in raising political capital for the future than they were in the minutiae of the present administration. The princes had been told that they could not rely on British paramountcy and would have to fit in with the new constitution after the transfer of power; this bald statement from the 1946 Cripps Mission was met with incredulity and dismay, not just by the rulers of the states themselves but also by their British political officers. The Sikhs continued to voice their concern about the possibility of emerging as a minority in the Punjab, and in the North-West Frontier Province another political anomaly gave cause for concern. The Red Shirt ministry was Muslim in character yet linked to the Congress Party. Its official line was to oppose the creation of Pakistan but on that score it did not have the support of the Pathan tribesmen who prided themselves on their political independence. When Nehru visited the province with the Red Shirt leaders, Dr Khan Sahib and Abdul Ghaffar Khan, he was given short shrift by the tribesmen in places like Peshawar and Razmak and was forced to cut short his tour. Everywhere in India, it seemed, communal polarisation and the consequent jockeying for political power had sharpened the need for a speedy constitutional settlement.

The greatest divide, however, was created by the strength and confidence of the Muslim League. Ever since 1940 and the demise of the Congress ministries in the provinces, Jinnah had been strengthening his hand; he emerged from the war as the natural Muslim leader and his party was the focus for the aspirations of the majority of Indian Muslims. By then it was almost as strong as the Congress Party and its leaders considered that their claims for political autonomy were as cogent as Nehru's. Jinnah knew, too, how to use that political leverage: when he refused to co-operate in the Cripps proposals for an interim government unless the League nominated all the Muslim members the talks were doomed to failure. Congress could not accept Jinnah's proposal, because it would then have had to concede its long-held claim to speak for a united nation. Moreover, Nehru made it plain that, once formed, the interim government would be a sovereign body whose actions would be free from the constriction of British rule. In protest Jinnah withdrew from the talks and instructed Muslims to take up the call for an independent Pakistan. He was also mindful of the need to include Calcutta in any eastern Pakistan that would be created. The result was a 'Day of Direct Action' which exploded into an orgy of bloody riot, murder and violence.

The first, and worst, riots began in Calcutta on the night of 15–16 August 1946. Black flags were flown from Muslim homes in anticipation of the following day's *hartal*, or general strike. To ensure that Jinnah's Day of Action would indeed be a day of civic inaction the Muslim government of Bengal had declared 16 August to be a public holiday and thus the scene was set for a series of murderous clashes between the Muslims and the Hindu community – which greatly resented the *hartal* that had been imposed upon them. The

first blows were in fact struck by the Muslims, who took to the
streets and cut down anyone who opposed them. Nikhil Chakravartty had given up his studies to turn to a new career in journalism
and by accident he walked into a Muslim political meeting. It was
only the presence of mind of some Muslim journalists which saved
his life – he was quickly ushered out and allowed to make good his
escape to the safety of the Indian Communist Party headquarters
where he was marooned for three days.

> I had never seen such devastation. Without a war hundreds of
> people were lying dead on the roadside – and still the fires burned
> all over the place. Many shops were being looted and many houses
> were burned down. On the third day I came back home where I
> found to my horror an old Muslim washerman being beaten up –
> civilised people who knew him were doing it.

Soon the Hindu bazaar areas were ablaze and the overworked
police and fire services were powerless to come to the assistance
of every victim. The Hindus outnumbered the Muslims two to
one, though, and as Stanley Taylor of the Indian Police recalls,
they were not slow to take their revenge.

> The scenes which took place in Calcutta were indescribable. The
> British were no longer the target of the rioters. The Hindu and
> Muslim communities waited in ambush for each other armed with
> every conceivable kind of weapon, and slaughtered men, women
> and children without restraint. Business came to a standstill and
> the streets were piled high with rotting corpses. The supply of food
> from outside Calcutta ceased, shops were looted, houses were
> burnt and thousands of people rendered homeless. A pall of
> smoke from burning houses hung over the city. It will never be
> known how many were killed; a conservative estimate put the
> figure at 5,000.

Young Das who had spent his war with the Rajputana Rifles, his
own regiment, found himself in Calcutta commanding a Punjab
battalion. As a former intelligence officer he was dismayed to find
that no one knew what was really happening in the streets or in
the surrounding areas.

> For the first couple of days we didn't know what was happening or
> who was doing all the mischief. During the day it was quite calm
> on the surface but it was at night that the troubles would start.
> There was a lot of arson, a lot of shouting and my battalion was

fully stretched: we used to patrol the whole night through to try to control the situation . . . the main thing was that it was a communal riot, one community wanted the other out because by then partition was expected and it was anticipated that the whole of Bengal would go to Pakistan.

Later, Das was to say that his involvement in the attempts to keep the two sides apart was 'the most unpleasant part of his military service' and that as a young officer his greatest dread had been the order to deploy Indian troops in aid of the civil power. In Calcutta that fear had become a hateful reality.

The communal fighting lasted ten days in Calcutta and was eventually put down with the help of the Indian and British armies. Forty-five thousand troops were involved in the operation, but by the time they had regained control Calcutta's dead belonged to the vultures or to the waters of the River Hooghly. Stanley Taylor suggests that 5,000 Indians lost their lives during the time of the Great Killing, as it came to be known, but other observers believe that it could just as easily have been twice that number or more, for there was no means of accurately assessing the high numbers of casualties. Even though the British community had not been attacked or its property destroyed, memories of the Mutiny had been rekindled and few families had been left untouched by the experience. Muslim and Hindu servants had suddenly disappeared, either to take part in the killing or to escape from it, and from polite suburbs large areas of the city could be seen blazing. To Sheila Coldwell, who had taken refuge with her husband in his firm's apartment in Clive Street, the scene seemed to spring from history's pages, Moscow burning before Napoleon's army.

We certainly did not feel safe and would have been attacked if the mobs had turned against us. There were Muslims coming off the ships in the Hooghly and walking up Clive Street, not knowing that anything terrible was happening. Before they had gone a few paces they were set upon by Hindus yelling '*Jai Hind*' who then butchered them on our doorstep. My husband phoned the police and got a police sergeant who was in a terrible state of hysteria and said there was nothing he could do. The Muslims and the Hindus were looting the city, he said, and setting it on fire and people were murdering one another. That was completely obvious to us; we saw it all. We lived in a Hindu area and at night, all night long, the people in the go-downs round about shouted almost like jackals, '*Jai Hind*'. In a high-pitched tone, it was really very frightening, the whole night long, '*Jai Hind*'. It was horrible, it really was.

Eventually British troops were moved into the city to clear away the rotting corpses, many of which had been festering for ten days in the hot August weather. Their deployment in Calcutta also helped to still the growing fears of the British community.

They marched down Clive Street and they were singing 'It's a long way to Tipperary'. I may be accused of sentimentality but we wept tears of joy and pride and a great thankfulness engulfed us.

It was a horrid, disgusting and thankless task and one which had to be repeated in the months to come elsewhere in the Gangetic plain. By the beginning of October the trouble had spread to the Noahali and Tippera districts of East Bengal where the Hindus were outnumbered ten to one. Lives were again lost on a large scale but here the main damage was done to the property of wealthy Hindus – houses, farms and crops were all destroyed in an orgy of violence. In Bengal, too, the troubles were exacerbated by agitators from the Communist Party which had gained control of many of the trades unions. Their main target had been the railway system, particularly the Bengal–Assam Railway, where strike had followed strike throughout 1946. They had also brought their influence to bear on plantation workers in the north and east of the province, paralysing production of tea and encouraging riots in rural areas.

For the police in Bengal it was often an impossible situation. Not only did each new day bring fresh problems as riots or demonstrations broke out in unexpected places, but the ensuing unrest threw hundreds of additional demonstrators on to the streets. Another problem was the use of the continuing communal unrest as a stick with which to beat the police force. The IP had always prided itself on its ability to stand aloof from racial or religious bigotry and in most states the police forces contained both Hindus and Muslims. Now, in Bengal, the men had to bear the brunt of abuse from a hostile Indian press and local politicians anxious to make political capital. Hindu policemen were criticised if they were ordered to break up Muslim disturbances or if they used excessive force in pursuit of their duties. Conversely, Hindu politicians turned on Muslim policemen if they were believed to have an anti-Hindu bias. It was a difficult task and one that was not always made easier by the intervention of the local politicians. In Chittagong, for example, the local District Magistrate, a Muslim, ordered all the officials and the police to fly Muslim League flags during the Day of Action; at the same time, Hindu policemen were forbidden to intervene during the day-long Muslim demonstrations.

Similar doubts about the impartiality of some politicians troubled Martin Wynne who was serving at that time in Amraoti City in the Central Provinces. During the Day of Action he had kept order by cordoning off the city and keeping the rival communities apart, but later he ran into a potentially explosive situation at Badnera, a railway junction on the Bombay–Nagpur–Calcutta line. There, the men of his Special Armed Force had opened fire on a rioting crowd, killing one Harijan (Untouchable) and wounding three Muslims. No warnings had been given and all the rules of engagement had been broken, yet Wynne was bound to admit that the forces' action had prevented further trouble by dispersing the crowd. A few days later the Prime Minister, Sri Ravishankar Shukla, a Hindu, came to Badnera to hold an inquiry, and although Wynne had met him previously during the war he did expect trouble.

> We greeted one another with pleasant smiles in recollection of our previous encounter. The Police were exonerated. Would they have been, I continue to ask myself, if the SI had been a Muslim and the injured Hindus? This was the only occasion during eighteen years that the Police in a district where I served opened fire, and it was in these grisly farcical circumstances that the record was broken. I should add that apart from this incident, no Hindu or Muslim police officer ever gave me cause to believe that he had acted less than impartially in communal matters.

Taylor makes a similar point about the standards of service and discipline of his own force in Bengal, even when they were sorely provoked by outside influences. They resisted all the blandishments of the Communists to undermine authority and stood firm in the face of riot, 'on duty for long hours, for months on end in intense heat or pouring rain'. Not for one minute, claims Taylor, did they ever think of following the example of their fellow countrymen who mutinied or went on strike in the Indian Army, Navy or Air Force.

The affair in Badnera was not the end of Wynne's political

trouble: it came next from a Muslim League minister who accused the Hindu policemen in his district of harassment and intimidation in rural areas which were predominantly Muslim. Wynne had the allegations investigated but these were found to be either untrue or exaggerated. Not content with the findings the minister raised the matter in the provincial assembly and Wynne was asked to reopen the investigation. Unwisely, perhaps, he began his report with a reference to Goebbels's claim that a big lie, frequently repeated, would soon be believed. His report then fell into the hands of the Home Minister, Sri Dwarka Prashad Misra, with unfortunate results.

> I should have remembered that with an elected Government in power my report would not stop at the IG's office and remain confidential. The Home Minister seized upon it and quoted it at Question Time; it even made the national press; but it destroyed any relationship I could hope to build with the Muslim community. Misra later apologised to me in a somewhat Laodicean manner, but the harm had been done.

Students, too, joined in the rioting and both Robins in Lucknow and Harrison in Madras had to deal with demonstrations which were usually more notable for their noise than for any damage to property or life. One notable, and faintly ridiculous exception happened to Robins when the Home Minister, a Congress Party member, intervened to address a riotous assembly on the university campus. To Robins's alarm, he would not accept police protection as he felt that it was an occasion for diplomacy and not force. Three-quarters of an hour later he returned to police headquarters with a broken head, having been beaten up by the crowd. 'Mr Robins, you take your police in there,' he ordered. 'And I don't care what you do to them!'

Alastair MacKeith, in the North-West Frontier Province, also found that threatening situations could be defused by sensing the ridiculous. Faced by an angry crowd in Kohat which was demonstrating on behalf of Pakistan, he was surprised to hear the cheer-leader suddenly reverse the slogan which was then taken up by the other demonstrators.

> The cry was 'Pakistan Zindabad – Long live Pakistan!' followed by 'Death to the British Government!' This would be chanted with monotonous regularity. So monotonous that the cheer leader got tired of them himself and thought that he would vary the

sequence. He shouted out 'British Government!' and there was a
great cry, 'Long live the British Government!' I was standing
there, saw the humour of the situation and burst out laughing.
Indeed, the whole crowd did!

MacKeith admits that he had to face little or no communal
hostility at this time; the main problems came during the period
of partition when Muslims, enraged by news of atrocities in the
Punjab, attacked Hindus who were attempting to flee to India.

To Wavell, though, the race riots which followed in the wake of
the Calcutta Day of Action were no laughing matter. After
visiting the city on 24 August 1946 he returned to Delhi firmly
convinced that what happened in Bengal could be repeated
elsewhere unless he could encourage the Congress Party and the
Muslim League to work together in the Constituent Assembly. If
he failed, the result would be chaos across the Indian subcontinent and in Wavell's opinion the British would be powerless to
intervene. His fears were not without foundation for although the
Indian Army had remained encouragingly loyal there were fewer
British troops in India at that time than there were in the whole of
Palestine, a country about the same size as a large Indian district.

Wavell's answer to the problem was a soldier's solution.
Basically he proposed that in India south of the Ganges valley
and the Indus delta power should be transferred to a Congress
government by 31 March 1947. In the Indus and Ganges valleys,
though, where the Hindu and Muslim populations were more
evenly divided, the Government of India would retain power
until 31 March 1948 by which time a settlement would have to be
reached. Meanwhile, preparations would be made to protect
British civilians, including if necessary the evacuation of women
and children. The alternative suggested was for the British to
start planning to stay in India for a further fifteen or twenty years.

Wavell went home to London to argue his proposals with
Attlee's Cabinet but he was allowed to return to India on 24
December without receiving an answer. Attlee balked at the idea
of announcing a date for the transfer of power and was against
mounting the operation in two stages, but he did give approval
for the laying of secret plans to protect British interests should
there be further trouble. The civil servant given the task of
working on the project was John Christie, who had to work under
the cover of secretary to the Viceroy's Honours Committee: in

this guise he could consult senior officers of all the services without raising any suspicions.

> Emergency plans for concentration, which already existed in every city, district and subdivision, were brought up to date; camps and depots were earmarked and arrangements made for stocking them with food, clothing, medicines and other necessities; transport and escorts were arranged. All had to be done without attracting attention. I was an especial thorn in the flesh of the Quartermaster General's branch of Army Headquarters, as the Commander-in-Chief, Sir Claude Auchinleck, later had occasion to point out to me; but I had all the co-operation I dared to expect from busy men for a contingency plan.
>
> Lord Wavell, naturally, took an interest in what I was doing: I reported to him from time to time, but was allowed to get on with the work without interruption. Wavell's awkward silences could sometimes be formidable, but I did not experience them when I came to report progress. He used to describe similar plans which he had caused to be prepared in Egypt during the war, and demonstrated with the aid of ink-pots and paper-weights on his desk.

Wavell nicknamed his plan Operation Madhouse, the withdrawal of the British from India province by province; Attlee on the other hand thought it a policy of scuttle unworthy of a great imperial power. While the Viceroy continued his efforts to get a working agreement between the Congress Party and the Muslim League the British Cabinet decided that a new initiative was necessary. On 18 December – while Wavell had been in London for discussions – Attlee had put out the first feelers to the man who would become the last Viceroy of India, Admiral Lord Louis Mountbatten. It was a brilliant choice. Mountbatten had proved himself to be an astute wartime commander with the panache for personal leadership, and in the first days of peace he had acted sensibly and liberally during the liberation of South-East Asia. He was also the King's cousin and enjoyed the kind of popularity that his contemporaries usually reserved for handsome Hollywood film stars. Attlee had good reasons for supposing that a fresh mind was needed to deal with a seemingly intractable problem and then for pushing through Mountbatten's appointment. What did him less credit was his treatment of Wavell, who was not told of the appointment and was given a short interval in which to quit India. A stay of execution was then granted to enable his daughter to be married and on 20 March 1947 he gave a farewell party for his staff and their wives.

> With a wry sense of humour and a twinkle in his only eye, he touched on recent events. He compared himself to King Nebuchadnezzar, 'who, as you remember, heard a voice from heaven, the equivalent in those days, I suppose, of a telegram from Whitehall. Some lines, which could be appropriate to my case, came into my head:
>
> > The banished monarch, now put out to grass
> > With patient oxen and the humble ass,
> > Said, as he champed the unaccustomed food,
> > "It may be wholesome, but it is not good."'

John Christie went on to serve Mountbatten but he, like many others present, thought that Attlee had behaved shabbily and that 'the manner of Lord Wavell's dismissal was not happy'.*

At Mountbatten's insistence Wavell was awarded an earldom but he continued to believe that, had he been allowed to remain in office, he could have reached accordance with the Indian leaders by the agreed dates. Paradoxically, his successor also demanded that a date would have to be fixed for the granting of independence – and Attlee had to consent to it. That he had turned down a similar proposal from Wavell seems not to have troubled him and later Attlee was pleased to accept the credit for the idea. Whatever else might happen, Mountbatten went to India with instructions that were unequivocal about the date of Britain's departure from the subcontinent: 'The date fixed for the transfer of power is a flexible one to within one month; but you should aim at 1 June 1948 as the effective date for the transfer of power.'

---

*On 31 March Wavell presented his final report to Attlee in 10 Downing Street. He was then ushered out of the room without a word of thanks and that night wrote of Attlee in his diary: 'He is a singularly ungracious person. I had no desire for an insincere little speech and was glad to be spared it, but it was not a good exhibition of manners.'

Chapter Six

A Lovely Time to Walk in Delhi

Mountbatten was a man who evoked a variety of responses both in those who met him and those who knew him only by reputation. Some fell under his easy charm; others thought him shallow and pompous. To his staff in Delhi he was a leader who brought directness and consistency to the task in hand. A working day of eighteen hours was not uncommon and men used to the calmer hours of Linlithgow's or Wavell's rule in India soon found that they were expected to share the burden. It had been agreed that Wavell's staff should stay at their posts until the new Viceroy had run his eye over them. When the time came for Christie to be interviewed, Mountbatten merely said, 'Planning an evacuation, are you? That's not my idea at all. I shall have to think about you.' Meanwhile, Christie was told to work with General Ismay, Mountbatten's Chief of Staff, and to complete the report. He quickly fell under the Mountbatten spell.

> For those who served with him at that time Lord Mountbatten was not only everything that history had recorded and will record of him, brilliant, inspiring, courageous, tireless; he was also a great leader, the perfect commanding officer. He drove his staff hard, but never harder than he drove himself, and whatever he asked one to do, it was as if he conferred a favour. At the end of the short time that I was privileged to work with him, I would have followed him anywhere.

In the interests of continuity, Christie and the other members of Wavell's staff were asked to stay on to become part of the Mountbatten team and the famous evacuation plan was eventually completed – only to be shelved. Later, as part of the Viceroy's twelve-man management team, Christie marvelled at the way 'ideas popped out of His Excellency's head like rabbits out of a warren' during the conferences which began each working day. Then it was 'the duty of his staff to catch them, and return the wilder ones to their holes before they had run too far'.

To men in the provinces and districts facing the turmoil of communal hostility Mountbatten's political manoeuvrings seemed to belong to another world. After all, had it not been the custom for provincial servants in Mogul times to utter the sentiment *Dilli dur ast* (Delhi is far away) whenever they were inclined to ignore some disagreeable command from the Peacock Throne? Yet even in the quiet places of India, where life proceeded at an even pace, and where communal bloodletting was not a problem, Mountbatten's appointment caused a few eyebrows to be raised. John Griffiths had gone out to India in 1937 to join the ICS and was Sub-Collector at Malappuram in Malabar early in 1947. He welcomed the announcement that heralded the end of British rule in India but, as he told his mother, he feared that the Attlee government might be falling into the same trap as the Congress Party – 'full of ideas and most pained when they find the ideas are not quite sufficient to meet the situation'.

> If we are going out the sooner we make up our minds the easier it will be. So we British Civil Servants are on the whole quite pleased with the announcement. If we just carried on the burden would fall on us; as it is, the responsibility is being shifted from our backs. The disgusting part is Wavell's resignation; it's funny how the solution for the Indian problem always seems to be, 'Try a new man – someone who knows nothing about it.' They send missions and have conferences but never seem to consult those with experience. I daresay we cannot do much but it is strange how politicians at home seem to think that a situation would be obvious to an untried and inexperienced man. Certainly Mountbatten does not know as much about India as Wavell.

Outside government and civil service circles opinion was just as sharply divided. At the time of his arrival anti-Mountbatten sentiment was quite strong; he was thought to be a playboy who knew little about India and to have used his political and social influence to replace a Viceroy who was plainly none of these things. How could a man so apparently unqualified, they asked, retrieve a situation in which Hindus wanted a unified India while the Muslims resisted the claim with violence, and in which parts of the country like the Punjab contained communal problems which were on the point of boiling over into civil war? Those were just some of the questions which civilians like Sheila Coldwell were asking themselves when Mountbatten arrived in India.

> I thought he was a very conceited man, full of his own importance and quite pleased to be the last Viceroy, with the emphasis on 'last'. At that time I didn't think that he was a man to be admired very much. He was in a difficult position, of course, because he was the servant of a government who knew absolutely nothing about India and who had no idea what to expect in India.

The British in India knew that the writing was on the wall but many could see no reason to accept the situation in the wholehearted and businesslike way recommended by Mount-batten. Far better, they reasoned, to play for time and try to preserve a united India; at the very least some areas of British influence could be preserved, the princes, particularly of the larger states of Hyderabad or Gwalior, could perhaps retain their independence, and most people wanted to see the Indian Army remain as a unified force. Mountbatten, though, was determined to see the thing through quickly, firstly because he had doubts about the ability of the British to prevent a communal conflagration, and secondly because his own style of leadership demanded a sharp tempo of progress. From the evidence of those who worked on his staff it is clear that his methods of operation were disarmingly simple: he would consolidate a point of negotiation as soon as it was gained and before the parties had found time to have second thoughts. That sense of urgency and commitment commended itself to men like Dr Taylor in Bombay's Wilson College who had been a supporter of Indian independence for many years.

> We were very glad that he came to India. He put aside all the old conventions of being Viceroy and all the uniforms and parades and so on. He was just an ordinary man and willing to meet people at their own level and this was a new idea. The pomp and circumstance were put aside and that really touched the Indians. What leapt at the heart of Nehru – and of Gandhi – was that Mount-batten and his wife, and I think his whole entourage, were prepared to put all that kind of thing to one side and deal with the

problem man to man. He was obviously a man of such extraordinary ability and charm; I mean he would charm anybody . . . the
only man he didn't quite charm was Jinnah.

Of course, this was the view of himself that Mountbatten was
anxious to promote and that was consolidated both by himself
and his many admirers later in life. There was a large element of
play-acting in Mountbatten's approach to the job; true, he threw
himself unstintingly into the tough, almost uncrackable, problems
thrown up by the ending of British rule in India, but he also
seemed to revel in the excitement at being centre-stage in the last
act of a great drama. For example, he made much of the fact that
he had been granted 'plenipotentiary powers' and that this
authority had allowed him to succeed where others had failed. In
the strict meaning of the phrase he had been given nothing of the
kind; all his major plans for a settlement had to be referred back
to London for agreement by the Cabinet and as his most recent
biographer, Philip Ziegler, points out, the phrase was never
mentioned during the period of Mountbatten's viceregality.
When questioned about the so-called powers later in life, Mountbatten would always claim that Attlee had granted them to him in
private and for security's sake had not minuted the agreement.
Nehru is supposed to have guessed that the new Viceroy had been
given fresh authority but such divination was hardly remarkable.
Mountbatten was a member of Britain's Royal Family and a
popular and glamorous war hero: even had the 'plenipotentiary
powers' not been conferred upon him, Mountbatten, the inner
man, certainly behaved as if he possessed them.

   Mountbatten was also fortunate in his wife, Edwina. Although
their marriage had seen its share of difficulties and disagreement
over the course of Mountbatten's career, Edwina seems to have
genuinely liked her time in India. Her close friendship with
Nehru is well known and there is little doubt that the mutual
attraction they had for each other helped to ease the passage of
the last days of British rule. As the Viceroy's wife she also shared
Mountbatten's appetite for hard work, at times rivalling her
husband in the effort she put into her public duties. Like her
husband she was unstuffy, committed to the task in hand and at
ease with everyone she met. There is also a suspicion that, like
her husband, she disapproved of Churchill's view of India and the

Indians. During the war Prem Bhatia had been attached to her staff while Mountbatten was Supremo and he had 'shivered in his pants' at her view of Anglo-Indian politics.

> I was travelling with her in her aircraft and I was the only Indian in her entourage. She found that I was sitting alone and walked back from the front seat and asked to sit next to me. She sat down and, after a few pleasantries, said, 'Do you know who stands between you and independence?' Even if I knew it I wouldn't have said the truth because I was wearing uniform. She said, 'I'll tell you. The man who stands between you and independence is Churchill.'

Later, in Calcutta, she invited Bhatia and others to a private dinner party at the Saturday Club; but when he arrived he was refused admission by the Indian staff. The story got back to Lady Mountbatten who immediately went round to Bhatia's residence to apologise personally. Such consideration was manna to the Indians who met her but it was not likely to go down well with the memsahibs in the clubs. The Mountbattens also made it a rule to cut from their invitation lists any Europeans who were rude in public to their Indian guests.

Having arrived in India, Mountbatten moved quickly. He met all the leading politicians and instantly struck up close relationships with them all bar Jinnah who, as Taylor rightly says, refused to fall under the Mountbatten charm. He had no need to: his mind had already been made up about the partition of India and the creation of Pakistan. Within a few weeks Mountbatten was already beginning to feel that although the Congress leaders paid lip-service to the idea of a united India, they too – with the exception of Gandhi – were moving towards the possibility of partition. Behind the scenes in Delhi John Christie had already started work on the administrative masterplan should such an eventuality come to pass.

> The objective was still to hand over power to the government of a united India. In all the cut and thrust of negotiation to this end, it became apparent to some of us that partition, before the word had been officially breathed or its possibility openly admitted (at any rate in the Viceroy's camp), was likely, however unpalatable, to be the solution. At a private lunch in the house of V.P. Menon, the constitutional adviser, six of us discussed the implications and decided that, since it is the duty of civil servants to protect their masters from being taken by surprise, we must have ready for the

Viceroy a contingent plan which could be laid before the political
leaders, if and when they should cut their Gordian Knot.

The plan, known as 'The Administrative Consequences of Partition', was a bold attempt to forecast what would happen to the
country's assets should India and Pakistan decide to go their
separate ways. Everything, from railway rolling stock to the
armed forces, from national art collections to the currency
reserves, from government papers to gold ingots, from prisoners
in jails to lunatics in asylums, had to be divided. To accomplish
such a Herculean task required not only tact and good sense; it
also needed stamina and a capacity for long hours of hard work.
To assist him in his task Christie enlisted two fellow ICS officers,
one a Hindu, H.M. Patel, and the other a Muslim, Chaudhuri
Mohammed Ali, who later became the Prime Minister of
Pakistan.

> I let them into the secret and we had a series of lunchtime meetings
> *à trois* in my house. They did most of the hard work; I did the
> editing, reconciliation and stitching together. Reconciliation in
> another sense was sometimes necessary, for the bargaining was
> tough and on several occasions a 'walk-out' by one or other of my
> colleagues was narrowly averted.

The pay-off for the civil servants came on 3 June 1947. By then
the Congress leaders had reached the reluctant conclusion that if
independence were to be achieved quickly then some form of
balkanisation was inevitable, and Jinnah had been forced to
compromise with a 'two-winged' Pakistan in the north-east and
the north-west of the subcontinent. Following a whirlwind time-
table of meetings and hurried agreements, the Viceroy's plans for
partition and the transfer of power were revealed in Delhi. The
new state of Pakistan would be formed out of the states and
provinces of Baluchistan, Sind, North-West Frontier Province;
India would comprise most of the remainder; the Punjab and
Bengal would be bisected and the princely states would be given
the opportunity to negotiate with one or other of the two new
states. Importantly, from Mountbatten's point of view, both new
countries would become dominions within the British Commonwealth, thereby emphasising their links with Britain and its Royal
Family. With dramatic effect Mountbatten then tabled Christie a
report which outlined the administrative consequences of the

plan which the leaders had agreed to accept. 'Now, gentlemen,' he said, 'this is what partition means. This is the job we must get down to at once and finish before the fifteenth of August.'

The plan having been agreed and announced to the world Mountbatten faced the press on the following day. Speaking without notes – like Roosevelt in his prime, noted one admiring American journalist – he laid bare the main points of the argument and then fielded questions both about the manner of the transfer of power and Britain's commitment to carry it through. Mountbatten would not have been the man he was had he not provided the occasion with one great dramatic moment. Asked when the transfer of power would take place, he replied casually, 'I think about the fifteenth of August.' Like all good storytellers, Mountbatten would claim that the date was pure inspiration, that it came to him out of the blue and that he fixed on it because it was the anniversary of his wartime appointment as Supreme Commander in South-East Asia. If we are to accept Christie's evidence, though, the Viceroy had already announced the date at the previous day's meeting of Indian leaders and there is evidence to suggest that, earlier still, Mountbatten had discussed the timing with Nehru and Jinnah and had proposed mid-August as the most suitable date. Come what may, the British would leave India seventy-three days later and it was up to him, his staff and the politicians to ensure that it really would happen. (After astrologers had warned that the date was inauspicious it was agreed that the transfer in India would take place on the midnight hour of 14 August.)

The announcement did wonders to concentrate the minds of the British community in India. For the businessmen – the box-wallahs – it was a case of facing up to the fact that most firms would be transferred to Indian or Pakistani ownership but that their expertise would still be needed. Killick Nixon's in Bombay, for example, was transformed from a private British partnership into a public limited company with an Indian board of directors. At the time, June 1947, Wilfrid Russell felt that there could be no place for him in the new set-up. 'I have come to the conclusion,' he wrote in his diary, 'that now we are leaving India, I have no wish to stay on in the emasculating and exasperating atmosphere of a Hindu republic.' Time was to prove him wrong, though, as Russell remained in India after independence to play a role in fashioning the future of the new country.

Similar fears invaded the British community in Calcutta – which Russell, incidentally, did not like, feeling that it was more like an eighteenth-century colony which had been cut off from the rest of modern India. Sheila Coldwell decided to stay on, an easy decision for her, 'because in those days we did exactly as our husbands told us'. Another kind of loyalty ws also involved. Her husband had served in the army during the war and his firm had kept his job open for him. In spite of the terror of the Calcutta riots in 1946 he was determined that his future should be with the new India.

> The writing was on the wall, obviously, and we did think about coming home. In fact, I was very keen to come home; I had a presentiment that something awful was going to happen. My husband was prepared to come back and did in fact try to get a job in Britain, but it wasn't easy at that time. His company had been very good to him right through the war and continued to look after him while he was in the army. They had been extremely generous. I think he felt that he owed loyalty to them – as people in those days did, a loyalty that has gone out of business now.

Generally, the jute managers stayed on too. The industry still needed them and there was no urgent necessity to think of leaving. Ron Fraser had lived through the worst of the Bengal riots 'without ever feeling nervous' about them; in the run-up to independence he was working near Barrackpore and never thought twice about where his loyalties lay. 'Most of our friends decided to stay on, too. And of course we had Indian friends, both in Calcutta and in the mill with whom we got on very well.'

The only serious change that George Robertson noticed was that the British could no longer involve themselves in attempts to stop communal hostility, of which there was no shortage of incidents in his part of Bengal. He, too, had decided that his future lay in India but he had to steel himself against the hatred and violence which erupted in the period before and after the granting of independence. It was as if Pandora's Box had been opened, and the authorities were powerless to intervene.

> It was something we had to stand aside from. We had to ignore it because we couldn't possibly allow ourselves to be embroiled in any communal trouble; we couldn't show ourselves to be siding with Mohammedans against Hindus or Hindus against Mohamme-dans. We had to be completely impartial . . . I saw people being

attacked in the streets. A lone Mohammedan chased by a group of Hindus, and being beaten to death. I saw another poor unfortunate Mohammedan being stabbed by six Hindus but there was nothing you could do about it. They had the army out but these were isolated incidents and the army couldn't possibly cope with everything.

A further problem was the continuing irritation of lightning strikes caused by fluctuating and often wildly conflicting rumours of massacres in other parts of the province, all at a time when the jute industry was trying to get itself back on to a peacetime footing.

The difficulties facing the police at that time are well illustrated by Robins's experiences in the United Provinces where he had been put in command of the Special Armed Constabulary after a spell of leave in Britain. Once the date of independence had been announced by Mountbatten there was a flurry of activity in the Punjab and Bengal as rumours began to fly about the proposed divisions of the communities. A large group of Sikhs had fled out of the Punjab to Dehra Dun where they began to cause trouble by threatening the lives of the local Muslim population. In turn, the terrified Muslims had decided to escape to the safety of Saharanpur; but having paid exorbitant fares to the local bus company they then found that the drivers were Sikhs who had no intention of leaving before dark. Robins was ordered by the Commissioner of Meerut to intervene as the local police force was exhausted after days of coping with communal riots in the city. This placed him in a dilemma as his men were supposed to be guarding a prisoner-of-war camp, but, taking a chance, he decided to leave a token presence and form a convoy using all the available policemen at his disposal. He then ordered the Sikh drivers to start their engines and to drive out of Dehra Dun: if there was any trouble, he reminded them, they would be the first to suffer.

Passing the outskirts of the city I could see the sugar-cane fields alive with Sikhs armed with swords and guns. They were livid with rage because they were losing their prey. They could see we were strongly armed and we got through. I carried on with the convoy through a hill pass, got them safely over that and then I left them, to continue to Saharanpur. I thought by that stage they were safe. I returned to Dehra Dun and next day I felt terrible when I heard a widespread rumour that after I pulled out with my men the

refugees had all been massacred. It proved a false alarm. They did
get through unscathed but it was a nasty moment for me when I
heard the rumour. Fortunately too, nobody had escaped from the
prisoner-of-war camp either, while I was using my men who should
have been guarding it.

With their forces overstretched and usually outnumbered by the
mobs, the IP officers did their best to stem the flood of communal
violence that erupted in parts of India in the weeks before
independence, but, all too often, like Robins, they could deal
only with isolated instances over which they could exert some
control. Unhappily, it has to be recorded that in some places – as
had happened in Bengal – Indian policemen actually joined in the
killing: this happened in Bharatpur where there was bloody
fighting between the Hindu Jats and Muslim Jats, or Meos. For
centuries the Muslims had lived in the Mathura district of United
Provinces which borders Bharatpur and their relationship with
the Hindus had been cordial enough. The tide of Hindu nationalism changed all that and when the Maharajah of Bharatpur
decided that his state should be cleared of Meos communal
rioting degenerated into civil war. The British IP officers did their
utmost to keep the Jats apart in the Mathura district but they
were powerless to intervene on one occasion when lorryloads of
Meos were massacred by the Bharatpur Police escort which was
supposed to be guarding a convoy on the way to Agra.

Incidents such as these obviously coloured British attitudes
when government servants came to consider their own positions
after the transfer of power had taken place. A number of IP
officers had been invited to stay on to serve India or Pakistan but
against those offers had to be balanced the difficulty of serving
the new dominions as a British 'mercenary'. Moreover, officers
from the Central Provinces, for example, had been told that their
services would not be required and they balked at the idea of
going to East Bengal or Sind which, they reasoned, would be like
foreign countries to them. Men began to weigh up their career
opportunities and to decide whether it would be worthwhile
remaining in their posts to serve a new government, possibly
under officers who had once been their subordinates. Even if they
were found to be suitable, British officers also realised that old
scores could be settled by politicians or colleagues who had once
disagreed with them, and the usual three-year contract on offer

was hardly a guarantee of continuing security. Another factor which they had to take into account was the payment of compensation and proportionate pensions at an age when most of them were still young enough to look forward to further employment. Because the British had given themselves a bare ten weeks to push through the details of the transfer of power government servants were suddenly brought face to face with an uncertain future. This was particularly true in the Indian Civil Service.

Mike Stuart was in Dacca in the months before partition and independence; it had been settled as the capital of East Pakistan and he decided to 'sign on the dotted line', to remain in his post and serve the new country. Great events might have been decided in Delhi where the administrative problems of creating two new dominions were hammered out, but for the ICS officers in the districts the time before the transfer was often taken up with difficult personal decisions. A number of options were open to them and because the ICS was a covenanted service these had been enshrined in two government White Papers. They could stay on in one or other of the two new countries, provided that they were acceptable; they could leave the service with financial compensation and a proportionate pension; they could apply for a transfer to the British Home Civil Service, or they could stay on to work for the British High Commission staffs which would be needed in India and Pakistan. Very few officers stayed on in India whereas a goodly proportion followed Stuart into Pakistan. The reasons are not hard to find. Pakistan was less well endowed than India in terms of civil administration. Many ICS officers preferred working with Muslims and were tired of dealing with an increasingly intransigent Congress Party. There was also a fear, not entirely groundless, that they might be placed in subordinate positions and be obliged to carry out disagreeable orders.

It was a difficult choice. Younger officers felt that they were not quite ready to come home and many of them were willing to throw in their lot with Pakistan. Not only was Jinnah's new state badly in need of a sound administration but there was a general feeling that it had received a raw deal during the division of the spoils. There was, too, an age-old feeling among some British officers that the Muslim races, with their simplicity of character and directness of speech, were preferable to the Hindus. Tall, upright, uncomplicated and conservative in outlook, they appeared to mirror British ideals of service and loyalty that were so often missing in the brasher Hindu nationalists.

India, though, was another matter. Continued service there could break the spell of loyalty to the raj and there was a growing concern that no one wanted to see the running down or possible destruction of such a noble edifice as the ICS with all its traditions of self-sacrifice and service. 'As far as I can see,' wrote Alan Flack to his wife from Muzaffarpur in Bihar, 'the sort of life one expected before the war has disappeared at least for some time. There's no use despairing about it. The only thing to do is to adapt oneself to the changed circumstances.' Flack had turned down the opportunity of working for Pakistan and his last days in India were spent haggling over the correct rate of compensation for his return to Britain. What he feared most, he told his wife, was to land a mediocre job in the Home Civil Service in London which would mean 'living in some back street and tooling off to a stuffy office every day'. Eventually he was allowed to stay on until September in order to complete his ten years' service which would give him compensation of £4,700 and a pension of £455 a year.

The fear of dropping standards of living troubled those who had grown accustomed to a life of relative ease and comfort: for them the prospect of living in semi-detached suburbia was a poor exchange for a spacious bungalow and a clan of servants at one's beck and call. 'I'm afraid I don't want a job in the Home Civil,' John Griffiths told his mother. 'My life of relative freedom has spoiled me for it.' For the ICS officer in particular such an exchange was doubly unwelcome, for in India he was very much his own man, often in sole charge of a huge district with manifold responsibilities; whereas in London he would have to work within the strictures of a civil-service department. Griffiths also noted the phenomenon of 'a kind of two-way evacuation' – 'we have people here who want to go home because they are afraid of the Indian situation, and others coming out becuase they don't like England.' As would become increasingly apparent, home-bound families who had spent the better part of their lives in India would not find it easy adapting to the tenor of life in socialist post-war Britain.

The problem was exacerbated for the men who worked in districts which fell victim to communal hostility because they had to witness the horrors of riot, violence and massacres. Many lived through those days with heavy hearts, aware that they dared not show any partiality to either side, yet anxious to see the transfer of power done well. In many places civil authority had broken down altogether and normal administration had become a thing of the past, while the machinery of partition was set in motion. Experiences could range from the ridiculous to the tragic: officers in Bengal, for example, had to oversee the strict division of office equipment; in the Punjab they had to organise the removal of whole communities, Hindus to India, Muslims to Pakistan. Concern about their own futures might have seemed out of place but with independence looming, it was, of course, impossible to ignore. Even in Delhi, where John Christie was entering the final lap, thought had to be given to what would happen after 15 August. The civil servants at the centre of government might have had their days taken up with redrafting constitutional niceties, arranging the plebiscites in Assam or the North-West Frontier Province, or investigating the bisection of the Punjab and Bengal, but family matters, too, had to be considered. Christie applied for the Home Civil Service and was offered employment by the Foreign Office, the lure being an immediate overseas appointment – in Lahore. Being at the centre of Indian administration he decided to hold off making a decision and was suitably rewarded.

> It was a new job of a quasi-diplomatic kind, to represent in Delhi a group of interests of which the chief constituent was Assocham – short for the Associated Chambers of Commerce and Industry in India – whose membership was predominantly, but not entirely, British. Their headquarters were in Calcutta, the commercial capital of India, but at an awkward distance from the seat of government. Mountbatten and Ismay, whom I had consulted, had encouraged me to accept this offer of employment, arguing that British business interests in India, which were considerable, would need a representative in the capital to advise them in the new political context.

The saddest cuts, perhaps, were reserved for the Indian Army. As happens at the end of any war, conscripted men wanted to return to civilian life and to pick up the strands of their private lives. Wartime emergency commissioned officers, British and Indian, wanted to be released, as did the many thousands of men who had swelled the ranks of the Indian Army during the war; conversely, the professionals wanted to return to peacetime soldiering, secure in the knowledge that they had all acquitted themselves well. The army in which they had served was the largest and most professional ever to have been raised in India. It had given valiant and fiercely committed service to the Allies throughout the war and despite the doubts of Churchill and others it had proved its loyalty and fighting abilities. In the first uneasy days of peace it had weathered the storm of the INA trials and had stood firm in coming to the aid of the civil power during the disturbances in Bengal, Bombay and the states of the Gangetic plain. Politics, though, had now intruded too deeply into its being, the loyalty of some units was in question and, in any case, Indian nationalism could no longer be ignored.

Sadly, because its integrity had been beyond reproach since the Mutiny, the Indian Army, like the other institutions of British rule, was to be divided up between the two new dominions. Regiments which included men of several races – each working in separate companies, yet in complete harmony with one another – were to be broken up so that both India and Pakistan could have their own sovereign forces. The decision caused a great deal of anguish and bitterness amongst the regimental officers. Men who had seen Sikh serve with Punjab Muslim, Meo Jat with Hindu, had to come to terms with the fact that the one institution which provided racial and religious solidarity in India was to be disbanded. Major Mohamed Ibrahim Qureshi, the regimental historian of the 1st Punjab Regiment, noted sadly that the division ended a great tradition, that 'what had taken two hundred years to build was dismembered in three months'.

> So ended that remarkable partnership in which Hindus and Muslims had served in mutual friendship and respect in the same battalion for nearly two centuries. This separation also severed the equally long and perhaps unique brotherhood in arms of the Indian soldier and the British officer, which had stood for so long the strains and stresses of war and peace in many lands.

Qureshi's regiment was allotted to Pakistan and the parting of the ways meant that its Sikh company was transferred to the Sikh Regiment and its Rajputs to the Rajputana Rifles, both of which had been designated as Indian Army regiments. Some regiments were spared, such as the Mahratta Light Infantry, the Sikh Regiment and the Royal Garwhal Rifles, which all went to India, but many others were divided, much to the sorrow and consternation of their officers and men. For those who lived through the days of the final parades the memory of those farewells to their brothers in arms still has the power to move.

> On the eve of partition there were big farewell parties. We all gave tearful farewells and final hugs of affection to our brothers who were going to Pakistan. I can't think of a single instance of bad blood being between the two. The Baluch, for example, had one company of Brahmins, one of Pathans and two of Punjabi Muslims but they all had to be separated after partition. Later there was some trouble in the Punjab but that was different.

Unfortunately a less pleasant experience awaited D.K. Palit when he assumed command of his new regiment, 3rd/9th Gurkhas, which had been transferred to the new Indian Army after independence. Although instructions had been given to all Gurkha regiments to hand over their property intact, the officers of the 9th Gurkhas had attempted to smuggle the regimental silver and mess funds back to Britain. Instead of dining off silver, Palit found that there were only tin plates in the mess. Then, when other items of equipment began to go missing, he took the only course of action open to him.

> I had to ask the British officers to leave. I ordered a jeep, had garlands put on it and then it was pulled out. It was a bad time
> . . . but when I wrote to the colonel of the regiment he hounded out all the British officers who had taken the silver and they returned every single piece. You can't really blame them, though. If the Chinese had taken over my battalion, say, I would have done the same thing.

The problem was that the British Gurkha officers felt frustrated by the way they had been treated. Not until 8 August had they been told their fate and the news had upset them: of the twenty-seven battalions only eight would be transferred to the British Regular Army, those being the two battalions of the 2nd, 6th, 7th and 10th regiments. The remainder would go to the army of India. It was a difficult period for those British officers who regarded the Gurkha regiments as home and, as Palit understands, they would have preferred to see all the Gurkha regiments remaining in British service.

The British had in fact hoped to keep the Indian Army in being
as a unified force which would then have served the two countries
and helped to ease the problems thrown up by partition. Mountbatten came to India determined to try to keep the unity which
Auchinleck thought was essential if large-scale communal
bloodletting were to be avoided. It was an attractive argument
but one that, under the prevailing circumstances, was impractical.
Jinnah was impatient for partition to proceed and that required
the division of the institutions; Congress was suspicious that
Britain still favoured the Muslim element in the Indian Army and
so Mountbatten reluctantly put in hand the break-up of the
Indian Army forces. (The body appointed to oversee the operation existed under the bland title of the Armed Forces Reconstruction Committee.) The move caused great bitterness,
especially amongst the British regular officers of the Indian
Army, many of whom still believed that there might be a role for
them to play after independence and partition.

Their traditional belief in the value of morale and *esprit de
corps* meant that the army was not just a career but a way of life,
their regiments not just a collection of individuals but a family.
The destruction of such a fine instrument, though politically
necessary, was for many of them a terrible betrayal. Even
Auchinleck, a loyal imperial servant, hated the task which had
become his lot but like everyone else he had to put aside personal
feelings and get on with the job.

Things were slightly better ordered in the Royal Indian Navy,
first, because it was a smaller and more intimate service and,
second, because it lacked a large British officer cadre. Some
British regular officers went back to the Royal Navy, some stayed
on for a while with the new Indian and Pakistani navies and some
chose the moment to retire. For the Indian officers, though, the
division of the RIN was a new beginning. Like A.K. Chatterjee –
in 1947 on a staff course at Greenwich – they believed that the
partition of the navy was the inevitable consequence of the
British leaving India. If there were problems, these were largely
logistic.

There wasn't much argument or bad blood about it amongst the
officers principally because the government had laid down that it
[RIN] would be divided two to one. That meant that India would
get two ships and Pakistan one, in that proportion. There was no

difficulty about it. What was difficult with us was that a lot of senior sailors were Punjabi Muslims and all of them went to Pakistan. We ourselves got very short of senior men and had to borrow quite a few from the British. We also lost in Karachi three big establishments, one of them HMIS *Himalaya*, the gunnery school, and the boys' training establishment. Having lost them we quickly had to put up with those things.

Commander Goord was the naval member of the Armed Forces Reconstruction Committee and he remembers that in one instance two frigates had to lie alongside one another at sea to enable the transfer of personnel to take place. The worst moments, as in the other military and civilian institutions, came with the partition of the establishments where it was not uncommon for pieces of equipment to be divided to the last office chair. Only the good sense of the supervising British officers and some of their Indian counterparts brought dignity to what might otherwise have been a mean-minded scramble. Stories abound of British officers looking on aghast as former comrades and colleagues bickered over the meanest and least important items, such as a reserve supply of uniform buttons.

All over the subcontinent events were crowding in upon each other as the deadline for independence crept ever nearer; Mountbatten marked the passing days with a special countdown calendar which showed how many days were left to complete the transfer of power. All of a sudden, domestic arrangements, long disregarded, had to be made immediately, passages had to be booked and plans made for the future. A shortage of merchant shipping added to the difficulties for, quite apart from the government servants and their families, there was a lengthy list of British servicemen awaiting passage home, and many of these had served for six years in India. Another task for John Christie in Delhi was to draw up plans for priority passages and to ensure that Mountbatten's plea for 'more ships for India' was heard in London.

Another job which I had in those days was a different kind of evacuation plan, not so secret. After six years of war there was a long waiting list of British and other civilians and their families, for passages to Europe on ships which were in short supply. Their needs competed with those of others, of army families and of special categories, such as the Polish refugees who had made their escape overland to India, where they had spent the duration of the war. All these urgencies had to be co-ordinated, and the arrival of passengers at the quayside so timed that not a square foot of scarce shipping space was avoidably wasted. I took a hand in this complicated process, and also had to see that H.E.'s voice was heard from time to time above the clamour for ships from many corners of the world.

Before the war the voyage to and from India had been one of the great charms of imperial life. Whether it was by P & O first-class through the Suez Canal or by a leisurely merchantman on the long detour around Africa, it was part of the Indian experience and one that few have ever forgotten. 'In those days it was *de rigueur* to dress for dinner and woe betide the rebel who argued that as a fare-paying passenger he had the right to wear what he liked,' remembers an IP cadet who first went out to India on the SS *Viceroy of India*.

Post-war conditions turned out to be rather different. The British merchant marine had lost 18 million tons of shipping to enemy submarines and only two-thirds of that loss had been made good by rebuilding. Liners and troopers were in short supply and many of those which worked the India routes had been converted to take even more passengers. Families had to share in cramped cabins, troopdecks were often overcrowded and, overall, conditions were spartan. There was a pecking order – senior officers tended to get preferential treatment – and in the lower decks an atmosphere of camaraderie and shared discomfort helped to lighten the burden of what was a long and slow journey. Most were just glad to be on the move and on their way home. When the 2nd Black Watch left Pakistan on the trooper *Empire Halladale* deck space was severely limited and exercise had to be confined to regular doses of Highland dancing, but the overriding emotion was the sheer pleasure of returning to Scotland, a job well done.

The voyage took place in an age when most travel was slow, crowded and tedious, even when the journey was made on the fast-developing air services which mushroomed into being after the war. Trooping to India by air was a recent novelty, confined mainly to RAF personnel at one end of the scale and at the other to senior officers and officials who had to make frequent trips between London and India. Mountbatten had made it a condition of his accepting the appointment as Viceroy that he be allowed to retain the services of his Avro York, MW-102, a relatively fast and modern civilian transport which he had used during the latter stages of the war. For the others who travelled by air it was something of a lottery. Called back to India for a combined operations exercise in January 1947 Commander Shaw found that his initial dismay at the sudden recall was softened by the ministrations of the BOAC staff who operated the prestigious flying-boat services from Poole.

> I left Launceston by train, on the morning of 8th January 1947 and, having reported to BOAC, went in a coach to the train in Victoria Station, where compartments were reserved for those flying on Service 13Q94, most luxurious travel and VIP treatment. We arrived at Harbour Heights Hotel, Sandbanks in time for dinner and, next morning, after an excellent breakfast, we went by launch to the converted Sunderland flying boat. We took off at about 1000 and had lunch flying over France at about 13,000 feet and landed at Marseilles about 1600, where we were taken to a hotel for the night. BOAC were most apologetic about our having to be called at 0530 the next day. We landed at Augusta in Sicily for lunch and then on to Cairo for another overnight stay.

The journey took five days in all – a far cry from the sea voyage with its different temperatures and constantly changing sea conditions. It was a far cry, too, from the journey undertaken by Tom Berry and other 'erks' who had to put up with a style of travel that would have been unthinkable were it not for the continuing wartime shortages. He left RAF Gransden Lodge in a converted Liberator bomber carrying twenty-six passengers, eighteen of whom had to sit in the aircraft's bomb-bay.

> The bomb-bay seats are canvas slings [he wrote in his diary on 29 January 1946] and we sit with knees almost touching. Wearing the Mae Wests and carrying a side pack it is difficult to move easily. I hope no idiot will accidentally or deliberately inflate the lifesaver. The prospect of escaping through the rear hatch in event of emergency is not something that calls for careful consideration. Because of my lack of inches I found it hellish difficult getting in. We hear stories of these flights going down in the Alps . . . The route is south over Reading and across the Channel and the French coast near Le Havre. The windows on

the bomb-bay are small and inaccessible. We see nothing and rely on information passed down by word of mouth from the crew.

His journey took much the same time as Shaw's but in place of the Sunderland's relative luxury, the Liberator offered only basic amenities, such as 'a funnel for peeing into up front', the constant roar of the engines and 'an indigestible block of dried oatmeal, a block of iron-hard compressed fruit, boiled sweets and chewing gum' served up as in-flight catering. It was a familiar story: the civilian airliners of the 1930s had been pressed into RAF wartime service; thereafter aircraft production and development had been confined to military types and it was not until 1944 that manufacturers could turn their attention to designing and building a new generation of passenger planes. The aircraft which flew on the India routes were either converted bombers or derivatives such as the Halton and the Sandringham, both of which were developed from surplus RAF aircraft.

The primary requirement was to get service personnel and their families home before the date of independence and they were given top priority. Even so, despite the rush to slim down the British presence, the traffic was by no means one-way only. At the big transit camps like Deolali, Malir or Mauripur there was still a constant toing and froing of drafts as replacements arrived to relieve demobbed wartime personnel. Their task was to maintain the British military presence which would cover independence and partition, for even though they would be disallowed from interfering in communal problems after 15 August they were still required to protect British interests. During the post-independence massacres many British servicemen worked selflessly in refugee camps and RAF transport squadrons did sterling work flying refugees out of dangerous trouble-spots. 31 Squadron, for example, flew scores of mercy missions, on one occasion uplifting a record number of 65 Muslim refugees on board a Dakota transport, and on another rescuing 1,859 men of the Wanu Brigade which had been cut off by Pathans in the North-West Frontier Province.

It would be misleading, however, to give the impression that the entire European population was on the point of leaving India in the period before independence. Many people were on the move, it is true, but many more had decided to stay on, not just as administrators and businessmen but also because they felt a sense of commitment to the country. In his novel *Staying On*, Paul Scott examined the plight of one couple who did decide to stay either because they felt at home in India and could not bear the thought of returning to post-war Britain or because they wanted to give the new India a chance before making up their minds. In their case, Tusker, the retired Indian Army officer, and his wife Lucy also had strong personal reasons for remaining 'amid the alien corn'; both had an exasperated love for India and its people. ('I'm happier hanging on in India,' Tusker tells Lucy, 'not for India as India but because I can't just merely think of it as a place where I drew my pay for the first twenty-five years of my working life, which is a hell of a long time anyway, though by rights it should have been longer.')

Similar concerns, though for different reasons perhaps, lay at the heart of the missionary community in India. Dr Taylor of Wilson College had no intention of giving up his post as he believed that his service was to India and the Indians, whether or not the British were in control. Similarly, Dr Winifred Bailey in Poona was committed to the development of women's medicine in the new India and was slightly surprised when her servants asked her for references shortly before independence. 'We looked at them and said, "Why?" They said, "You're going, aren't you?" And we then said, no. They didn't differentiate between ourselves and the British Raj.' While acknowledging that these were simple people who were unaware of the changing events, Winifred Bailey did approve of what was happening. 'It was high time that they were thinking for themselves and not being ruled by someone else. I was not only pleased, but thankful that it was happening.'

There were other signs in the territory. Morton, the police officer, finally concluded that the time had come to leave India when the Hindu students of Punjab University demanded to be allowed to fly the Congress flag, and not the Union Jack, on the occasion of the Governor of the province presiding at an academic convocation.

The students won the battle and no British flag was flown. I was however struck by the spectacle of a young nationalist mounting the roof of his college to hoist the Congress flag to the accompaniment of a bugle fanfare. The youth was quivering with emotion and I thought – 'Well, it really is time that we quit and leave them to sort themselves out.'

In Bombay Wilfrid Russell was struck by the new mood of self-confidence he encountered amongst his Indian colleagues or their guests at Rotary Club lunches. They might have had fears for the future but these were as little when set alongside the exhilaration of imminent independence. On one occasion Russell listened to an Indian doctor explaining – quite optimistically – that no amount of industrialisation could raise agricultural standards, that inefficiency would be as widespread as before, but at least it would be an Indian problem. 'I don't think he was trying to please me,' he noted. 'He certainly didn't. What a topsy-turvy place it is, exasperating yet somehow charming, uncomfortable yet satisfying, utterly divided yet in a mysterious way a country rather than a continent.' Like others Russell was also aware of the differing and contrasting emotions that had been unleashed by the knowledge that independence was near at hand: 'an amazing phenomenon, this burning desire for independence, this love of England, this hate of English people, this idealism about India.' It was almost as if the anticipation was as exciting as the impending event.

A sense of expectancy, leavened by no little apprehension, also dominated dealings with the leaders of the interim government. The decision for partition having been accepted, there remained innumerable problems to be solved, many of which would have to wait until the post-independence period. Some of these were nuts-and-bolts matters, like the question of whether or not the Union Jack should adorn the new countries' flags; others were more serious and potentially explosive. The question of the partition of Bengal and the Punjab was put into the hands of an independent commission headed by Sir Cyril Radcliffe, a lawyer in whom Mountbatten rightly placed a good deal of faith.

Success in all things was an important part of the Mountbatten image. Nehru had fallen under its spell and even if Jinnah had not, there appears to have been at least the basis of some mutual respect. With the princely states it was a different matter. The more astute leaders might have seen that the writing was on the wall when Churchill, their chief supporter, lost the 1945 general election, but their fears for the future had been assuaged by the appointment of Mountbatten, a scion of the British Royal Family. As it turned out, though, it was to be the Viceroy himself who was to persuade them to accede to the new order, despite all their misgivings. Using his personal charm to good effect, and overriding those IPS officers who opposed him, Mountbatten managed to persuade the Indian princes that their best option was to sign an 'Instrument of Accession' which would bind them to India or Pakistan while allowing them to retain their sovereignty. Much of the donkey work might have been done by V.P. Menon who argued for the formula which offered this unexpected route to reconciliation, but it was Mountbatten's performance, resplendent in admiral's uniform, at the Chamber of Princes on 25 July which finally won them over. Three weeks later, by 15 August, only three states had not fallen in with Mountbatten's plans – Hyderabad, Jammu and Kashmir, and Junagadh.

As with the difficulties facing the boundaries commission there was a liberal use of scissors and tape in Mountbatten's handling of the princes, but with the days ticking by any hesitation could have been calamitous. During that hectic period Prem Bhatia was working for the *Tribune* and he was an interested observer of the events which were unfolding in Delhi. Although he realised that the British administration ran the risk of making errors in their haste to transfer power, he believed at the time that Mountbatten was right to push through the major details with such vigour.

> Mountbatten was a soldier, a clear-headed person. He had an objective which was to leave India in peace as a going concern. For all I know he may have had instructions to encourage partition but I think by the time he came on the scene partition had become inevitable. I was in Lucknow in 1946 and the leaders of the Muslim League were totally irreconcilable to the idea of India. If Mountbatten precipitated it, if he expedited the operation, I don't think he did wrong . . . I have no time for people who blame Mountbatten, as if he were a sinister agent of the British government.

With the benefit of hindsight, many people, British and Indian, have reached different or opposing views about Mountbatten's role and these will be discussed in a later chapter. At the time, the preparations for independence, however speedily they were arranged, were just part of an overall plan that had to be implemented and few could afford the time to consider them calmly or rationally. The increasing communal violence also helped to concentrate people's minds. Not only had it forced the politicians to compromise, it had also convinced officials that there could be no going back, that Britain had to achieve the transfer of power before there was civil war or administrative breakdown.

Some idea of the nest of vipers which lay below the surface can be glimpsed in Radcliffe's boundary commission. Already, by August, violence had been flaring up in the Punjab and the impending announcement of the awards only served to heighten the tension. Against the advice of his officials, including Christie, Mountbatten decided to withhold Radcliffe's findings until the day after independence, 16 August. In that way, he reasoned, any pain caused by the announcement would be soothed by the nationwide rejoicing. Inevitably, though, there were leaks,* Radcliffe having completed his task by 9 August, and the people most vexed by the impending partition were the Sikhs who inclined, naturally, to India. In the ensuing chaos Sikhs turned on their Muslim neighbours on the Indian side of the border where the worst atrocities were committed in debatable lands like Ferozepur and Gurdaspur; in return, Muslims attacked Sikhs before they could escape from the new Pakistan. Whatever Radcliffe's findings, no one was going to be truly satisfied and the result was going to be misery for the people of the Punjab. Amongst the more extremist Sikh nationalists the call for a Sikh homeland became more strident and four decades later it has still not been laid to rest. Ismay's Sikh adviser, Major John McLaughlin 'Billy' Short, a former Indian Army officer, was recalled to India to help with the problem and, prophetically, he saw nothing but trouble in the years to come.

> Owing to the close intermingling of the population, this [partition] will tend to set up strife in two halves of the Punjab which will probably spread and spread till gradually the whole of Northern India is involved in turmoil and there may be up to 50 or 100 years of anarchy such as we have been seeing in China in our lifetime.

Short knew what he was talking about. He had been a member of the Cripps Mission in 1946 and was trusted by the Sikhs, even by their fiery leader Master Tara Singh.

*Pakistani historians have suggested that Mountbatten discussed the findings with Nehru and amended the awards in India's favour. There is no evidence to support their argument.

Another problem which troubled the Viceroy was the protocol of the transfer of power, especially his own position thereafter. Because both countries would remain within the Commonwealth as dominions, they would have a governor-general and, privately, Mountbatten assumed that he would be invited to occupy that post in both India and Pakistan. Nehru certainly welcomed the idea but to Mountbatten's chagrin Jinnah would not agree. He preferred, instead, to become Governor-General of the new Pakistan himself and was unmoved by those who told him that he was removing from Mountbatten the crowning glory of his reign as Viceroy. Reluctantly, London agreed to the appointment and urged Mountbatten to stay on as Governor-General of India only, even if that ran the risk of showing a degree of preferment to the new Hindu nation.

As to the actual ceremonies which would mark the transfer of power, Mountbatten was desperately anxious that they should be well handled and that, as far as possible, there should be no cause for any demonstrations of ill-will against the British. To that end he ordered that there should be no ceremonial flag-lowering on the night of 14 August in case the formalities allowed opportunities for the Union Jack to be insulted. In this wish he was not altogether successful as it was normal for the British flag to be lowered each evening at sunset and raised again the following morning. In Karachi and Delhi the Union Jack might not have been much in official evidence but elsewhere the drama of the situation seemed to demand the ritualistic lowering of the British flag on the evening of 14 August and the breaking of the flags of the new dominions the following day. In fact, the parades, ceremonies and official gatherings were a necessary piece of theatre to mark the transfer of power and Martin Wynne in Amraoti was not alone in noting that pageantry and tradition triumphed over every other emotion on the morning of 15 August.

I was proud to attend in uniform and salute the new flag as it was raised to replace the lowered Union Jack, and to watch my police, no longer my police, march past under their new SP. A few days later my wife, infant son and I were on our way to Bombay. We were seen off at Badnera on the Bombay Mail by many friends, Indian and European. The train's first stop was at Akola and there was Harnam Singh, now SP Akola, to garland us and say farewell.

Within an hour or so I had left the Central Provinces for the last
time.

Scenes like these, familiar to anyone who lived in India at the
time, were to be repeated as the British began the long process of
saying goodbye.

A sense of drama enveloped the parting of the ways. As the
Viceroy could not be in two places at once to preside over the
official transfer of power it had been agreed that Independence
Day would be marked in Karachi on 14 August and in Delhi a day
later.

Huge crowds greeted the viceregal plane when Mountbatten
arrived with his wife and entourage in Karachi on 13 August. The
occasion could have been marred by a threat to Jinnah's life but
both men agreed that the formal procession and the official
opening of the Pakistan Constituent Assembly should go ahead as
planned. Understandably, perhaps, there was a certain coolness
between the two men; Christie recalled that Mountbatten took
little trouble over his speech and was content to leave the wording
to him. 'I had not done this sort of thing for years,' he remembered, 'and was out of practice. My wartime efforts for Lord
Linlithgow had been influenced by Winston Churchill's style,
which somehow would not be quite appropriate in the mouth of
Lord Mountbatten.' When he read the draft Mountbatten was far
from happy but as there was no time to change it he had to read it
with a few choice emendations. One phrase of Christie's did stick
in the memory, though, for when Mountbatten came to collect his
speeches, he chose as the title, 'Time Only to Look Forward', an
echo of the words Christie produced for him to use in Karachi.

> We who are making history today are caught and carried on in the
> swift current of events; there is no time to look back – there is time
> only to look forward.

The threat on Jinnah's life never materialised but it had been
real enough to discomfit the security services. When the party
returned to Government House the new Governor-General
turned to Mountbatten and thanked God that nothing had
befallen him. The Viceroy returned the compliment; a moment of
real warmth between those two very different men.

If the atmosphere in Karachi had been happy and excited then
the celebrations in Delhi were to border on the ecstatic. That it

was a tumultuous occasion owed much to Nehru's ability to seize the moment. The scene in the Legislative Assembly in New Delhi shortly before midnight on 14 August was an impressive sight and Nehru made the most of it. Speaking in front of his fellow countrymen, all dressed in a bewildering variety of dress, khadis and saris, military uniforms and formal suits, he chose the occasion to make history. 'Long years ago we made a tryst with destiny,' he told the rulers of the new India, 'and now the time comes when we shall redeem the pledge, not wholly or in full measure but very substantially. At the stroke of the midnight hour, while the world sleeps, India will wake to life and freedom.'

Then just before the midnight hour, the unearthly sound of a conch-shell horn, glittering in rose and purple, heralded the dawning of a new age. After three hundred years of British presence, and less than a hundred years of direct British rule, India had claimed her freedom. Outside the building, in the broad and capacious avenues of the capital city, Indians swarmed into the open spaces, oblivious of time and the falling monsoon rain, anxious to do homage to the new nation.

Above all, it had been Nehru's speech which had caught the imaginations of his fellow countrymen. This was an Indian celebration and they were determined to mark it in style. Like countless thousands of others who lived near Delhi, Inder Malhotra walked into the city – in his case the ten miles from the village where his father was stationmaster – in order to witness the moment when independence would be given to his country. Even at the age of seventeen he could not fail to be impressed by the drama of the moment and as the clock struck midnight he found to his surprise that along with many others he was weeping. Then one other thought struck him forcefully: 'Gandhi was nowhere around. We were aware that he was a much bigger man than Mr Nehru – although he was the cynosure of all eyes – but Gandhi was far away in his *ashram* in Calcutta. Next day in the paper we read that he had told a foreign correspondent that "I have no message to give on independence because my heart has dried up."'

Malhotra's thoughts were shared by A.K. Damodaran who stood in another part of the crowd where the shouts were not for Nehru or Mountbatten but for Gandhi. 'Where is our Gandhi?' they asked one another and Damodaran suddenly realised that

for many ordinary Indians Gandhi's absence was more important
than the presence of everyone else.

In spite of the forebodings occasioned by Gandhi's absence
from the official celebrations, the sights and sounds in Delhi were
to remain with the two young students for the rest of their lives.
Before setting out for Delhi Malhotra's socialist ideals had been
enraged by a neighbour's daughter who described the excitement
as 'Mr Nehru's Coronation'; forty years after the event he had
come to the conclusion that she might have been more perceptive
than he was on that famous day.

> It was a strange moment of transference, the whole struggle of the
> past sixty years had ended in a great reconciliation, despite the
> bloodshed and despite the partition . . . there were refugees
> everywhere; all up Connaught Circus was covered by people
> sleeping in the open or pushing their pushcarts and other belong-
> ings. Some chaps were even washing and bathing at public taps.
> But despite that the atmosphere was one of great elation. There
> were some people saying 'This is not independence but destruc-
> tion' but they were very few and were shouted down.

Kushwant Singh was in that Delhi crowd too. He had come down
from Lahore a few days earlier and thrilled to Nehru's words
which were broadcast to the crowds outside the Legislative
Assembly building.

> He had a great way with words and he took trouble over his speech
> even in moments like Gandhi's assassination. I have no doubt that
> after shedding the necessary tears he sat in his study to write an
> historic speech for the occasion. There is nothing spontaneous
> about his 'tryst with destiny' speech; it is extremely well created
> and polished and sums up the event in really felicitous words.

The paramount feeling was one of tremendous excitement that
India had become independent but Kushwant Singh also remembers the upsurge of goodwill towards the British. Stiff-upper-
lipped army officers were picked up and carried shoulder-high
through the streets, drink flowed in the smart Imperial Hotel as
Indians gladly embraced their British rulers of yesterday and the
whole of the city seemed to be ablaze, not just with the lamps that
burned all night but with an overwhelming sense of pride,
gratitude and happiness.

We see them standing there amongst the crowds in the streets,

walking proudly shoulder to shoulder with their fellow countrymen, the young men and women, students like Singh, Malhotra
and Damodaran. Das, the soldier, sits in his office quietly
listening to Nehru proclaiming freedom at midnight; while in the
Legislative Assembly building, grave in his formal suit, Frank
Anthony, the Anglo-Indian leader, rises from his seat to hug
India's new leader. It was a moment which no one could forget,
even those whose hearts were broken by the partition of the India
they loved. 'There was tremendous rejoicing in the chamber,'
recalled Badr-ud-Din Tyabji, the Muslim ICS officer who had
thrown in his lot with Hindu India. 'I had been Indian all the time
and believed in the place of Islam in India. It was part of my
heritage.' But it was outside in the streets that the excitement was
most tangible. As A.K. Damodaran remembered, it was 'a lovely
time to walk in Delhi'.

The following day Mountbatten was sworn in as constitutional
Governor-General of the new dominion of India. Once more the
scenes in the Durbar Hall were as full of pageantry as they had
been in the past but all present were acutely aware of one striking
difference: this was an Indian occasion for the Indian people. The
mood was matched outside, for when Mountbatten left the old
Viceroy's House to witness the ceremonial raising of India's flag
all his carefully arranged programme of pomp and protocol
disappeared beneath the mass of seething humanity which had
crowded along the route to Prince's Park to witness the historic
event.

'Frankly, I've never seen so many people, they must be here
literally in their hundreds and thousands,' reported an excited
Wynford Vaughan Thomas of the BBC. 'A great, swarming,
excited, cheering, enthusiastic Indian crowd, here to celebrate
the climax of the day's excitement in New Delhi – the hoisting of
the new flag of the Dominion of India.' To the sound of blaring
car horns and joyous shouts of '*Jai Hind!*' Mountbatten, Britain's
last Viceroy and India's first Governor-General, passed the
serried ranks of assembled soldiers – Sikhs, Garwhalis, Rajputs,
Gurkhas – and waited for the ceremony to proceed according to
plan. It was not to be. So dense was the crowd that he could not
get down from his carriage and could only stand there and salute
as the flag was unfurled, the three bands of saffron, white and
green with the Wheel of Ashoka in the middle.

(By one of those contradictions which run through India's history, the national flag was designed by a Muslim, Badr-ud-Din Tyabji. Originally the tricolour was to have contained the spinning-wheel symbol (*charka*) used by Gandhi but this was a party symbol which Tyabji thought might strike the wrong note. After much persuasion Gandhi agreed to the wheel because the Emperor Ashoka was venerated by Hindu and Muslim alike. The flag which flew on Nehru's car that night had been specially made by Tyabji's wife.)

As the national flag unfurled over Prince's Park the great monsoon clouds which had piled up overhead sent a sudden shower of rain over the Red Fort and Wynford Vaughan Thomas noticed a rainbow breaking out over the night sky, 'a symbol of the future hope and prosperity of the future Dominion of India'. Ending his emotionally charged broadcast with a description of the happy scene, Vaughan Thomas claimed that Mountbatten had been cheered by the Indians as no other viceroy had ever been. Others were less certain. At home in Edinburgh, A.P. Hume, by then working in a 'soft and essentially useless' job in the Scottish Office, caustically asked his father, 'I wonder how he knew!'

Similar scenes were enacted that same day in Karachi when a dignified Jinnah, the new Governor-General of Pakistan, inspected a parade of his military forces under the command of their respective British commanding officers – Commodore J.W. Jeffard (Navy), Lieutenant-General Sir Frank Messervy (Army) and Air Vice-Marshal A.L. Parry-Keane (Air Force). The city was *en fête* with flags of the new dominion flying from every public building and millions of lights burning in the windows of offices, public buildings and private houses. Wilfrid Russell had spent the past weeks at home in London but he had been determined to celebrate the 'famous day' with friends and colleagues who would be making their homes in the new Pakistan.

> Sitting on an old Ford surrounded by a cross-section of Indian Muslims, all restrained, yet fervently happy, as far as I could tell, I felt the tears coming to my eyes. It was all so sensible and friendly with real comradeship between the new and the old, real under-standing on both sides. Pray God it will last, as I am sure it will if Jinnah is spared for another ten years . . . from a purely

superficial glance it looks as if Pakistan has decided to be discreetly but staunchly friendly to England both out of sentiment and self-interest.

The feelings of togetherness and sentimentality noted by Russell were reinforced the next day when Jinnah attended a Dominion Day service in Karachi's Anglican cathedral. In the first bright dawn of independence it seemed to Russell and his colleagues that nothing would ever be able to break that remarkable bond of fellowship and goodwill.

Independence parades and ceremonies were the order of the day throughout India and Pakistan on Saturday 15 August 1947. These could range from simple commemorations in isolated country areas to grander affairs in the larger towns.* On the day itself John Griffiths was acting Collector of Malabar, having decided to throw in his lot with the new Indian Civil Service. His first task had been to arrange the independence celebrations at Calicut, and although his memories of the actual ceremonies are vague, he does remember that he turned in his mind to history: 'I felt myself part of a long line which began with Vasco da Gama and passed through Clive and Munro and the old Collectors of Malabar, and ended with me.' After the Union Jack had been lowered for the last time he retrieved it and took it into his safe keeping so that it could be buried with him when the time came. Today, the gesture seemed to be a quixotic one. 'So much has passed on with time since then that the gesture would be meaningless today. I shall leave the flag behind me, if anyone should care in the future to gaze on it and reflect.'

His speech at the flag-raising ceremony in Calicut could not have been typical, for he chose to praise the great contribution of the Indian political leaders.

My personal view is that every Indian who fought to assure an Allied victory in the recent war has made a great contribution towards hastening the day of Indian freedom. Let us however leave that aside and pay our tribute today to Mahatma Gandhi and

---

*At Lucknow the ceremony was doubly poignant for it was there that the British community had survived a terrifying siege during the Great Mutiny of 1857. Ever since, a British flag had flown from the masthead of the ruined residency as a symbol of British defiance: it was unthinkable that an Indian flag should replace it. When the British sappers took down the Union Jack for the last time, they cut down the flagstaff and cemented over the base so that no other emblem should fly over that historic place.

Pandit Jawaharlal Nehru, men who have represented the Indian
people in this struggle for freedom and have typified before the
world the spirit of India. Mahatma Gandhi is, as others have said
before me, such a man as India alone could produce and embodies
in himself that universality of outlook and sense of perfection
through suffering which is peculiar to India. Gandhiji has long
been the keeper of the conscience of the Congress Party and it is
significant that even today he dwells on the success of Independence rather than on the joys. As we say in English Mahatma
Gandhi is a man of sorrows and acquainted with grief. Let us
therefore pay our humble tribute today to Mahatma Gandhi,
Pandit Nehru and other leaders of the Indian people.

To Griffiths and to many others in southern India where there
had been little or no unrest the transfer of power was largely a
peaceful event. People had gone about their business as usual,
the police and the administration had remained loyal and it
seemed as if the changes were being introduced by some outside
agency far away. Only the sight of two Brahmin lawyers, dressed
in conventional black, and 'dancing down the aisle in suppressed
excitement', was an exception to an otherwise orderly and
matter-of-fact kind of day.

In Bombay, the city whose recent history was inextricably
bound up with the independence struggle, the celebrations were
as wild and as exhilarating as anything in Delhi. Lights burned
there, too, all night, people crowded into the streets, ships' sirens
hooted in the harbour and from the temples millions of rose
petals were cast into the air. Everyone, it seemed, wanted to be in
on the act. To Dr Taylor independence was the proper end to the
imperial process and he was overjoyed when a distinguished
Wilsonian came to celebrate the occasion in the small hours of the
morning.

I shall never forget the actual night of independence. Bombay just
went wild. The Chief Minister, Mr B.G. Kher, was down at the
Secretariat at midnight for the celebration. Fortunately it was a
fine night, though in the middle of the monsoon. But his first act as
Chief Minister of a state in this newly independent India was to
come to Wilson College and there, between 1.30 and 2 o'clock in
the morning we had a little tea party. He spoke of his affection for
the college and insisted on going up to the hotel and finding his old
room. 'This is what it means to me,' he said. 'My roots are here.'
He then thanked all his old teachers who had helped him along the

road. When that was over nobody went to bed. I found myself on top of Malabar Hill with a party of students drinking lemonade at 3 o'clock. It was a time to remember.

For Taylor it was a great moment in history, a day of celebration. Other British families were bound to feel regrets. They held quiet dinner parties far away from the sounds of rejoicing which had erupted in the night outside; for them the chimes at midnight played a requiem for the passing of an age. Sheila Coldwell was in Calcutta where there were genuine fears that the communal violence of the previous year would erupt again in the wake of the independence celebrations. It was exactly a year since the notorious Day of Action when the Muslims had taken to the streets to massacre Hindus, but this time there was no hostility and observers in Calcutta compared the calm to the Christmas truces which had taken place on the Western Front during the First World War in 1914. Instead of fighting one another, though, excited crowds swept through the Governor's official residence, ransacking it and destroying or disfiguring the effigies of British rule. It was an undignified end to British rule with Burrowes and his wife having to take to the river to escape by motorboat. The thought came to Sheila Coldwell that Burrowes's departure was a poor way to finish off this chapter in Britain's history, one which seemed to mock the ideals of Clive and Hastings. 'The pictures were broken to bits and all the lovely furniture. It was a small calamity in comparison to the dreadful things that were happening elsewhere, but it was all thrown away.' She was one of the British community in Calcutta who considered herself to be in mourning when the time came to mark the emergence of the new India.

> We went to various parties to which I didn't want to go because I hated the whole idea. The Union Jack was pulled down and the Indian flag was put up; we had drinks all round. It went completely against the grain with me because I didn't think it was right. I hated it all and loathed every minute of it.

But for every Sheila Coldwell in Bengal there was at least one George Robertson who took to the streets to celebrate. 'It was practically impossible for traffic to get through the streets, so if you had to get anywhere you had to walk.' Passing through the crowds Robertson was greeted by joyous shouts of '*Jai Hind!*'

Unabashed, he replied in similar vein, noting that 'everyone seemed to be quite happy about it'. Commander Goord was trapped by similarly emotional throngs. In August 1947 he was still in Delhi, having presided over the division of the RIN between India and Pakistan and he, too, found the celebrations profoundly moving.

> It was impossible for any Englishman that day to be unaffected by it. To see one's national flag replaced by another is bound to wound one's pride, but the real pleasure, goodwill and enthusiasm of the vast crowds was such that one could feel nothing but goodwill towards them and their future. On all sides the past was forgotten.

Goord, Robertson, Russell, Taylor and many others all found many good reasons to be gratified by the response to the independence celebrations. Relief and pleasure, though, were bound to be mixed with a certain sadness and a regret for times which had passed and which would not come again. For those leaving India, especially, it was a time of farewells, of taking leave of servants and subordinates who had given years of faithful service and who were often bewildered by the departure of the British. All over the country soon-to-be-familiar scenes were being acted out as the sahibs and their mems were taken to the railway stations, begarlanded with flowers as servants and friends waved goodbye, perhaps for ever. Jack Morton left Lahore with a specially printed tribute which spoke of the benefits to the Indian Police Service of his 'highly proficient parts'. 'We shall miss your dignified figure,' it continued, 'your inspiring personality and your rich cultured habits.'

Even the tribesmen of the North-West Frontier Province who had spent much of their time and energies battling against British authority were incredulous at the turn of events. 'Do you mean that, after beating the Germans and the Japs, you are going to be chased out of India by Hindu lawyers?' they asked the officers of the Frontier Scouts. Most of the units – Gilgit Scouts, Khyber Rifles, Kurram Militia and other famous formations – were inherited by Pakistan and with a Muslim government in power the frontier became relatively peaceful.

More than anything else, though, the celebrations belonged to the people of the new dominions. Prem Bhatia was in Lucknow on 15 August, a day which he remembered as being completely euphoric. Along with around a hundred thousand of his fellow countrymen he listened in awe and excitement as the Chief Minister of the United Provinces, Pandit Govind Ballabh Pant, spoke to them about his hopes for the new India. Afterwards, he was invited to tea with Pant, a man whom he had come to regard as a father-figure, 'a big man in every sense, physically as well as mentally'. Aroused by the emotional inspiration of Independence Day Prem Bhatia boldly told the Chief Minister that his speech had been fine as far as it went, but he was surprised that it did not contain any anti-British sentiment. That would have been acceptable to the crowd, he added, as it was well known that Pant had been the victim of police brutality at the time of the Simon Commission. So severe was the beating he had received that Pant had been left permanently disabled.

'You can't even hold a cup of tea. You have to drink out of a glass with both hands,' he was told. 'And you have no ill-feelings? I'm surprised. I would have liked to hear you say something nasty about our past rulers.'

Pant's answer showed the measure of the man. 'All that's in the past,' he replied, 'Gandhiji told us to forget the past.' His temper rising, Prem Bhatia retaliated with his own story about the British brigadier who had thrown him out of a railway carriage during the war.

That's not very much, said Pant. Look what happened to me. I started life as a lawyer and on a visit back to my village I met an English subaltern as I got out of the bus. Seeing me dressed in Indian clothes he asked me to carry his bags. 'You didn't do that!' Yes, said Pant and at the end of the job he gave me two annas. 'Why did you do it?' Don't get upset, he said, I did it deliberately to prepare myself to throw the British out. Let me see how far they will go to humiliate us. The subaltern was a stupid young man – I didn't mind it. Pant's story brought tears to my eyes; here was a truly great man.

Later, after the first heady excitement of independence had died down, Prem Bhatia woke to the reality of partition: part of his family's property was in Pakistan and it was to be many years before he saw it again. It was then that Pant's message became clear – independence brought responsibility and commitment. There was no time to dwell on past miseries; as Christie had spoken for Mountbatten, now there was time only to look forward.

Chapter Seven

The Punjab Massacres

The celebrations to mark independence had no sooner ended than one of the greatest mass migrations seen this century had begun. Partition might have brought Pakistan into being as a contented Muslim nation but for many individuals the division spelled only fear, disruption, misery and widespread death and destruction. Even before independence there had been carnage in the Punjab and in Bengal; now that they felt themselves to be their own masters, the inhabitants also believed that they were at liberty to protect their own homelands or to rid them of neighbours who had suddenly become aliens. In the Punjab the Muslim majority was pro-Pakistan while the Hindus and Sikhs saw their worst fears being realised with the province's division between the two new dominions. Most politicians, British, Indian or Pakistani, feared that there would be violence; few could have realised how terrible the massacres would be. At Malir, near Karachi, Claud Moir, a company commander with the 2nd Black Watch, noted laconically in his diary: 'The great day has dawned and four hundred million Indians have got freedom to kill each other without the freedom to call upon the British to protect them – which is just about what it amounts to.' It was as if Pandora's Box had been opened and the British guardians were powerless to help.

Although it had been agreed that British military units would not be used to quell communal fighting after independence, some measures aimed at containment had been taken. A Punjab Boundary Force was established to control the disturbances that were expected in the wake of the announcement of the Radcliffe awards; commanded by Major-General T.W. 'Pete' Rees, and based largely on the 4th Indian Division, it was conceived as a neutral body which would attempt to maintain law and order along the new frontier in the Punjab.

From the very outset, though, it was only a makeshift force. Professional and impartial it might have been but it was hopelessly small and overstretched. When trouble had first flared up in the Punjab the Governor-General, Sir Evan Jenkins, had told Mountbatten that peace could only be kept by a minimum military force of four divisions: under his command Rees had only 55,000 officers and men, well under the number required. In its favour, many of the men were Gurkhas who were not affected by the communal divide, and its British officers had lengthy experience of Indian affairs. Peter Pearson, a major with the Somerset Light Infantry, was seconded to Rees's force and he remembers going into action almost immediately after assembling in the Lahore area.

> While the advent of Independence was heralded almost universally throughout the newborn twin dominions by rejoicing and inter-community fraternity, Lahore, which was predominantly Muslim, was preparing for it in an entirely different way. Bitter rioting broke out in the city on 14 August accompanied by widespread arson, and hundreds perished.

The riots continued into the following day and erupted with even greater fury once the Radcliffe awards had been disclosed. The award which angered the Pakistanis was the inclusion of the Gurdaspur District in East Punjab while the Indians were furious that the Chittagong Hill Tracts, a remote Buddhist area, had been granted to East Pakistan. None of the leaders repudiated the awards but they did cause enough displeasure to fuel the resentment felt by the ordinary people. 'A night curfew had been imposed previously,' noted Pearson, 'and the city was continuously patrolled by lorryborne troops. Public administration and utilities virtually collapsed.' Pearson soon came across another phenomenon which was to become disgustingly familiar: the trains which were the means of escape for the hordes of refugees trying to flee to their own side of the border became death-traps, held by Sikh *jathas* on one side and Muslim gangs on the other.

The partition ordered by the Boundary Commission was

always going to cause problems. In a moment of optimism Mountbatten had compared it to the division of Ireland in 1922 – quite forgetting that the Irish political solution had come about after two and a half years of bloodshed and much material destruction. What had happened in Ireland, though, was to be but a drop in the ocean as far as the Punjab was concerned. The awards pleased no one, and although the leaders were bound to accept them the same strictures did not apply to the ordinary people of India and Pakistan. In the eastern Punjab Sikhs began systematically butchering Muslims while in the west Muslims turned on Hindus and Sikhs in some of the ugliest massacres witnessed this century. It is still not possible to compute how many people died when Muslims, Sikhs and Hindus found themselves caught on the 'wrong' side of the Punjab frontier and tried desperately to escape. Half a million seems to be the most widely accepted figure – a high proportion of the five and a half million refugees who were on the move during that hate-filled September month. Many of them died from natural causes, from disease, starvation or despair while on the march or in the transit camps but many more were the victims of the kind of slaughter witnessed by Richard Sharp of the BBC.

In the company of a patrol of the Punjab Boundary Force he had arrived in Shaikpura, about twenty miles west of Lahore, 'the usual Punjab town with the attractive Mogul fort on the outskirts and the broad tree-lined avenue of the civil lines.' It was in the heart of the old town, though, in the narrow streets of the bazaar that the idyll seen by Sharp from the main road was to turn to nightmare. For centuries a mixed population of Sikhs and Muslims had lived in harmony in Shaikpura and that happy state of affairs might have remained but for the advent of Muslim refugees on the run from India. With them they had brought rumours of the massacre of Muslim innocents and within hours of their arrival this quiet Punjab town was 'soaked with the stench of death'. The military patrol drove into the bazaar but it was far too late, the Muslims had done their worst. Sharp warned that this was 'a horror story, unpleasant to listen to and even more unpleasant to relate', but his relentless narrative does much to explain what was happening in the hearts and minds of the population on both sides of the new frontier.

The fires were still burning, there were dead bullocks lying in the centre of the road and not a soul stirred in the streets; over everything drifted that unescapable filthy smell of putrefaction and blood. You would have sworn that in this dreary wasteland no Sikh could have survived and yet we did come across them. Some thousand had barricaded themselves into a high school and although the shooting was now over, nothing could persuade them to venture out again. Our brigadier rapped at the door and he parleyed with them, and at last, assured that they were no longer in any danger, they did start slowly to come out into the shattered street again. A more pitiful broken-hearted body of people I've never seen. They dragged out their wounded, and they were wounded with horrible wounds, caused by the slashing of knives and the stabbing of spearheads. Where could they put them? Well, they just dragged the wounded out on to the roadside. And it was in the heat of an Indian afternoon and the first thing that happens when you expose wounds to that heat is the flies come. The flies came in filthy swarms and covered the wounds with a dark swarming mass.

Worse was to follow. As the soldiers began to tend the wounded Sharp was sidetracked by a distraught Sikh father who wanted to find his children. He led them back along the street to a narrow alleyway in which stood a row of one-storeyed houses each with a small untidy garden in front. Normally it was a place which rang to the sounds of domesticity, but on this day of massacre it had become a charnel house. Dead bodies of women and children sprawled everywhere, cut to pieces, the remains lying in pools of congealing viscera and blood. 'The poor fellow went on calling but of course nothing answered him in these houses of the dead. And then the monsoon winds started driving in clouds of hot choking dust. From the waste plot outside the dust rose in a cloud and as it drove towards us it brought with it all the smells of the disturbed town, a fetid mixture of burnt rags, decayed flesh, garbage.'

Modern times have seen sufficient examples of man's inhumanity to man for us not to quail at such descriptions; the Nazi concentration camps, civil war in Biafra, the wars in Vietnam, the Lebanon are all sharp reminders of our capacity to lose our reason in mindless violence. What happened in the Punjab was no different in the scale of horrors, but to outside observers like Sharp there was an intensity to the ferocity which passed understanding. Friends or neighbours of long standing turned on one another simply because one was Hindu, the other Muslim: logic and common humanity found themselves being replaced by fear, panic and hatred. For a while it seemed as if the whole world had gone mad as stories began to emerge of the wholesale slaughter of refugees, of trainloads of men, women and children meeting ghastly ends, of the burning alive of communities in their homes and places of worship, of death, destruction and rape. Even if some of the stories have been exaggerated with the passing of the years, even if some of the figures have been overblown, there can be no doubt that in the Punjab at least, India and Pakistan were born to a baptism of fire.

India was no stranger to communal violence but during the years of British rule its outbreaks had been largely contained by the authorities. In the Punjab, at the time of partition, those same officials were powerless to intervene. To begin with, the violence erupted on such a scale that Rees's Punjab Boundary Force was often unable to put itself between the warring communities; another problem was that nobody really understood its causes or where it was likely to break out next. Long-standing religious or political differences were one cause, panic and fear another; criminality added its quota as did a tendency to violence among certain sections of the Sikh and Muslim communities, but the dynamics of their malignancy were impossible to fathom. Within days of independence the Punjab had become ungovernable and appeals for peace from Indian, Pakistani and British officials were lost in the winds of hate that blew through the province. Kushwant Singh saw Lahore, the 'Paris of the Orient', ablaze and men and women being killed in its streets. The memory still appals him.

> It was totally out of control. No one suspected there was so much bestiality in human beings, that they should rise against innocent people and slaughter women and children on both sides. The savage in all of us is under the skin. It doesn't take much to do the most diabolical acts of violence. So there is nothing surprising that we saw it in 1947.

With its echoes of John Buchan, who held that civilisation is a thin veneer, 'with a very narrow line between the warm room and the savage out of doors', Kushwant Singh's sentiment goes straight to the heart of the matter. No one, not even the

pessimists, of whom there were plenty, could have foreseen that
law and order would have broken down so quickly or that so many
lives could be so needlessly lost. In the Punjab madness did reign as
the terror multiplied and men lost control of their passions. In the
old days, the IP, backed up by battalions of British or Gurkha
riflemen, would have put a stop to the troubles, but the old days
were in the past; now it was India's and Pakistan's responsibility.
That they were unable to do anything says more about the
emotions that had been unleashed in the Punjab than any inability
on the part of the politicians or the administrators.

Naturally, because it was such a cataclysmic event in their recent
history, there is a tendency for Indians to speak of 'human frailty'
when talking about the massacres in the Punjab; more dramatically some have admitted that it was necessary to spill blood
before the two nations could spring into being. Prem Bhatia,
whose family lost their home to Pakistan, describes it as a time
when people went mad and every act of violence multiplied to turn
in upon itself.

> Who wants to leave his home? My mother didn't want to; the
> Hindus in what is now Pakistan were smoked out and the Muslims
> on this side were no better treated. People acquired a certain vested
> interest in evicting Muslim and Hindus because they thought it was
> a vicious circle, that if they were going to lose their homes they
> might as well prepare to occupy homes on the other side. It was
> beyond control at that stage.

The pragmatists, though, are inclined to believe that more could
have been done to prevent the excesses, that the arrangements to
police the border were inadequate and that the refugees could
have been given better protection. It is an attractive argument and
one which still has a number of supporters, but it would have been
a difficult policy to adopt. Britain dared not intervene militarily in
the affairs of the two new dominions and India and Pakistan lacked
the wherewithal and the commitment to co-operate in a policy of
containment. To have been able to do so would have required tact
and understanding, two virtues which were sadly lacking in the
relationship between Karachi and New Delhi after the Radcliffe
awards had been announced. Both governments were suspicious
of the findings and both felt that Britain favoured the other. Those
tensions led to the disbandment of Rees's Punjab Boundary Force
on 29 August with each country taking over responsibility for

policing their side of the frontier. It was not a foolproof solution but it was the only one that worked as both armies reported to a Joint Defence Council which provided regular military liaison between the two countries. Further help was given by Mountbatten who chaired an Indian Emergency Committee to deal with the problem, but it was not until the end of September that the last massacres petered out as the refugees made their way over the Punjab frontier into whatever promised land awaited them.

In the midst of all the mayhem, when the very heavens seemed to be falling around the people of the Punjab, there were stories of stoicism and courage which saved many lives. European families protected their servants from rival mobs, often hiding them beneath the seats of their compartments in refugee trains; in some villages the call to violence was ignored in spite of intense provocation and on the whole the morale and discipline of the regiments of the old Indian Army stood firm. Also, it has to be recorded that the presence of the remaining British officers of the army and the ICS in the Punjab gave much-needed confidence and moral support in the first days of independence. This was especially true of the men who served in the area bounding Lahore, Amritsar and Ferozepore.

One of the most hair-raising episodes – which happily ended in lives being saved – took place near the village of Digru on the branch line between Ludhiana and Ferozepore. A train of Muslim refugees was derailed by a group of some five hundred Sikhs who would have undoubtedly slaughtered the helpless passengers, had it not been for the presence of two Indian Army officers, Majors Derek Harington Hawes and R.A.M. Major. That they happened to be on the train owed more to luck than anything else; that Harington Hawes was able to take command of the situation speaks volumes for his cool nerve and powers of leadership.

An officer with the 14th Punjab Regiment, Harington Hawes was serving as secretary to the Resident, Punjab States in Lahore, and was due to demit office at midnight on 14 August. His adventure began the following day when he travelled down to Simla by road; he was due to return to Lahore by train two days later. Despite the growing evidence of massacres along the line and the heavy refugee traffic he was able to take an overnight train to Ludhiana where he transferred to the Calcutta–Lahore mail which ran on via the Ferozepore branch line. After a considerable delay, during which Harington Hawes's suspicions were aroused by the sight of the Sikh passengers drifting away from the station, the mail left at midday with an escort of six sepoys from the Punjab Regiment. Two hours later it reached Moga, the centre of a turbulent Sikh area where dacoity had long been endemic, and there it halted because the next station down the line, Digru, would not give the clear-line signal. Undeterred by the confusion, Harington Hawes persuaded the driver to take his engine down the line with himself and a sepoy acting as guards; they found nothing amiss and returned to Moga to collect the rest of the train. Although the stationmaster protested that it was a violation of the company's rules Harington Hawes insisted that the mail continue its journey and in the late afternoon it was eventually allowed to proceed. It had only gone four miles at snail's pace when it was derailed and ground to a halt: Harington Hawes was relieved to see that although the engine and the three leading coaches were off the line the train was still in an upright position and that nobody had been injured.

> When the dust had subsided and we had collected our wits enough to look around, we saw that we had been derailed at a spot where thick patches of *seroot* grass grew close to the permanent way on each side. What is more, it was soon clear that the grass concealed a large body of men; for suddenly there was a loud shout of '*Wah Guru ji ki fateh!*' (Victory to the Guru), the Sikhs' war cry. This was answered by a confused yell from the passengers in the train, a blend of fear and answering challenge, and by a fusillade from the train guard, who started to fire at random into the grass. As rounds might be precious later on, and uncontrolled firing is of little value, I ordered them to stop.

Taking stock of the situation, Harington Hawes's first move was to consolidate his forces – as well as the six sepoys armed with .303 rifles, he enlisted a Pakistan Air Force officer and two young Hindu RIASC officers all armed with service revolvers, and amongst the passengers emerged another Indian Army major with his wife and daughter. They were armed with a sporting rifle and two shotguns and were prepared to use them. Major Major was on his way out of India to start a new life in East Africa and the train carried all his family's worldly goods. At the time, though, the British officers' first consideration was to get the passengers away from the train to a position which could be defended more easily. Harington Hawes went ahead to scout out the station at Digru and, finding it deserted, decided that the best plan would be to make a stand there. It was then that Mrs Major found that she had to play once more the traditional role of the unflustered British memsahib.

> I suppose all the Sikhs thought we should all be laid out but instead of which we were all bright and perky and stepped out of the train and rather astonished them I think. There were so many women and children – as a matter of fact, they were really marvellous, they kept absolutely quiet, they never cried, they never moaned, they never did anything. While we were all waiting about, wondering what would happen next, a Pathan sepoy came up to me and said, 'Memsahib, here is my wife and little girl. I leave them with you. Will you look after them? It doesn't matter about me. I'll go somewhere but I do want you to look after my wife and little girl.' Of course, I took them.

As the Majors' belongings were trapped in the guard's van they decided to abandon them and to save lives instead – in addition to her Pathan family Mrs Major picked up a lost child who was howling her heart out by one of the carriages. That meant abandoning her only suitcase and the Majors lost everything they possessed in the ambush. With dusk falling they began shepherding the anxious refugees along the track to Digru, no easy task with the armed Sikhs gradually closing in to loot the train.

Digru offered a good defensive position because the armed men could be posted on the station roof to cover any attacks from the surrounding countryside. During the evening the Sikhs looted the train and, having done so, an advance party, variously armed with rifles and *kirpans* (swords), approached the station. As the small party on the roof braced themselves for the expected onslaught Harington Hawes played his ace. Calling up one of the sepoys, a Sikh, he ordered him to open fire, even though the range was a good two hundred yards. In the distance, one of the Sikhs fell and, chastened by the accuracy of the fire, the others ran off.

> This fluky shot had a marvellous effect, for not only did it put the rest of the enemy to flight, but it also raised the morale of our own people who shouted in triumph. It was indeed remarkable that this young Sikh soldier had fired on his own people, and more remarkable still that his shot had found its mark.

Nevertheless, in spite of the reprieve, it was a long and anxious night before dawn brought safety with the arrival of a relief train and a party of sepoys of the Jat Regiment from Ferozepore. During the course of the siege, when morale was at its lowest, both Major and Harington Hawes heard a 'real cry from the heart' from the young pilot officer who said that he had been through five years of war only to die on a station roof in the Punjab. 'For my two days of freedom,' he confided, 'I'd rather have five hundred years of slavery.' Even for the experienced Major Major, it had been a terrible glimpse into the horrors of the Punjab massacres.

> I've never had such a frightful experience, expecting at any moment to shoot my own wife and daughter and to see women and children slaughtered in front of me – this would undoubtedly have happened had we not been there.

As the relief train pulled into Ferozepore the British passengers could not avoid noticing the monolith commemorating the victory of the Army of the Sutlej over the Khalsa during the Second Sikh War of 1848–9. General Sir Hugh Gough's force had been outnumbered three to one and his triumph had led to the annexation of the Punjab. In that quiet moment, as the train passed by a monument to a guardianship that was already slipping into history, it seemed to Harington Hawes that the wheel had once again come full circle.

In another incident, witnessed by Peter Pearson, British good sense again managed to win the day over religious fanaticism. On 20 September a special train carrying British and Indian service families arrived in Lahore from Rawalpindi en route to the Deolali transit camp at Bombay. It was escorted by 150 men of the 16th Punjab Regiment under the command of Major H. Maclean. The driver, a Muslim, refused to take it on to the next stage of its journey to Amritsar because he had heard that an earlier train had been ambushed at Harbanspura further down the line. Morale amongst the British passengers remained high, despite the delay, because they were homeward bound, but the Indians were naturally apprehensive. While the authorities argued about what should be done Maclean hit on the happy expedient of finding an Anglo-Indian driver who was prepared to take the train over the two-mile border stretch where so many refugees had perished. The ruse worked and a Hindu crew then took the train on to Amritsar, a distance of some thirty miles which took twenty-six hours to cover. 'Perhaps this was just as well,' recalls Major Pearson, 'since fifteen hundred Muslims had perished during the night at the hands of a Sikh *jatha* in one of the bloodiest train massacres of the transition; among the dead was the British officer commanding its escort.'

With so many people on the move it was inevitable that some British citizens would also be caught up in the mayhem. The 2nd Black Watch were the last British regiment to leave the frontier and when they pulled out of Peshawar on 10 August they had to leave behind a rear party which was quickly cut off owing to the paralysis which hit the railway system after the transfer of power. Nevertheless, in spite of the disquiet they felt at leaving their colleagues behind, the Highland regiment made a brave show of their departure, marching down to the cantonment station with drums and pipes playing. There they were met by the pipes and drums of the 1st Royal Garwhal Rifles who played them off to the tune of 'Highland Laddie', an apposite enough gesture as the two regiments had become friends during their internal security duties in the province. It was a long and tiring journey across the Sind desert and the battalion's A, B and C companies were given a grim foretaste of the horrors to come when their train, the second to leave Peshawar, was held up for twelve hours outside Lahore while a bloody communal battle raged inside the station. So concerned was the regiment about the dangers and discomfort of the journey that they had been able to persuade the authorities to transport their families by air to Malir, a task undertaken by RAF Dakotas of 31 Squadron.

Arrangements had also been put in hand to use RAF aircraft to airlift the rear party which had remained in Peshawar to complete the handing over of the cantonment to the Pakistan Army. The party consisted of six officers and sixty men under the command of Major A.D.H. Irwin and they were faced with a lengthy period of handover, a task made more onerous by the knowledge that all communications with the outside world had ceased. The handover took much longer than expected, too, because most of the Sikhs and Hindus were more concerned with making plans for their own escape and it was during that period of tension that the Black Watch men were forced to be silent witnesses to a communal massacre.

Early in the morning of 7 September they were awoken by a
fusillade from the area of the barracks which housed two Indian
Army regiments, the 3rd/8th Punjab Regiment (Muslims) and the
19th Lancers (Sikhs and Hindus). This was followed by intermit-
tent firing which lasted for a few minutes. After ordering his own
men to take cover and posting armed pickets Irwin hurried down
to the orderly room of the 3rd/8th Punjab Regiment where he
found that two Muslim soldiers had been killed after 'an unfortunate misunderstanding' between armed patrols of the two regiments. All might have been well had the army been able to
contain the incident but the news spread quickly to the world
outside the cantonment and by midday some two thousand
tribesmen and civilians appeared, as if from nowhere, to take
their revenge on the men of the 19th Lancers. Earlier in the day,
the brigade commander, Brigadier J.R. Morris, had stopped the
Indian and Pakistani troops from mutiny by driving through their
ranks in a jeep and ordering them to cease fire, but nothing could
stop the carnage that followed. Writing to the regimental depot in
Perth a few months later, Irwin painted a graphic picture of the
horrors which his men, perforce, had to witness.

> Firing commenced at about 1230 and by 1300 hours the canton-
> ment was swarming with tribesmen in lorries, tongas and on foot,
> intent on the murder of all Sikhs (in particular) and Hindus (as a
> sideline) and the looting of all shops owned by them . . . during
> the afternoon, further tribesmen entered the city and by evening
> the Sikh quarter was burning furiously – the whole night sky
> glowing crimson. The authorities considered that it would never be
> known how many perished in the flames, for we were told that the
> tribesmen not only surrounded the burning area and prevented
> anyone from leaving but they even drove people from other
> quarters into the area.

The troubles continued into the following week when tongaloads
of tribesmen swept into the cantonment to wreak their revenge
on the Hindus who worked in the canteens. Some accepted the
Black Watch's offer of protection – they were hidden in barrels in
the barrack's go-down – but those who tried to flee never made
good their escape. In one of the worst incidents the canteen
manager, a Hindu, attempted to get away disguised as a Muslim:
he got as far as the gates to the officers' mess where he was
recognised and murdered – 'a particularly messy proceeding

during which he was shot seven times and then finished off with a meat cleaver'. It was not until 15 September, eight days after the riots had begun, that most of the rear party were able to make their way to Malir by RAF Dakota.

Aircraft had been used to good effect during the Bengal famine of 1942 but they really came into their own as savers of life in the Punjab and on the frontier. Thousands of refugees were rescued during the airlifts and although the Dakota aircraft could only carry limited payloads the RAF and RIAF were able to carry out several notable mercy missions. Because the emphasis had to be on saving civilian lives, British servicemen, like the men of the Black Watch in Peshawar, were given a lower priority. The same was true of British subjects who were considered to be in relative safety outside the main trouble-spots, in places like Kashmir.

This was one of India's real pleasure gardens, a lotus-eating paradise of sunshine and breathtaking scenery. At its capital, Srinagar, visitors whiled away their time in the comfort of the houseboats on Lake Dal, for by law only a Kashmiri could own land in Kashmir. It had been the playground for a succession of invaders and the British had been no exception, filling the lakes and rivers with brown trout from Scotland and building a suburban golf course in the meadows of Gulmarg. With its cool fresh air, green pastures and coniferous forests Kashmir was a cherished holiday resort; it was far removed from the stifling heat of the plains below the hills and in 1947 it had the added attraction of being a safe haven. Not only was the state cut off geographically, but its ruler, the Maharajah Hari Singh, had contrived to hold himself aloof from the political scene. A Hindu who ruled over a state that was predominantly Muslim, he had refused to listen to Mountbatten's argument that Kashmir should become a part of Pakistan; instead, he decided to hold out for independence. Like any other weak and vacillating ruler he hoped that the problem of aligning himself to one country or the other would go away if he refused to have anything to do with it. Within his state there were many others, British subjects included, who inclined to the same view.

Some of them were permanent residents but many more were visitors who wanted to be out of British India at the time of the transfer of power or who simply wanted to have a last holiday in agreeable surroundings. In May 1947 Feh Williams, the wife of

Brigadier T.E. Williams, Auchinleck's Director of Military Operations, had gone up to Gulmarg with her young daughter and infant son. It was a normal routine holiday and to begin with they encountered no problems whatsoever. But as summer passed into autumn life began to get more difficult.

> Halfway through September I came down from Gulmarg to join my friend Cynthia Cheeseman who had two children, a dog and a Hindu bearer in a boarding house on the lake in Srinagar. By then there was no possibility of hiring a taxi or bus and such planes as were able to fly into Srinagar were already overbooked. By then, too, we were well into October and it was beginning to get cold. We wondered if we were to face a winter there and what we were to do about our dwindling finances. There was still no communication from either of our husbands.

Their holiday was to have a dramatic ending. Shortly after their arrival in Srinagar a senior army officer turned up at the club with twenty RAF buses to evacuate all British women and children who wanted to be taken to Rawalpindi. His appearance in Kashmir caused considerable offence to the maharajah but whoever had ordered the evacuation must have known that trouble was afoot. On 24 October, encouraged by the government of Pakistan, hundreds of Pathan tribesmen swept into the vale of Kashmir to spark off a tribal invasion of Hari Singh's state. The maharajah's private army was too small and ineffective to put up much resistance and it was weakened further by desertion and by the murder of many of its Hindu officers. All of a sudden it seemed that the Pathans, traditional enemies of the British on the frontier, would deliver Kashmir into the hands of Pakistan.

The invasion started alarm bells ringing in New Delhi. Auchinleck wanted to send in British troops to protect British subjects who were natural targets for the Pathans. Mountbatten refused to countenance any interference, arguing that such a move would only embroil Britain in a border war between India and Pakistan. Privately, though, he insisted that if Indian troops were used then Kashmir would have to concede to India. That decision taken, V.P. Menon flew to Srinagar on 26 October and having obtained Hari Singh's signature of accession, India was left free to intervene on Kashmir's behalf. By the following day a massive airlift had begun, civilian Dakotas flying in Sikh troops and then bringing out the more vulnerable refugees. At the same time RAF planes joined in the airlift and according to Squadron Leader David Penman this was one of the most testing periods of 31 Squadron's last days in India. By then his squadron was based at Mauripur with a detachment at Chaklala in Pakistan.

On 29 October eight aircraft took off for Srinagar in the Kashmir valley to evacuate British citizens. We took on petrol in jerry cans as there was none in Kashmir and a ground party to organise the evacuation. We left Chaklala at 7 a.m. and in perfect weather flew down a pass between mountains 14,000 feet high and covered in snow. We had no oxygen to clear the tops and at that time in the morning the mountains were a beautiful sight. In the Kashmir valley smoke and flames were rising from burning villages and the battle line was only sixteen miles from Srinagar. We had been warned to keep as high as possible until above Srinagar and then to circle down. The airfield was 5,500 feet above sea level and without runways, very dusty and very cold. We landed at 8.15 a.m. and found the runway swarming with Sikh troops and refugees. We had to wait until 11 a.m. for our passengers to be sorted out. Many arrived with large quantities of luggage and furniture and had to be told that only small amounts could be taken. In some cases they elected to stay and face the future in Kashmir. By 11.50 my aircraft was loaded and with fifteen passengers aboard I was back in Chaklala an hour later. A quick refuel and I was back in Srinagar at 2.25. Six of the other aircraft were still on the ground because of the difficulty in parting passengers from their belongings. Eventually all aircraft were loaded and I was last to leave at 4.25 p.m. with nineteen passengers and a newsreel cameraman who took films of the hills and the crew as we made our way back for a night landing, made more hazardous by the appearance of cows on the runway which necessitated an overshoot and delay until they were cleared.

Dangerous those flights might have been but they were not as arduous as the long journey by bus which Feh Williams and Cynthia Cheeseman had been forced to make before the invasion had begun.

Five a.m. next morning saw a motley collection of women, children, cats, dogs, parrots, retainers and a sprinkling of men embussed and wheels moving. We pulled away on a glorious golden morning, the sun gleaming on mountains already crowned with fresh snow – the world a blaze of colour, red, gold, bronze

and pale yellow. Tears sprang to my eyes as I knew I was saying
goodbye; that never again would I see this most beautiful country.
The journey down the pass was a never-ending nightmare. We
finally reached our destination, a boarding house in 'Pindi at 9
p.m. that night, to find ourselves in a far worse plight in Pakistan
than we had been in Srinagar. We had, too, the added anxiety of a
Hindu ayah and bearer and my ten-month-old son had gone down
with dysentery.

Their hardships had, in fact, only begun, as the families could not
stay long in Pakistan and were required to return to India. The
suggested solution – train to Karachi and then onwards by ship to
Bombay – was turned down by both women, not only because it
was a roundabout route but also because it would mean leaving
their Hindu servants in a Pakistani refugee camp. This Feh
Williams would not allow: 'I had taken her to Kashmir and I
would take her back to Delhi with me. I had previously suggested
to my ayah that she should abandon her sari and pantaloons and
that I would supply her with European clothes. She could be a
temporary Christian Eurasian, just whilst we travelled. It was no
good, she would not agree; although she was a small frail little
woman she was also a very brave and courageous one.'

Having heard that a military convoy was about to leave for
Delhi, Cynthia Cheeseman decided to flag it down on the main
trunk road. It was late at night and she only had a small pocket
torch; nevertheless, the convoy stopped and the officer in charge
agreed to take her bearer into India so that a message could be
passed to her husband, an officer with the Rajputana Rifles.
Miraculously, the message got through to him in Delhi. Then
there was a further piece of good fortune.

I heard that a senior general from Delhi, whom I knew, had come
up to 'Pindi for a conference and was dining that night at Flagstaff
House. Very quickly I wrote a letter to my husband – the one and
only chance I had of contacting him. I told him what had become
of us, where we were and of the proposed plans for evacuation
from 'Pindi. That if the worst came to the worst our friend Cynthia
would take our children, together with hers, to Delhi. That I
would remain with our ayah and that, hopefully, we would find our
way back to Delhi in due course. That I refused to abandon her to
the refugee camp. Having sealed the letter and addressed the
envelope I set off in the dark, with a torch, to Flagstaff House,

dressed in a cotton skirt and blouse, walking shoes covered with dust. At Flagstaff House I rang the bell: before me appeared an immaculately dressed bearer who looked askance at the figure before him.

Refusing to be deterred by the rules of protocol Feh Williams insisted that the letter be given to the general. It was, and a few days later her husband was able to raise the matter during Auchinleck's morning 'prayers' – as the daily morning meetings at GHQ in Delhi were known. Although all the senior officers, including Brigadier Williams, realised that there were more pressing problems on the agenda, Auchinleck was sufficiently moved by the plight of the 'wives in Kashmir' to order them to be evacuated by air. By then it was mid-November and an uneasy peace had returned to Kashmir. By then, too, 100,000 Indian troops were in the state and, having abandoned his country to Nehru, Hari Singh had abdicated in favour of his eighteen-year-old son, Karan Singh.

The phlegm and determination showed by both women had served well not only their own families but also their servants. Others were not always so lucky. George Robertson's brother, David, was also a jute manager in Bengal and he had to face the dilemma of what to do with his one Muslim servant after partition. Eventually the bearer took matters into his own hands by deciding to escape to East Pakistan – which was, for him, unknown territory. He set off into the night and from their verandah David Robertson and his wife could hear shrieks and screams from the bazaar as the enraged mobs chased their man. Against all the odds he managed to get away to safety and to the Robertsons' surprise he turned up again a year later, unharmed, and was welcomed back into their employment. Just as Cynthia Cheeseman had known that her message would eventually get through to her husband so too did the Robertsons' bearer realise that his job would be waiting for him if he were ever able to return to Bengal.

Sadly, many other servants who found themselves on the wrong side of the border at the wrong moment in history were not so lucky and many British families returning home were upset when news percolated through to them of the murder of a much-loved ayah, bearer or sweeper. That more lives were not lost in Bengal owed much to the pervasive influence of Mahatma

Gandhi, who had moved to Calcutta before Independence Day. There he had taken up residence in one of the city's many poor districts, living amongst the Untouchables and the dispossessed and threatening to fast to death should violence break out. Miraculously, there was no repetition of the mass murders that had disfigured Calcutta a year earlier and the whole province of Bengal remained reasonably calm.

For those who had served India well the massacres were a grievous blow. Many ICS officers, embittered by the stories coming out of the Punjab, felt that their work had been in vain and that despite all their efforts the two new dominions were sinking into a morass of violence and terror.

> Lots of people here are depressed and miserable about the transfer of power. The whole show is now so utterly corrupt that the educated classes feel that it can't go on. The Punjab is an absolute inferno and is still going strong. Thousands have been murdered and 10s and 100s of thousands of refugees are streaming about. There has been a lot of arson. It will take generations of work to put things straight. There are fearful floods in Chittagong, many lives have been lost and famine is starting. There has been trouble in 'Pindi and the Frontier: 'Pindi has been isolated for days.

Alan Flack also told his wife that he felt that Britain had made a terrible mistake in not ensuring the safety of the population of the Punjab before handing over power. His was a common enough sentiment at the time and with the passing of the years it was to grow stronger still. Even a senior civil servant like Sir George Cunningham, the Governor of the North-West Frontier Province at the time of independence, claimed in a letter to Lord Halifax that the 'opinion of most sensible people out here [is] that the trouble was enormously aggravated by the speed with which everything was done'. While admitting that there was some truth to Mountbatten's contention that both sides were so completely irreconcilable that, whatever happened, there would have been bad blood, Cunningham clung to the view that Britain was partly responsible for the carnage.

> It has been quite appalling and I doubt if anything commensurate with it has ever happened in history. Even if a quarter of the stories that one hears of massacre, starvation and worse horrors are true, it would be bad enough. Lahore has a feeling of misery about it, even now: hundreds of graves in the refugee camps,

lorries moving about full of the most pitiable human beings, and a general atmosphere of hopelessness. So far we have been spared these troubles up here [North-West Frontier Province], as there has been no big influx of Muslim refugees . . .

In his reply to Cunningham's letter Halifax was inclined to agree that the acceleration of independence from June 1948 back to August 1947 was the principal reason for the massacres and it is on that point that people start to differ. One argument has it that Mountbatten rushed through independence far too quickly, thus creating the tensions which led to violence in the partitioned territories; the other claims that the unrest was simmering below the surface of Indian society and would have sprung into being whatever the date of the transfer of power. With the benefit of hindsight it is easy to fall into step with the feelings of many an ICS officer who believes that the massacres could – and should – have been avoided, but the question remains, how was this worthy goal to be achieved?

For one thing, there were too few British troops in India – Montgomery had suggested that a minimum of six divisions would be required to hold India by military force – and Auchinleck had resisted the idea that more might be sent. But even had there been sufficient manpower it is extremely doubtful if the British government would have allowed troops to be used in that way in countries which were now independent. (An added problem was the reliability of the men in India, most of whom only wanted to get home.)

One solution would have been to make greater use of the Indian and Pakistani armies, especially as a Joint Defence Committee still existed under Field Marshal Auchinleck. This argument has an attractive ring to it because on paper a unified command would offer impartial assistance to the two governments in holding the peace in the Punjab. Mountbatten had hoped against hope that the Joint Defence Committee would ensure unity of command for the first two years of independence but the truth of the matter was that once partition had taken place the armies, too, wanted to be divided and to create their own traditions and loyalties. Older officers might have lamented the breaking up of the old Indian Army regiments but for the younger men the division only offered a challenge that had to be accepted.

Those of us who felt politically that partition was something we didn't want still believed that we should have our own army. Certainly I wasn't amongst those who felt that the two countries should have one army – that was said not only by ordinary people but also by very eminent soldiers in India. It was a totally unreal idea. I was quite prepared to start reconstructing from our share and to build a new Indian Army. At no time did I think that the two armies should stay together – as a lot of people thought at that time.

By then Palit had transferred to the 3rd/9th Gurkhas, his own regiment, the 1st/10th Baluch having been transferred along with its other four battalions to Pakistan. Shortly after the Independence Day celebrations he had been walking in Delhi when a friend collared him with the words, 'Get that bloody thing off!' It was only then that Palit realised he was still wearing his Baluch Regiment shoulder flash and that he could have been lynched by an angry crowd which was rioting further down the street. After years of serving in a battalion which had mixed companies, the strength of the communal rioting in Delhi came as a shock. True, the Indian Army had supplied a sense of unity under the British but now that had gone. 'There had to be a parting of the ways. Those companies of Sikhs, for instance, stationed in Peshawar, they had to come out to India and those companies of Pathans located in Hyderabad, they naturally had to go to Pakistan.'

General Das was another refugee from the recent past, but his loss was perhaps more tangible than Palit's enforced transfer from the Baluch Regiment. His family home was in Lahore, now it was in a foreign country and as a result his relatives had fled to stay with him in Delhi. Food was in short supply during the September riots and he remembers that 'it wasn't that our accommodation was small but we couldn't get food. The only things we had to eat were the rations I was getting – we had to share them all.' As happened to many others caught up in the same situation, Das was eventually compensated with the gift of land in India and ten years later he was able to build his own new house in Delhi. Having provided for his family his prime concern was to help in the rebuilding of the army he served and to try to heal the wounds caused by its partition.

With so many units in a state of reorganisation following partition it is not really surprising that the army's aid to the civil power was often patchy. Because of the divison of matériel, some regiments and units were short of transport or petrol, others were in the process of reorganising themselves; those with Punjab Muslim companies still in India could not act and neither could the Pakistan regiments which still contained Hindus or Sikhs. Yet in the midst of the undoubted chaos, many lives were saved by the faith and discipline of the new Indian Army.

> My first memory as I came into the Punjab was of an unending stream of people moving in both ways – trains stuffed to the brim with people riding on top and long convoys moving on roads. The Muslims were going west and the Hindus and Sikhs coming east: we had to arrange camps along the route and also to see that the two columns didn't meet or impinge on one another in any place because if they had there would have been absolute mayhem. So, different routes had been prescribed for those coming in and those going out. Where the trouble started was when trains from Pakistan used to come in with only dead people and bodies. This would enrage the local population and so when a train carrying Muslims going west came this would be attacked and the passengers killed. When the same train got to the other side exactly the same thing happened, so it was a vicious circle. Our job mainly was to see that these attacks didn't take place and, by and large, once we got sufficient troops into the Punjab we were able to control it and to some extent we stopped or minimised the number of incidents that took place. You couldn't stop it entirely because trains are easy targets.

General Candeth believes that the violence would have been much worse but for the presence of the army – by then he was a brigadier serving in Jullundur. The trouble was that few people in authority could determine where the disturbances would take place, or more importantly, they could not always understand the dynamics of group violence. What seems to have happened in the Punjab was an established pattern of crowd behaviour in which large groups of people lost their sense of personal responsibility and behaved in a violent and irrational manner. First there would be a period of heightened tension brought about by rumours of Muslims killing Sikhs (or vice versa) and the subsequent reprisals. The stories were usually exaggerated and out of proportion to what had happened, but they helped to breed a siege mentality. Thus, when the refugee trains arrived in a locality the second stage would be reached with the rapid spread of the rumour, causing panic and fear. Thirdly, the mobs would act with extreme violence and individuals would lose themselves in a collective fury which the victims would be unable to withstand. Once that had started it was very difficult to stop. Given the scale of the territory to be protected and the unpredictable nature of the attacks, it proved exceptionally difficult for the Indian Army – or any army – to provide complete cover for the refugees.

Once Mountbatten had arrived in India to push through the British decision to abdicate power speed had to be of the essence. To have delayed the transfer would have been to court disaster on an even larger scale because the tension would surely have increased and then the violence might well have been aimed at the British. As it was, the massacres were confined mainly to the Punjab and there were very few instances of British people being involved. When they were harmed it usually happened because they were in the wrong place at the wrong time. Unlike later transfers of imperial power in places like Malaya, Aden or Cyprus there was no long-drawn-out guerrilla or terrorist war against British subjects or British property and as Nikhil Chakravartty points out, in that sense the British handled the matter well.

> After all, the whole chain of circumstances was such that it was not like the French getting defeated at Dien Bien Phu and then withdrawing. It is a testimony to the astuteness of British imperial ideologues that they could handle it so carefully . . . in this part of the world the British behaved like a very wise and far-sighted imperial power. They had lost their strength because at that time the centre of gravity had passed to the Americans.

This is very much to the point, because after the transfer of power the massacres had become a problem for the Indian and Pakistani governments. Although the British might have felt a moral responsibility they were powerless to act and as A.K. Damodaran reminds us they were also relatively safe, even in the hot-spots of the Punjab.

> The only visible and safe and unhateable non-adversary group was the Europeans, the English. It was a funny situation: this was a psychological volte-face. The Europeans could wander about any bazaar because neither Hindu nor Muslim would kill them. We had this very odd situation where the dislike of decades of pretty

bad oppression by individuals and administrators was forgotten in the bazaars and streets because it was diverted between Hindu and Muslim. That, of course, was only part of the story; there's really not much hate in the movement – except in the terrorist groups in the corners.

Few Indians who were caught up in the violence remained unaffected by it. Damodaran was able to retire to the calm of his native Kerala after celebrating independence in the streets of Delhi. 'The moment I crossed over from Nagpur to the south, the moment I crossed into Madhya Pradesh [Central Province] it was another world . . . there wasn't a single anti-Muslim incident in Madras. We had this huge hinterland of tranquillity towards this terrible crisis which the Pakistanis did not have.'

As was the case with so many of his fellow countrymen the violence in the Punjab came as a complete surprise. Damodaran had complete faith in the province's secular tradition and had underestimated the strength of the passions aroused by the rivalry between the Hindu and Muslim sectors of the population. Until the 1945 general elections the agrarian-based Unionist Party had dominated Punjabi politics, but during the war the Muslim League had worked hard to win over the support of the Muslims in the province. Not only did they convince the peasantry that their future lay with Pakistan after the British left, but they also won the votes of the Muslim political and religious leaders. Support for the moderate Unionist Party dwindled and as independence approached the Muslim League could claim to speak for virtually all the Muslims in the Punjab. All these facts were known and understood but because the Punjab had such a strong secular tradition, and because it had been by tradition a recruiting ground for the army, the hope persisted that there would be little trouble. The flashpoint came with the migration of the peoples.

Compare this with Bengal: there was migration, certainly, though not to the same extent. The refugees came but they settled along the border. There was some violence in East Bengal but not on the scale that would lead to mass migration . . . all the refugee settlements were along the border and when the situation improved in East Bengal they trickled back. But the Punjab Hindu, he'll go all the way across the frontier to settle down. When I came to Delhi it came to me as a shock that a migration on such a large scale had taken place.

With his background in Marxist ideology Chakravartty, like other Communist Party members, stood aghast at the spectre of peasant turning on peasant in the Punjab. As a young man he had placed no little importance on the view that the independence struggle was as much between the peasantry and the landlords as it was between the Indians and the British, yet here was a conflict which bordered on civil war. The Calcutta Riots which he had witnessed the previous year had shown him how illusory was that aim yet he still retained a belief in the essential humanity of the peoples who were most affected by the partition. Had they not been forced to move, ran his argument, then the Punjab could have remained as trouble-free as Bengal. (Chakravartty is also inclined to the view that the right-wing Hindu party, Rashtriya Swayamsevak Sangh, fomented much of the Hindu unrest in the Punjab. As a party it was weaker in Bengal.)

Chakravartty's hope was a forlorn one, for once the British had imposed a communal divide on India and then withdrawn their responsibility for implementing it, there was bound to be trouble. Throughout the period of their rule in India the British had controlled communal hostility by imposing superior force, both civil and military. Trouble had been kept at bay with a mixture of practical politics and control of the armed forces and the police. By redrawing the boundaries in the Punjab in a way which did not always reflect group identities, Radcliffe's awards had paved the way for future problems. Only by introducing a ruthless partition or by employing strong central authority with autocratic powers could the problem have been solved, and neither application was possible in 1947.

Nehru's response was one of horror and dismay. To him the riots in Delhi in September were a personal affront and he took to the streets around Connaught Circus in a vain attempt to shame the rioters into submission. Such was the power of his personality that his appearance was usually enough to halt the mayhem but as All-India Radio producer P.C. Chatterji recalls, no sooner had Nehru left than the trouble broke out again. In such tense circumstances he could hardly be the one-man boundary force that Gandhi was in Calcutta.

Gradually, like a relief ship pulling away from a troubled country, the massacres in the Punjab receded into the distance and died away. The migrations of the peoples which had triggered them off were at an end and although riot, arson, rape and murder were still to be part of the vocabulary of Indian political life the worst was over by the year's end. India had indeed been given a baptism of fire but, as General Palit points out, there was a sense of fatalism surrounding the whole sorry episode. It was perhaps a necessary experience, an outcome of independence which had to be endured.

> The Congress leaders never took the idea of partition seriously. They couldn't believe that India would be partitioned and therefore my own opinion is that they didn't work at it. When it came it was too late to go back and fight it . . . how the local communal troubles were stirred up by politicians or local thugs I don't know. How much it was because of the basic intolerance of the Hindu, not his aggression, but his non-acceptance of anything outside his caste – that's a very cruel aspect of Hinduism which people don't realise because it's a very soft and non-xenophobic religion but it's a very intolerant one – I also don't know. But I think that, politically, in the first thirty years of independence it was necessary for us to have a strong centre, though we have a fragile system. In Nehru's day the strength of the centre established us as a nation.

Without that strong centre in September 1947 the problem of coping with the massacres in the Punjab was bound to be acute; but a grain of comfort can be found in the fact that the violence did not spread elsewhere into other areas where Hindu, Muslim and Sikh lived together in close proximity.

Despite the difficulties which had threatened to engulf the fledgling dominions the immediate aftermath of independence was not just coloured by the red of the blood that flowed in the Punjab. For Nikhil Chakravartty it was a time when the positive and the negative aspects of life became hopelessly jumbled, a violent and turbulent period which, events notwithstanding, was a happy time. He had noticed the signs first in November 1945 when he witnessed in Calcutta a student riot in support of the INA officers undergoing trial in New Delhi. Sitting in a teashop he saw the crowds assembling for the mass meeting and demonstration and decided to cover it for his newspaper. No sooner had he left the shop than there was the sound of shots being fired as the police arrived to break up the crowd.

'Now it struck me: normally whenever there's police firing people run away from it. It's a natural instinct to take shelter. But on that particular day they ran towards the police to overpower them.' To him this was the beginning of a new India, a positive sign that the people wanted to take their destiny into their own hands – even at the risk of their own lives. It came as little surprise to him to find the negative aspects of that new-found independence in the killings in the Punjab.

Not everyone, of course, responded to the calls for violence and there were numerous examples of Hindus and Sikhs aiding fellow villagers who happened to be Muslim, and of people on the Pakistani side of the border refusing to be drawn into violent reprisals on escaping refugees. In Delhi, Dr Ram's family had to intercede on behalf of the Muslim workforce in their mills. Once again the main problem was the arrival in the community of wild rumours about the massacre of Sikhs in places like Lahore and Rawalpindi; as these began to spread Ram's Sikh workers turned on their Muslim workmates. To prevent a massacre, the Muslims were locked up in a secure part of the factory and when the tumult died down they were transferred to the Rams' Pakistani factory in Lyallpur. 'They couldn't stay in a factory in which the Hindu and Sikh workers were emotionally surcharged so, in a sense, they lost their jobs.' Ram's Lyallpur factory was managed mainly by senior Muslim officials who were forced to quit Delhi in 1947 and it remained in his family's hands until the Indo-Pakistan war of 1965.

Ram's family also helped in other ways. Muslim friends of the family were taken into the safety of his home in Curzon Road where there was less chance of them being attacked by the mobs. By the end of September the army and the police had secured most of the areas of the city in which trouble was expected and a sense of normality had returned to the capital. The arrival of Madrassi troops had also helped matters; like the Gurkhas they were considered to be reasonably neutral, thus justifying Mountbatten's order to Muslim officers and officials to keep a low profile after the transfer of power. Badr-ud-Din Tyabji, for example, had felt safer carrying a pistol during that period, even when he visited the comparative safety of the Gymkhana Club.

Human nature being what it is, though, many Muslims carried on as usual in India while in Pakistan Hindu army officers remained loyal to the government they now served. P.C. 'Tiny' Chatterji's brother, a brigadier in the Indian Army, had taken his

Baluch troops, mainly Pathans, back to Pakistan; they had served with him throughout the Second World War and although they knew that he had opted for India they continued to obey him even when they encountered fierce rioting in Nowshera. After a four-month-long silence he turned up in Delhi on Christmas Day 1947 and was surprised to find that his family had given him up for lost. 'He pooh-poohed it all, it was utter nonsense. Never did he have any fear that his Muslim troops would not obey his orders or that he was in fear of his life.'

Some controversy still surrounds the role played by Mountbatten in the handling of the crisis. After giving his blessing to the disbandment of the Punjab Boundary Force on 29 August he had left Delhi for a well-deserved break in Simla. Four days later an appeal arrived from V. P. Menon saying that the situation in the Punjab was out of hand and that Mountbatten's return to Delhi had been demanded by the new government. This was not strictly true as Menon had not discussed the matter formally with his colleagues, but it was too strong an appeal for the Governor-General to resist. On 5 September Mountbatten was back in Delhi to establish an Emergency Committee under his chairmanship. Although he was careful to maintain the fiction that Nehru was officially in charge Mountbatten worked the committee as if it were running a war. Matters were put in hand to return civil order to Delhi, guards were put on the homes of political leaders and foreign diplomats, arrangements were made to collect and bury the dead, medical aid was rushed into the refugee camps and protection was given to the convoys and refugee trains. In a sense, Mountbatten did assume dictatorial powers but that firm intervention was badly needed both to restore the morale of Nehru's government and to persuade Jinnah that he was not acting against Pakistan's interests – for the threat of a large-scale conflict in the Punjab was never far away. By chairing the Joint Defence Committee in a calm and neutral way Mountbatten certainly helped to maintain a tenuous peace between the two countries during that tense and difficult period.

Once the emergency was over the Indian leadership felt ill at ease about Mountbatten's intervention in the matter of the Punjab massacres. Although they had welcomed his help there was a lingering feeling that they had, perhaps, failed in their own duties. According to the evidence of new District Magistrate

Govind Narain, the new Indian administration could have controlled the situation if it had shown firmness and resolution. At
Aligarh the returning Hindus were segregated and put under
close guard before they could spread their stories amongst the
villagers. In that way the local Muslims were safeguarded and
there was no trouble in the district. 'The thing that I recall with a
lot of pride,' he says, 'is that the Indian administration, with a
leadership that was great at that time, was able to solve most of
the problems in the course of time. That's a source of great
satisfaction because the service was depleted of many talented
people, the British having gone home and the Muslim officers to
Pakistan.'

As a further precaution Narain had neutralised the Aligarh
student population which had been a hotbed of discontent before
independence. If there was any trouble on the campus, he
warned, then he would not hesitate to send in the police, but if all
were calm he would not interfere. Wisely, the students took him
at his word – after the Independence Day celebrations he had told
the crowds that to save the life of one Muslim he would be
prepared to sacrifice a hundred rioting Hindus. Having imposed
strict control over Aligarh – with the support of the government –
Narain did not expect any trouble from his charges and was
mightily, and understandably, pleased when the students and the
Hindu population kept their peace.

Narain succeeded where others failed – and Aligarh was a
potential centre of communal strife – because he ruled his district
with a firm hand and eschewed democratic niceties. Too often,
faith in basic human decency or a belief that one-man-one-vote
would be a cure-all permitted violence to take a grip as tribalism
took over. Against anarchy, gangsterism or infectious hysteria,
democratic government – as understood in the Western European sense – was powerless, especially in areas where its agents,
the police and the army, offered only limited resistance. All the
institutions in the world could not halt the racial and religious
antagonism in the Punjab, where the violence escalated through
fear and the desire for revenge. It was a madness, albeit
temporary, but it provided a clue for the causes of other
post-colonial conflicts which started in similar fashion – Biafra,
Uganda, Sri Lanka.

Few people in authority could escape censure for their part in

allowing the massacres to happen. The British drew up boundaries which did not always agree with tribal or religious divisions;
many Indian and Pakistani politicians stood guilty of whipping up
antagonism amongst ignorant peasant people; the people themselves abandoned reason and submerged themselves in hatred
and villainy. And was not this the country which worshipped
Kali, the wife of Shiva who took her dead body on his shoulders
and whirled through the world in an orgy of violence and
destruction? This is the goddess with devilish eyes and a garland
of skulls who can only be propitiated by daily sacrifice. Her
presence, too, was felt in the Punjab in September 1947.

Chapter Eight

Going Home

The last to go were the soldiers of the British Army. Their forebears had been in India from the very beginning of the British presence, first acting as guards to the possessions of the East India Company and then fighting the wars which would bring the native states into the empire. From those early forces had grown the Indian Army, manned by the martial races and officered by Europeans. Sometimes they fought alongside British battalions – the first companies of the 39th Foot, later the Dorsetshire Regiment, had landed at Madras in September 1754 – and until the Mutiny their loyalty had never been questioned. After 1857, though, it became the custom to keep British troops in India on a ratio of one to three and British regiments began arriving in India on a large scale, often spending up to twenty-one years at a time in the country. In turn India became an important part of army life. It provided ample space for training and also the opportunity to fight the kind of tribal warfare which became part of the lore and mystique of British India. Soldiering in India came to have an emotional and sentimental significance that had no equal in any other part of the empire. Right up to the very end those links were considered to be sacrosanct by those who regarded India as the army's second home if not its true one.

There was hardly an infantry regiment in the British Army which had not served in India, for ever since 1825 regiments had divided their forces into companies for service abroad and service at home. In 1870 Edward Cardwell, the Secretary of State for War, had introduced the linked-battalion system to further the process and in 1881 his successor Hugh Childers cemented the new framework by permanently linking the units into two-battalion regiments.

Thus a regiment like the Somerset Light Infantry, whose history is inextricably bound up with India, would have its 1st battalion in India while its 2nd battalion would train for home duty at the depot in Taunton – or vice versa. For the men on twelve-year engagements there was the opportunity of serving six years in whichever battalion happened to be in India. (Some men volunteered to spend the whole of their service in India.) The Somersets' connection with India had begun in 1822 and the title 'Jellalabad' in their cap badge commemorated the regiment's heroic behaviour on 7 April 1842 when the forces of Akhbar Khan were routed at Jellalabad during the First Afghan War. Between the end of the Mutiny and the end of British rule, a period of ninety years, one or other of its battalions was invariably stationed in India. The 1st battalion had spent the Second World War there, firstly fighting tribesmen on the North-West Frontier, then acting as riot squads in Delhi during the Quit India movement in 1942 and finally serving with the 7th Indian Division during the fierce fighting against the Japanese in the Arakan. It was, therefore, right and proper that it should fall to the Somersets to be the last British troops to leave India in February 1948.

In the last days of the raj British servicemen had been withdrawn from operations in support of the civil power and instead began their preparations for departure. By then the Somersets were in Bombay where there was little public disorder following the independence celebrations; when rioting did break out in the Crawford Market the battalion had to remain in barracks while the Gurkhas, the independent force, took control of the situation. By then, too, the battalion was down to some three hundred men and their final seven months in India turned out to be relatively easy and quiet – their last involvement in Indian affairs had been putting down a riot instigated by Indian signallers at Jubblepore the previous year, but that, as Michael Ryall recalls, was not caused by politics. 'Rather it was against conditions of service. As a company commander I had something like twelve hours' administrative training but we had hours of riot drill. We had to form up in squares – it was almost like a repetition of the Napoleonic Wars in a modern battlefield.'

In the month before the transfer of power the battalion also had a new commanding officer in John Platt who had first come out to join the Somerset Light Infantry in 1926 and whose career had subsequently taken him all over the world. His first task had been to organise his men for an Independence Day parade. They were the only British troops taking part and it was an agreeable occasion, the salute being taken by the Governor-General of Bombay, Sir John Colville, and the Chief Minister, B.G. Kher, fresh from his nostalgic return to Wilson College. Platt could not help noticing that his men drew the biggest cheers from the crowd, many of whom were in tears because the British were going.

In the days that followed he had to put in hand something less pleasant – the paying off of the battalion's Indian workers, many of whom had given a lifetime's service to the regiment. The worst moment for Platt was having to face the regimental contractor, Kher Mahomet, whose family had looked after the Somersets for over a hundred years. To him and his forebears had fallen the task of providing the battalions with all their needs on their arrival in India; now it fell to John Platt to end that historic connection.

> He couldn't understand why we were going. What's more, he faced a bleak future without us – he had produced all the services for the regiment, the tailor, the shoemaker and the laundry. In fact he did everything. Just before we left he came into my office and said, 'Sahib, what am I going to do?' I could only say, 'I'm awfully sorry but I can't help you in any way.' He was losing his whole business.

In other respects the battalion's last weeks in India were one long round of parties, receptions and ceremonial parades during which nostalgia for the past and a desire to get back home to families and friends were the chief – and usually rival – emotions. Christmas Day 1947 was marked by the long-standing tradition of the officers, warrant officers and sergeants bringing early-morning tea to the corporals and privates and later the whole battalion sat down to 'a superfeed of turkey, pork, mincepies and plum pudding'. So exceptional was the meal that Platt was moved to remind his men that they were unlikely to find such abundance at their next Christmas meal in England. The battalion also paraded for Sir John Colville at the ceremony when he demitted office and his successor as Governor-General, Sir Maharaj Singh, was sworn in at the Durbar Hall in Government House. For the officers there was the opportunity to indulge in field sports, hunting with the Bombay Hounds and Jackal Club and duck shoots at Mahdmeshwar; for the men there were sports and games with the other units of 29 Brigade whose headquarters had been moved from Delhi to Bombay. The rest of the time was spent packing and making special arrangements for the safe transport of the substantial quantity of regimental silver which would accompany the battalion back to England.

By the beginning of February the last British troops, commanded by Major-General L.G. Whistler, were on the move. The remaining companies of the 1st Essex Regiment and the 1st South Staffordshire Regiment left on the *Empress of Scotland*, leaving only two regiments in the subcontinent – the Somerset Light Infantry in Bombay and the 2nd Black Watch in Karachi. Some interested observers felt that the honour of being *ultimis ex Indis* should fall to the Scottish regiment because of its connections with Lord Wavell – he had served with the 2nd battalion – and because it, too, had historic links with India. Eventually it was decided that the 1st Somerset Light Infantry should be the last to leave because they had been in India longer than any other regiment. The date for their departure was fixed for 28 February and it was agreed that the 2nd Black Watch should leave Karachi two days earlier.

The job of licking the officers and men of the Somersets into shape for the final parade was the responsibility of Regimental Sergeant-Major Bartlett, who spared no one in getting things right. During the war he had trained recruits in the United Kingdom and was considered to be the right man for the job – which is in many respects the top post in an infantry battalion. Everyone had to play a part, even the Regimental Quartermaster-Sergeant, A.F. 'Jack' Frost, who had not worn boots for years, and an army catering corps sergeant who changed his badge for the stringed bugle-horn and mural crown of the Somersets. According to Frost it was all done at frenetic speed: men had grown used to dressing sloppily during the war, wearing only shorts and plimsolls, and there was a shortage of the traditional light infantry green beret. These had to be borrowed from the Gurkhas and by the last week of the month the colour party was ready to rehearse on the historic landing stage – the Apollo Bundur – in front of the Gateway of India where the parade would take place.

On the day before their departure the battalion and its belongings were loaded on board the *Empress of Australia* which then moved into the Bombay roads to allow a quick and easy embarkation once the ceremonies had been completed. 'Jack' Frost's wife was the only Somerset wife on board and because she had to remain with the liner she missed the ceremony, much to her lasting regret. Their final duty had been to put down their dog Judy along with the other mess pets, no one being prepared to leave them to the mercies of the Bombay civic authorities. Then at dawn on Saturday 28 February the regiment prepared to say farewell to India on behalf of the British Army.

They made an impressive sight. At 7.30 a.m. the Somersets' colour party and escort under the command of Major F.M. De Butts changed into their ceremonial dress at the Yacht Club – drill shirt and shorts, white gaiters and belts, green berets – and made ready to march on to the Apollo Bundur. Peter Pearson carried the King's Colour and Michael Ryall the Regimental Colour. With bands playing and colours flying, the regiments of the Indian Army took up their positions to say farewell to their British comrades-in-arms. Looking back from the Gateway, on the right stood the guards of honour of the 3rd Indian Grenadiers, the 2nd Sikhs and the Royal Indian Navy; on the left stood those of the 3rd/5th Royal Gurkha Rifles, the 1st Mahratta Light Infantry and a further guard from the Royal Indian Navy. Later, John Platt was to remember the vivid contrast between the smart white naval uniforms and the red puggarees of the Sikhs with the plainer khaki drill uniforms and green berets worn by his own men.

At 9 a.m. the guests began to arrive in the seats which had been specially prepared for them; only five hundred tickets had been issued but many thousands more ordinary people had crowded around the perimeter to watch the event. Among the guests were B.G. Kher, Sir Maharaj Singh, General Whistler and Major-General D.R. Bateman, the GOC, Bombay Area. As soon as the Governor-General was seated the colour party and escort marched on parade to the Regimental March, 'Prince Albert's March', played by the band of the Royal Indian Engineers. They were received by the Indian guards of honour with a Colour Salute and by the crowds with a great cheer of enthusiasm and approval.

Then followed the speeches, the first from Sir Maharaj Singh
who spoke of the sense of comradeship and honour which had
always existed between the armies of the two countries. True, he
added, there had been political differences but those were in the
past; instead he preferred to remember 'the manly comradeship
existing between the soldiers of our two countries cemented by
the trials and hardships of two Great Wars, yes, and by the
success in many a battle against militant fascism'. He was
followed by General Whistler whose father had once been
Governor of Bombay. There was one other link between the two
men who were sharing the platform for the last time – both had
been educated at Harrow together: a curious commentary,
thought Platt, on the recent history of British rule in India and the
Indian struggle for self-rule.

The highlight of the ceremony was the presentation of a silver
model of the Gateway of India which Platt was asked to accept on
behalf of the regiment.

> I was presented with a silver model of the Gateway of India from
> the Indian Army and also with a picture of a Gurkha winning a VC
> and, thirdly, with a flag of India. They were presented by General
> Bateman who was commanding the Area. Alongside him stood
> Brigadier D.S. Brar who was an Indian. I'll never forgive General
> Bateman, because an opportunity for an Indian officer to have
> given those things was lost, and yet he did it. I thought it very
> tactless.

As if to make up for the lapse, Platt's reply of thanks ended by
making specific reference to India's new-found independence.

> We depart with mixed feelings. On the one hand we look forward
> to seeing again our own country and families; while on the other
> we are most reluctant to leave behind so many good friends and
> your great country which our Regiment has known and served for
> so long. At the same time we are happy for you in your new-found
> freedom; and I take this unique opportunity of wishing you all
> good luck, Godspeed and *Jai Hind!*

And then it was all over. The bands played 'God Save the King'
and 'Bande Mataram', the Royal Salutes were given and
answered, the Indian guards of honour presented arms. Major
De Butts gave the orders: 'Outwards Turn', 'Inwards wheel –
slow march', and the whole escort trooped the colours to the tune
of 'Auld Lang Syne', down the centre of the parade and through

the Gateway of India to the waiting launches, paying compliments to the Governor of Bombay as they passed. The whole manoeuvre was carried out with the utmost precision and it was captured for posterity by the newsreel cameras of Movietone News to become a motif for the final departure of the British from India. 'Of course, the reason was they wanted to show the world that we were not being kicked out of India,' claims Platt. 'We went out with the Indian Army presenting arms and presenting us with gifts to commemorate the occasion.'

For the men of the Somersets' colour party and escort the departure from India was one of their proudest moments. 'The sun was in our eyes as we walked down the steps of the Gateway of India,' remembers Peter Pearson, 'but we could see tears in everyone's eyes.' As the launch pulled away, the colours billowing in the breeze, the crowds rushed forward, oblivious of the police, to shout their final farewells to the last British troops to have manned a garrison on India's shores. Above them, still in their positions on parade, the bands of the Indian Army continued to play 'Auld Lang Syne': incongruously, the chorus of this deeply moving Scottish song of farewell and fond remembrance was taken up by thousands of Indian voices. And still the chorus rang across the water as the *Empress of Australia* slipped her anchor and headed for the open sea. After 126 years the Somerset Light Infantry were finally going home.

By then the men of the 2nd Black Watch were also on the high seas. Like the Somersets they had not had an operational role since the transfer of power and had become instead guests of a dominion whose government wanted them to leave as soon as possible. During the war the battalion had seen extensive service in the Middle East and in Burma and in the post-war period it had been stationed in Peshawar, engaged on internal security duties during the referendum in the North-West Frontier Province. Since independence they had been at Malir cantonment, a dry and dusty place, and although plans had been made to bring the battalion home early, it had been agreed by the Pakistani and British governments that they should stay on until all the European families were clear of the country. Only 500 regulars remained in the 2nd battalion and their future was uncertain, for the post-war reorganisation of the army decreed that they should be reduced to cadre form, with the officers and men being split up amongst the other regiments in the Highland Group. After 170 years of unbroken service the 2nd Battalion Black Watch would be returning to Scotland to disband. It was a sad moment in the regiment's history and the commanding officer, Neville Blair, admitted that he had to keep his men especially busy as no one dared think too hard about what the future might hold for them.

Unlike the Somerset Light Infantry in Bombay who, according to Major De Butts, were little more than 'a transit camp for the waifs and strays of the British Army in India', the Black Watch were kept in shape almost until the very end. At the height of the trouble in the Punjab they were ordered to train for airborne operations and two mock-up Dakotas were built for that purpose. Various rumours flooded around the camp, the most popular being that the battalion would be flown to Delhi to quell rioting, but no more was heard by the end of October. For the most part the problem was keeping the men occupied. As the battalion was still reasonably well manned the companies took part in several 'schemes' to keep the men up to the mark – range practices, night marches, river crossings and village clearing operations being just part of the daily routine. Various sporting fixtures were played against the other units with whom they were brigaded, there were field sports for the officers and, being a Highland regiment, the pipes and drums were much in demand at social occasions.

Although depleted by demobilisation the pipes and drums of the Black Watch still put on a brave show. At the end of December they played at the farewell parade for British troops in Pakistan, General Whistler taking the salute, and at Hogmanay they welcomed the arrival in Karachi of the cruiser HMS *Norfolk* whose crew also had a pipe band. However, it was for farewells at the docks that the battalion's pipes and drums became chiefly known as they played off the last British units to leave Pakistan. On 14 December 1947 the 1st Royal Scots, which had also been part of 235 Brigade, left for Edinburgh, marching down to the docks with bayonets fixed and pipes and drums playing. For an hour or more the pipes and drums of the Black Watch played alternate sets with the Royal Scots, who played from the deck of their troopship. As the ship slipped away from the quay the Black Watch pipes broke into 'Dumbarton's Drums' and from the swiftly departing trooper came the strains of 'Highland Laddie', both bands playing the other's regimental march to say farewell.

At other times the Black Watch pipes and drums would break
into the mischievously named tune, 'How Happy We Have Been
A' Together'.

And that indeed seems to have been the mood of the time.
Neville Blair admits that he was sad to be leaving a country which
had such strong links with his regiment, both because that
association was being ended and also because he knew that his
own battalion was about to lose its identity. Shortly before
leaving Karachi, though, he heard that the War Office had
changed its mind once more. 'News has just been received that
amalgamation with the 1st battalion is now our destiny; not
reduction – for which we are all thankful,' he noted at the time.
'The future of the battalion's property is thereby partly solved,
and its proud history will not be forgotten.'

One problem remained in Blair's lap. Because his battalion was
to be amalgamated he had to reduce the numbers of his regular
soldiers, 250 of whom were due to be posted to Middle East Land
Forces where they would serve with the 1st Argyll and Sutherland
Highlanders. On the other hand, if the remaining men could be
kept in India they would stand a better chance of being sent to the
Black Watch's 1st battalion; accordingly a plot was hatched to
keep as many of the regiment's regular troops as was possible.
Men were given local leave, sent on courses where there were
vacancies or were drafted to help the Quartermaster, Captain H.
McL. 'Nobby' Clark, prepare his final audit for the day of
departure. A shortage of available shipping also helped the
battalion to keep itself more or less intact and by the time that the
day of leave-taking dawned – 26 February – Blair had over two
hundred men under his command.

Initially the battalion had hoped to leave Karachi without any
fuss and Blair was against having an official send-off. The
government of Pakistan was adamant, though, that the event
should be celebrated and Major-General Mohammed Akhbar
Khan, senior officer Pakistan Army, succeeded in persuading the
Black Watch that they should leave his country with colours
flying, bayonets fixed and pipes and drums playing. And so the
scene was set for the last British troops to leave Pakistan.

Their day began at 9 a.m. when a convoy of trucks took the
battalion down the three-mile stretch of road from the Malir
cantonment into Karachi where they were due to line up at the

assembly point in the grounds of St Catherine's School. What began as a routine exercise nearly turned into a disaster because, unusually for that time of year in the Sind, the heavens opened, visibility was reduced to nil and almost all of the trucks stalled in the sudden downpour. It was a soaked group of men, Blair remembers, that began the march through the streets of the Empress Market into Elphinstone Street where they were due to say farewell to Dr Jinnah. But the pipes and drums put new heart into the men, and to the cheers of an enormous crowd they paraded down Elphinstone Street. Even when the music stopped the crowds kept on roaring their approval and it was their enthusiasm, above anything else, that stuck in Blair's mind as he marched at the head of his column of men.

> I was absolutely astounded by the reception. The crowds were vast and the police had to clear them away while they went on cheering . . . to see amongst those crowds proud old turbaned Pathans saluting the colours was really quite something. I shall never forget it.

Outside the Governor-General's house the battalion formed up in line and when Jinnah appeared he was accorded a Royal Salute. In his speech of farewell he made the customary remarks about the spirit of friendship which traditionally existed between the military men of the two countries; then, for a moment, he lost composure and broke down. 'I couldn't believe that I would ever be entitled to a Royal Salute from a British regiment,' he confided to an embarrassed Blair. Eight months later, Pakistan's spiritual leader and guide was dead from cancer of the lungs.

The civil ceremony over, the battalion then embussed for the military farewell at the docks. Their own pipes and drums were silent now but at the dockside waited the massed pipes and drums of two battalions of the Baluch Regiment and the 2nd/16th Punjab Regiment. Also waiting was another huge crowd which had assembled to watch the Black Watch marching off their colours. With the men formed up in hollow square, facing the ship, the *Empire Halladale*, the speech of farewell was read by General Akhbar Khan and then a begarlanded Blair asked permission to continue the parade. As the battalion presented arms the colours were marched out of the hollow square and the colour party took up station to the flank and in front of the

Punjab Regiment's guard of honour. The guard presented arms, and with the massed pipes and drums playing, the colours were slow-marched up the gangway into the grey side of the ship, whereupon the battalion's flag broke at the ·yardarm. It was a simple and impressive ceremony, bringing to an end ninety-six years of service in India. Touchingly, the last set to be played by the massed bands was the slow march, 'Will Ye No Come Back Again?'

> Will ye no come back again?
> Will ye no come back again?
> Better lo'ed ye canna be,
> Will ye no come back again?

To everyone present it seemed that the Pakistan regiments had got it absolutely right, Lady Nairne's sentimental chorus for the lost cause of the Jacobites ringing down the years to mark the Highlanders' farewell. Isabel Blair was already on board the *Empire Halladale* with the other wives and she remembers that 'the Scots were blubbing like babies'.

After the Lord Mayor's Show came the street cleaners . . . one reason why Blair had asked permission for the colours to be paraded was that once they were on board the trooper the battalion had officially left Pakistan. The ceremony over, the officers and men had to complete the loading of their equipment, while back at Malir 'Nobby' Clark had to work at breakneck speed to complete his audit: the Pakistan Army might have waxed sentimental at the Jocks' departure but they insisted that every piece of equipment on loan to them had to be accounted for. Ironically, the task was to take two days and it was not until the morning of 28 February, while the Somersets were parading in Bombay, that the *Empire Halladale* set sail from Karachi.

The *Empire Halladale* was a Glasgow-registered ship with a Glaswegian crew who enjoyed having their fellow countrymen on board. Physical exercises, usually so necessary for troops on a sea voyage, were soon replaced by Highland dancing, with everyone joining in, and the pipers were much in demand. It became an instant custom of shipboard life for the pipes and drums to play requests from the passengers and at every port of call topical tunes were played: 'The Barren Rocks of Aden' for example, when the ship arrived in the sultry heat of Aden harbour. Three weeks after departure, on 20 March, the whole battalion paraded at dawn to catch their first glimpse of Scotland as the trooper lay off the Tail o' the Bank before slipping up the Firth of Clyde into Glasgow's King George V Docks. A fine drizzle was falling and there was a nip in the air but spirits were soon raised by the strains of the pipes and drums of the Royal Scots who were on the dockside, playing their old friends back to Scotland. The following day, the battalion disembarked and boarded the waiting train which would take them back to Perth and home. 'As we wormed our way out of the Glasgow greyness,' noted Blair, 'it was good to see the green fields, the light and shadow of the woods, and the familiar contours of Ben Halton and Uamh Bheag.'

All that remained in the following days was to parade through the city of Perth for a civic welcome at which the salute was taken by Field Marshal Earl Wavell, and then it was all over. The 2nd battalion went into suspended animation, the officers and men went on leave and the final preparations for amalgamation were put in hand. Colonel Blair spoke for many when he ended his command with the thought that 'Perhaps we should take heart from a quotation associated with Mary Queen of Scots, "In my end is my beginning".'

The country to which the Black Watch were returning was very different from the Scotland which the older regulars had known in pre-war days. Then its industries had seemed moribund; now, there was a new sense of hope in the air. Coal, a staple indigenous industry, had been nationalised by the Labour government in 1946, a Forestry Commission had been established to plant one and a quarter million trees within fifty years, schemes for the construction of new towns had begun and arrangements were being made to clear slums in big cities like Glasgow and move the overspill to places elsewhere. War, the creator of change, had brought a measure of prosperity, too, to Scotland's heavy industries, and although unemployment was still well above the national average, many people had money in their pockets. At that time, social security combined with rapid economic growth seemed to be the cure-all for the brave new post-war world.

Yet, despite the surface prosperity enjoyed by the people of Scotland and by those in the rest of Britain, the country as a whole was beginning to lag behind its allies and former enemies. The war had cost Britain £3,000 million in debts, exports had fallen below their pre-war levels and loans from the United States of America had helped to weaken the value of sterling. Many of the industries, including coal-mining, were not particularly productive or competitive and transport and communications were suffering from a lack of planning and investment. Rationing was still in force and some foodstuffs were in short supply: one of the first lessons learned by Claud Moir was that when he asked for, and was given, a glass of milk, he was robbing his hosts of their supply for the day.

To a very great extent the army is normally insulated from dramatic social changes but, going on leave, the men of the Black Watch could not fail to notice the differences that had come about in their absence – and for many this was their first sight of Scotland for ten years. From leading a life of relative ease in Pakistan where food was freely available and cheap, they found themselves having to cope with the shortages of post-war Britain. Even those posted to West Germany, where the 1st battalion was stationed at Duisberg, found themselves forming an army of occupation in a sullen and defeated country. In time Germany came to be regarded, somewhat tenuously, as the army's successor to India, ideal for training with the regiments kept apart from the civilian population, but even the most enthusiastic promoters of that theory had to admit that it lacked the conditions, the climate and, it has to be said, the mystique.

Scenes similar to those that welcomed the Black Watch awaited the Somersets when they arrived in Liverpool on 17 March. John Platt noticed immediately that the publicity surrounding the regiment's departure from India had turned them into celebrities in England. 'My God, it's the Somersets,' he heard more than one porter exclaim as the train left Liverpool for the long journey to Taunton. Even though they arrived at their headquarters well after midnight a surprisingly large number of people had gathered to greet them, and those numbers were swelled the following day when the regiment exercised its right to march through Taunton with band playing and colours flying. 'So ended a series of ceremonies such as few regiments can have taken part in before,' noted Platt at the time. 'We were very lucky to be the battalion selected to be the last out of India, and can only hope that the tremendous publicity afforded us will enhance the good name of the regiment and encourage many more men from the County to enlist in it.'

It was a timely reminder, because the regiment's future had been far from certain. At the time of the transfer of power the Somersets had been told that their next destination would be Malaya where they would form a Light Infantry Brigade with the King's Own Yorkshire Light Infantry. Then came word that the battalion was to be reduced to cadre form, with its regulars being posted elsewhere within the Light Infantry Group; and just as Blair's men had to conspire among themselves to preserve their identity, so too did the Somersets in order to have sufficient men on parade for the farewell ceremony in Bombay. Eventually the post-war reorganisation of the British Army decreed that the 1st Somerset Light Infantry should amalgamate with the regiment's 2nd battalion on their return to Britain in 1948. After Taunton the regiment went into a training role at Bordon in Hampshire: it was to be a sea-change after life in India.

> I don't think you knew you were saying goodbye to that kind of life. Civilians probably felt it more than the army but we did notice changes notwithstanding – instead of one servant per man we went back to one servant for four officers.

Michael Ryall admits today that the return to England turned out to be 'a bit of a shock' but feels, too, that the changes were cushioned by the fact that he was a young man with all the resilience of youth. In any case, his regiment was very much a self-contained unit; it took all its possessions with it wherever it went and insulated itself against the influences of the outside world. As there was little petrol to be obtained for travel or many consumer goods on which to spend one's pay, the regiment concentrated on peacetime soldiering. 'You go out of one room in which you have been living, you go into the next,' he explains. 'You haven't shed anything or had any traumatic experience until you get to the next one.'

One change which Ryall and other regular officers could not avoid noticing was the introduction of peacetime conscription. National Service had become a feature of life in Britain and over two million young school-leavers were destined to spend up to two years of their lives in the country's armed forces. Because the army needed an increased manpower to fulfil its global strategic obligations it benefited most from the scheme, and the Somersets were no exception to that rule. When it went to Malaya in the

1950s some 70 per cent of the regular battalion's strength came
from National Servicemen and they contributed significantly to
the army's success in winning that difficult counter-insurgency
war. Conscription also meant that the Somersets, like other
regiments, could not always fulfil Ryall's hopes that the army
would return to the comparative isolation of 'real soldiering' in
peacetime as it had done in 1919 after the First World War. In
turn, National Servicemen wondered at many of the regiment's
Indian customs and were mystified by the 'Hobson-Jobson' words
and phrases which peppered the vocabulary of their immediate
superiors.

There were several other equally far-reaching social changes in
the country, and, as Ryall suggests, these made the greatest
impact on the returning British civilians. A programme of
innovations in the social services had been instituted by 1947;
there was a 'free' health service, a policy of publicly assisted
house-building had been introduced, the school-leaving age had
been raised to fifteen and there had been widespread nationalisation of Britain's major industries.

> There was still an amount of rationing which was a little bit
> depressing. I can remember the first glimpse I had of national-
> isation was suddenly seeing a railway engine with British Railways
> written on it. What was British Railways? I had never heard of it.
> It had always been the LNER, LMS and so on. So I was coming
> back to a place which had changed in many ways. One of these was
> arriving by air and looking down on the south of England and
> seeing tarmac everywhere. When I left there were still quite a few
> country roads which had not been tarred at all. Looking down on
> England from the air there was this pattern of tarred roads
> everywhere – even tiny farm roads had been tarred. I supposed
> that this was a legacy of the war, moving troops hither and thither,
> but that was my first impression.

It was not just from the air that Alastair MacKeith noticed
changes; on the ground, too, he had come to terms with a Britain
that seemed to have altered out of all recognition. Everywhere
there were long queues – for shops, to buy railway tickets, to see
the doctor – and people waited patiently, or resignedly, in them.
To MacKeith it seemed that here was a country exhausted after a
long war: 'There was a lack of spirit about the place, perhaps the
spirit had been expended in the war.' For a while he turned his

hand to schoolmastering but it was not a success and the recollection of a fuller life in India and Pakistan drove him abroad again in the colonial service.

Given the changes that had been wrought by the war it is hardly surprising that many older families returning from India tried to insulate themselves from the reality of everyday life. Large parts of Britain – London, Merseyside, the Midlands, Clydeside, Tyneside – had been devastated by war damage and continued to bear the scars; in other areas new industries were changing the face of the landscape; even the countryside appeared different, with new forms of farming being introduced. It became common, then, for older imperial servants to choose areas which had experienced the least change, and towns as different in character and climate as Budleigh Salterton, Cheltenham and St Andrews became havens for retired ICS and army officers. Very often, they did not always like what they found. In stark contrast to the relative luxury of life in India almost everything in Britain was rationed. In 1948 the basic weekly allowance per person was 13 ounces of meat, 1½ ounces of cheese, 6 ounces of butter and margarine, 1 ounce of cooking fat, 8 ounces of sugar, 2 pints of milk and 1 egg. More exotic items such as alcoholic drinks, chocolate or tinned fruit were even harder to come by and depended on a points system. Clothing, too, was rationed, with the result that people tended to look drab, and currency restrictions meant that holidays abroad were well-nigh impossible. The nation might have been healthier and fitter as a consequence, but the absence of items that people had taken for granted in India was often a hard cross to bear.

For those who had left Britain in the 1920s or in the early 1930s there were other obvious changes, many of which were as disagreeable as rationing. While the war had not been the great arbiter of social revolution that many Labour supporters hoped it would be, a wind of change had been felt in some corners of British society. The trades unions enjoyed a greater bargaining power and workers' earnings were higher than ever before; and if a man disliked a job he could change it without fear of losing his livelihood. Leisure activities had become more easily available once more, football and the cinema being especially popular, and young people had begun to express their individuality. Teddy Boys, wearing pale imitations of Edwardian dress, began to

appear in the streets and popular music of the kind introduced by
the Americans during the war years was rapidly making inroads
into British youth culture. True, National Service forced thousands of young men into the armed forces but this polarisation of
the nation's youth only served to break down barriers, albeit
temporarily, between teenagers from different social backgrounds.

Not everyone, though, was affected in the same way or to the
same degree. Whereas the younger returning India hands were
hardly dismayed by the sudden change in their lifestyles, those in
middle age frequently found difficulty in adjusting to a world
without servants or the other familiar trappings of the good life.
This was especially true of the burra memsahibs, the women who
had obeyed to the last letter the social conventions and petty rules
which had dominated life in British India. During the years of
their pre-eminence, and depending on their positions, they had
ruled over a household of servants, lived in large roomy houses
and had reflected their husbands' importance by taking precedence at countless balls, receptions and levees. Even the most
junior wife had others over whom she could rule the roost. The
colonel's wife was a *grande dame* in any society, but below her the
senior majors' wives took precedence over the captains' wives
and they all looked down on the box-wallahs' wives who, in turn,
felt themselves to be a cut above the wives of the jute-wallahs.

Not every English middle-class woman stuck so rigidly to that
social pattern but there was no denying that the memsahibs, often
deprived of the company of their children, frequently lonely and
homesick, did pay close attention to the rules of precedence and
used their husbands' position to establish their own. During the
war, many of their beloved conventions had been put to one side
but in the more rarefied atmosphere of the government and the
administration the Mrs Hauksbees and those of her ilk held out to
the very end.

To come back to what were in effect reduced circumstances
was a shock for the older woman. Domestic help, in the shape of
a maid or a daily help or both, was still possible but there were
bound to be moments when ordinary household tasks had to be
done unaided. (My mother, for example, had never cooked for
herself before she came back home to live in Britain.) To be fair,
most adapted quickly and for some, like Sheila Coldwell who had

gone out to India as a young woman, the transition from burra memsahib to Scottish housewife was simply a matter of picking up the threads of a past life.

> I'd been brought up in a frugal but comfortable house with good Scots servants and had been brought up by my mother to know what was what. She had a great saying: even if you don't have to do it, you must know how to do it. So, really, to come back to this country I was able to do most of the household things that were necessary. In Scotland I think we'd been brought up to know how to do these things. I was never one of those people who had never boiled an egg – which was the boast of many memsahibs. Some women had been out for so long, or their families had also been brought up in India, and they had never known what it was to do anything for themselves.

Sheila Coldwell also relished returning to the 'grey skies' of her native Scotland; although she had loved India and her time there she had never really regarded the country as home. And therein lay one great comfort for those who were returning from British India: at the back of their minds was the clear realisation that they would not stay on and end their days there. Home for them was Britain. One went home on leave every five years or so, one's children went home to school, one's people lived at home and it was one's intention to go home to retire in the shires, the West Country, Wales, Scotland or wherever. Home stood for everything that was good – and British. 'Life in India is horribly artificial and meaningless,' wrote Alan Flack to his wife after she had gone home in 1946. 'It's just sozzling in the club and general scandal mongering or petty romance. There's nothing real about it at all.' The shock of leaving India was cushioned, therefore, by the knowledge that at one stage or another the British simply had to come home. And, it has to be admitted, there can have been very few British residents who did not understand that the end of the raj was in sight after the Second World War.

Curiously, it did not take long for the people of Britain to shed the connection with India. The memories lived on in those who had lived there, and became rosier as the years passed by, but to many people a chapter had been closed. Far better, they reasoned, to concentrate on matters at home; in the brave new world of the welfare state it seemed rather presumptuous or quaint to think in terms of the kind of imperial grandeur represented by the British Raj. The dilemma seemed to be, what then to do with the rest of the empire, for although Britain had surrendered her power in India and Pakistan she still ruled over, or had suzerainty over, large areas of the globe. Eighty-five countries made up the British Commonwealth, an amalgam of older developed countries, mandated territories and colonies held together by some of the trappings of the old imperial system. To this shaky edifice Attlee's government tried to bring a semblance of order with the introduction of a number of schemes aimed at bringing economic, social and political progress; but it was all too late.

A Colonial Development Corporation was established, for example. It had money to spend and earnest young men were dispatched to Africa charged with bringing the British colonies into the twentieth century, working as technocrats in places where their fathers had served as administrators. In a world in which the imperial ethos was being attacked by the emergent countries and discouraged elsewhere, it was one of the final throws aimed at preserving British influence. The ideals were bound to remain unachieved, of course. Just as Curzon and Gandhi had forecast all those years ago, the end of British rule in India was the true harbinger of the end of empire. In the wake of the transfer of power Ceylon became a dominion and Burma an independent country and, further east, both Malaya and Borneo were earmarked for early independence.

India, though, had lain at the heart of the British imperial system – not only was it the largest overseas possession, but it provided a cornerstone for Britain's power and authority in both the Middle and the Far East. Once India had been granted independence the very foundations of the empire were shaken beyond repair. There was no longer any military need to guard the old lines of communication yet Britain refused to surrender her expensively maintained bases in Egypt, Palestine, Aden, Cyprus and Malta. In the changed circumstances of the 1950s and 1960s those bases became increasingly wasteful anachronisms. They also caused considerable problems to Britain's armed forces whose men found that their presence was only a goad to the people whom they were supposed to be protecting. During the retreat from empire, as had happened during its expansion, it was the army that had to bear the brunt of the decisions taken by the politicians.

Palestine was the first to go in 1948, after a short and bloody campaign waged by the Arabs and the Zionists: by leaving them to fight it out Britain gave further notice that she was not prepared to copy the French and fight to keep control over her colonies. Kenya, Egypt and Cyprus followed a similar and equally dreary pattern as Britain struggled to maintain her old influence over the lifeline to the eastern empire. The end was not long in coming. In the face of fierce local opposition the army held a tenuous peace while the politicians argued until it was time to go. The bands played, the Union Jack was lowered and speeches of friendship were read to the cheering crowds – just as had happened on that August night in 1947. That same year, 1947, the British forces in Egypt moved into the Suez Canal Zone, only to withdraw finally in 1954; Cyprus was abandoned in 1959, Kenya in 1963 and Malta became independent under the British Crown in 1964. Sometimes the British left hurriedly, as happened in Aden, while the marines, with cocked guns, covered the last retreat from the familiar contours of Steamer Point.

The withdrawal continued throughout the 1950s and into the 1960s. Nigeria, Ghana, Sudan, Uganda, Tanganyika, all won their independence, but all too often that freedom was lost again in civil wars as the peoples fought over previously imposed boundaries to protect familiar group identities. The older imperial servants at home in their retirement might have shaken their heads at such goings-on, which would have been unthinkable in their day, but by then there was a new mood in Britain as far as imperialism was concerned. Whereas it had once been the done thing to nod approvingly at Curzon's confident statement that 'after Providence, the greatest instrument for good the world has ever seen' had been the British Empire, it became fashionable to mock that agent of power and authority. By the 1960s students of politics or history would hoot with laughter at the notion of a small handful of British administrators ruling large tracts of the world and issuing orders to the people who lived in them. Gradually, imperialism became a dirty word and it was trendy to sneer at the economic exploitation of Africa and Asia, to excoriate those who had administered the system of colonialism and to attack Britain's reluctance to give independence to black states long after she had given it to white ones. In short, public opinion – as represented and formed by teachers, politicians and modish writers – turned its back on the idea of empire and chose, instead, to view it in the monochromatic simplicity of black and white. The Poona colonel became a stock figure of fun, a butt for facetious writers for whom it was easier to create a caricature than a genuinely rounded character with all the virtues and the failings of common humanity. Similar fates befell the memsahibs and the planters, and the box-wallahs came to represent all that was wrong with the raj, supposedly exploiting the country and robbing the people of their wealth.

The old empire was becoming increasingly troublesome, too. There was a time when imperial skirmishing had been a matter of pride and readers had thrilled to tales of derring-do in barbarous corners of the distant globe, victories against feeble native opposition had been proof of the nation's greatness and the notion of Britain acting as an international policeman was considered to be neither irrelevant nor absurd. The transfer of power in India had been achieved without using military force to cover the withdrawal but elsewhere the keeping of the peace was fast becoming an irksome responsibility. There was little glory to be gained in fighting colonial actions against committed terrorists; instead, the British Army became skilled in low-intensity operations, fighting counter-insurgency wars against ruthless opposition. Between 1947 and 1967 the army was involved in maintaining law and order in major hot-spots like Palestine, Malaya, Kenya and Aden, as well as in less publicised areas such as the Gold Coast, British Honduras, Singapore, British Guiana, Hong Kong, Nassau, the Cameroons, Jamaica, Kuwait, Zanzibar, Borneo, Uganda and Mauritius.

It was into that world that the last trickle of British residents in India made their way back home in the 1960s. George Robertson had stayed on until 1966 and returned to Scotland to live in St Andrews where, to his surprise, he found that, apart from the climate and the absence of servants, little had changed: the social round of golf and bridge was very similar to the one he had enjoyed in India. Ron Fraser, another jute manager who had stayed on, also found little difficulty in making the last journey home. When he had first gone out to India the journey had been long and expensive and young men were expected to commit themselves to their work. In a very real sense a young man could go out to India a boy and return on his first home leave a grown man, for when he said goodbye to his family it was a separation which could last several years.

In the post-war world all that changed with the advent of modern air transport. The pioneer wartime routes flown by the Royal Air Force had expanded into regular civilian services and as airliners became more powerful and more sophisticated so too did the journey times shrink. No longer was it necessary for families to be separated for years at a time. Once upon a time wives had to choose between their husbands and their families; now the children could be sent home to school but, thanks to air travel, they could go out to India for their holidays.

For those who stayed on in the aftermath of the transfer of power in India and Pakistan and who did not come home until later, the sense of dislocation was less pronounced, if it was noticed at all. They had been able to keep abreast of the developments which had taken place in British society and home was a well-trodden and familiar place in a way that India or Pakistan could never be. Besides, their children were growing up in a new kind of Britain in which there was a renewed spirit of innovation and an openness to invigorating ideas. The 1959 general election had ushered in the age of 'You've never had it so good', with the Conservatives being returned to power under Harold Macmillan. New appliances in the home and factory provided easier working conditions and increased leisure time, and rising incomes meant that people had more money to spend. By 1961 the average weekly wage for men over twenty-one was £15 7s 0d (£15.35) and although retail prices had risen by 15 per cent between 1955 and 1960, the products of the new technology – radios, record players, television sets, washing machines – were still relatively cheap in relation to the nation's spending power. The introduction of hire-purchase had also made those products more generally available to those who lacked the inclination to save for them, as their fathers' generation had done for their own comforts.

With the easing of financial restrictions and the arrival of a shorter working week – half-day working on Saturdays, for example, had begun to be phased out – British society began to throw off many of the restrictions which had been imposed during the Victorian period. The wider availability of cheaper wirelesses and gramophones aided the pop music revolution, clothes for young people became more colourful and less formal, student grants helped more young school-leavers to go to college or university, holidays abroad became possible with cheaper travel and the relaxation of currency controls: all these changes encouraged young people to believe that a new period of high living was there for the taking.

Hardly surprisingly, the new affluence in Britain was most noticeable to the people who lived closest to the poor of India and Pakistan – the missionaries. Both new dominions had welcomed their presence and even in Pakistan, which was essentially an Islamic state, the Christian Church was allowed to pursue its activities in comparative freedom. As they were often at the sharp end of many social and medical problems facing the people they served, the new hedonism in Britain frequently struck a sour note. Whenever Dr Winifred Bailey came home on leave she often felt that she was visiting a foreign country.

> For one thing, to us, there were exaggerated standards of living. One felt that people had far more than they needed. Increasingly, over the years, the thing that disturbed me most I think was that violence seemed to be increasing so much and, unfortunately, that was what you noticed when you came home. I remember one time when the Mods and Rockers were battling on the Brighton beaches, and just arriving you felt, 'Help, if this is what the country has come to, it's pretty awful.'

Moving around the country visiting friends Dr Bailey was relieved to find that, in other respects, little had changed amongst young people, that what hit the headlines was not the norm. Nevertheless, the conspicuous consumption was difficult to accept, the fully stocked supermarkets and 'the amount of money being spent only for people's own comfort and way of life'.

Dr H. John Taylor experienced similar feelings when he finally retired in the mid-1960s. 'Coming back to this country after forty years, one noticed very great differences. The wealth and the affluence struck me very much after the poverty I had experienced in India.' He had been due to come back home on leave in 1939 but the deteriorating situation in Europe had dissuaded him from making a move and it was not until 1948 that he enjoyed his first furlough. Even at that early stage some of the changes in British society disconcerted him. People seemed to be less interested in what happened in the outside world and more concerned with events in their own backyards. Once the mention of India had been enough to spark off a lively conversation; now friends and acquaintances paid scant attention to an imperial relationship that was rapidly fading into the past. Quite simply, he and others found that people in Britain were so wrapped up in their own lives that they had little interest to spare for what was happening elsewhere.

Another person who was to leave India in the wake of independence was the illustrious figure of the Governor-General. Originally, Mountbatten had agreed to stay on only until April 1948 but he came under pressure, from both Indian and British government leaders, to extend his period of office. It was a great temptation, for Mountbatten clearly relished his gubernatorial role and warmed to the excitement and colour that surrounded his position. He also felt that he was performing a task of the first importance, but against that he was aware of the dangers in any course of action which would tie him to India. Given his close friendship with Nehru and his own autocratic way of doing things, the charge of paternalism would never be far away. He had also managed to lose the confidence of Pakistan and in both domin- ions there was a growing belief that he had been partly respon- sible for the state of anarchy that had existed in the Punjab. Inder Malhotra, for example, felt that Mountbatten was guilty of writing history as he went along and that, had he decided to stay on in a position of authority, he would have found it impossible not to bring his influence to bear on Nehru's government – to its disadvantage. There was growing enmity between Nehru and Patel and Malhotra felt that Mountbatten's friendship with the Indian leader would do Nehru great harm in the long term.

From his own letters it is clear that Mountbatten did regard himself as a history-maker but he was too shrewd and ambitious a man to want to gild his lily by committing himself to India. He had promised his mother, on being appointed Viceroy, that he would be home by June 1948 and he was determined to keep his word. By then he had performed a final service to India by helping to keep the country calm in the aftermath of Gandhi's assassination on 30 January 1948. Arriving at the scene of the murder, Birla House in New Delhi, he had stilled angry claims that it was a Muslim act of treachery with the retort, 'You fool, don't you know it was a Hindu?' Only later did he admit to his press secretary, Alan Campbell-Johnson, that he had been unaware of the religion of the assassin, a Hindu fanatic called Nathruam Godse. Nevertheless, it was an inspired moment, one that belonged to the great tradition of British phlegm in the face of impending disaster. The Indians loved him for it and were sorry to see him go. Certainly no other British imperial servant can have witnessed such heartfelt regret as he did when he surrendered his office on 21 June 1948.

It turned out to be one of the last great imperial occasions in India, equalling the Independence Day celebrations in the mass of Indians who swarmed into the streets to say farewell to the man who had steered their country towards independence. For the final time a representative of the British people paraded along the historic highway of Chandni Chowk with the crowds cheering him for all they were worth. Kenneth Ryden, a former officer in the Royal Bombay Sappers and Miners, was in the capital at the time, working in a civilian capacity, and he found himself invited to Mountbatten's farewell party in the guise of a press correspondent. It was a glittering occasion, one which appeared to match the mood of the moment, for with Mountbatten's departure, Britain was taking her final leave of the old British Raj. Ryden had left India at the end of the war and although he had been saddened by the carnage which had disfigured the Punjab and Calcutta, he sensed, too, a new feeling of optimism. Carried along, perhaps, in the Mountbattens' tide of popularity, British people were still greatly respected, especially those who had served previously in India, and Ryden could not help noticing that even in the Delhi Gymkhana Club where he was staying, 'we were still well regarded. It was still essentially a British club with very few Indian members – although that was changing and they were being admitted in droves.'

Christie, too, was glad to note that the British who had cast in their lot with the new India were still held in some esteem. Although he had entertained doubts about his decision to stay on, the atmosphere in post-independence New Delhi convinced him that he had made the right decision.

Great friendliness from Indians immediately surrounded us. I believe that the appalling aftermath of partition had shaken their confidence and the realisation that some British people had enough faith in India's future to elect to stay in the country had helped to restore it. In fact there were many who shared our faith, and the number of British in India, so far from diminishing, was to increase over the next few years.

Because he had been required to resign his high office on the day before independence the celebrations had been something of an anti-climax for Christie. 'A dividend on our work had been declared,' he remembered. 'Nevertheless, the stock of some of us, though far from deflated, was feeling just a trifle "ex-div".' True to form, Mountbatten had jollied along Christie and other staff members to return to their posts, unpaid and unhonoured for a few weeks more; and just as typically, one of his last acts had been to visit Christie to present him with a specially inscribed silver cigarette case.

With Mountbatten's departure India became less of an issue in the British press. At the height of the period surrounding the transfer of power *The Times* had published 1,479 stories on India in 1947. By 1950 these had dropped to 680 and five years later, in 1955, there were only 406. It was not as if India had not provided newsworthy stories in that period; on the contrary, there were continuing problems over the princely states and border clashes with Pakistan over the question of Kashmir, but as a subject in its own right India had lost much of its glamour and its mystique. As an independent country it would no longer capture the eye of news editors as it had once done in the heyday of British rule.

Yet for all that the old days of the raj were rapidly passing into history, the memory of that time could never be entirely forgotten by those who had once lived in India. John Rowntree had left the Forestry Service in 1947 and had come home to a Britain which he felt to be 'too confining, too full and altogether too insular. It was, perhaps understandably, preoccupied with its own recent past and present troubles which we ourselves had not shared.' To him, England might have been a green and pleasant place, but it still took time to accept that after having held down a responsible and well-paid position in Assam, he had become a mere number on the National Insurance Register. 'I was, in some ways, more homesick for India than I had ever been for my own country and the homesickness was to stay with me for a long time.'

For him, it was like living in a vacuum and as was the case with many others like him, the remembrance of India was to cast a long shadow over the years of his retirement. 'You can take a man out of the forest,' ran the motto which had been engraved in his office in Shillong, 'but you cannot take the forest out of the man.' Even amongst those who had been too young or too busy to think about the recent past when they first returned home, the years to come would bring the realisation that India was never to be far from their minds.

Chapter Nine

Staying On

Of course, not everyone was going back home to Britain. Those who had jobs in India or Pakistan would stay on to help the businesses and industries of the new dominions, and the missionaries saw no reason to abandon their charges just because two new regimes had come into existence. For them life would continue in much the same tenor as it had done before. There were bound to be changes, some to be regretted, others to be accepted as part of the developing scene. Everything remained 'much the same as before' for George Robertson, who had decided to stay on in Bengal. 'I had been with the job for some considerable time and I had no desire to go anywhere else. Also I had been promoted and didn't see any reason to leave.' In his social life he noticed a greater participation by his Indian colleagues but that, too, was something he welcomed as a good thing.

His fellow Dundonian, Ron Fraser, had also decided to stay on in Bengal. In his eyes the changes were gradual and more concerned with material things. Conditions in Calcutta began to deteriorate, the traffic became more chaotic, Firpo's, the famous restaurant with its P & O decor, closed down but this was, after all, a city which even an admirer like Geoffrey Moorhouse had described in exasperation: 'The poverty of Calcutta is an affront to the dignity of mankind and a mocking tell-tale against the achievement of nations.' But Fraser liked India and the Indians too much to want to leave just yet. Like Robertson he found that most of his friends had decided to stay on too, thus providing him with a congenial society that had been greatly augmented by the inclusion of Indian friends, old and new. 'I liked India and the

Indians very much. In fact I felt just as much at home in India as I did in Britain.'

Another reason why the jute-wallahs wanted to stay on was that life was undeniably good in India. There they could enjoy a style of living which would not have been possible in post-war Britain with its food shortages, lack of housing and absence of servants. All these benefits were available in India and Pakistan and as the new governments were not anxious to kick the British out of their countries, many families were made welcome when they decided to stay on. This was quite remarkable considering the strength of feeling that had been laid bare during the independence struggle, but the truth of the matter was that the transfer of power had been accomplished with such goodwill on both sides that no one who cast in their lot with either India or Pakistan entertained many fears for the future.

The most difficult lesson to learn, perhaps, was that they were no longer living in a British enclave. The agency for which Sheila Coldwell's husband worked still had substantial interests in India: there might have been a larger number of Indians in middle management but the top brass were still British. The Coldwells' family life had gone on much as before – 'our servants were wonderful and we had a lot of very good Indian friends' – but she did notice a subtle change which made people think before they uttered an opinion.

> I think we had to be more tactful. My husband had various government connections and when he made a speech he had to be very careful because the Indians are sensitive people. If he felt that they were in the wrong – as they often probably were – he had to choose his words carefully. Before partition we were the government and then it was much easier to say what you thought.

There was a natural tendency for Indians to turn immediately to the British managers when there was a crisis and as Sheila Coldwell's husband discovered there was nothing to be gained by apportioning blame or criticising unduly harshly. For him – as for most box-wallahs – and their Indian colleagues, it was very much a relearning process as they turned their energies to the development of India's economy.

One of the criticisms made against the raj is that when the British pulled out they left India without the resources needed to control a modern country. There is some truth in the claim, for the agricultural methods of feeding the nation were primitive and underdeveloped. Most of the people were poor, too, a survey in 1949 revealing the unpalatable truth that the average annual income was Rupees 260, or some £25. Behind that statistic lay a story of people living well below the basic subsistence level, eating a bad diet and living in dreadful conditions without hope of state assistance. In many rural areas of India and Pakistan poverty and despair were endemic – just as they had been for centuries. Before there could be any significant change new methods of farming had to be introduced – new technology and equipment, redistribution of land and better access to water supplies – but the problem of agrarian development was not to be tackled until the early 1950s. In that respect, India was indeed a backward country, one in which hardship and poverty were part of the daily grind.

However, unlike many of the African colonies which received their independence two decades later, India did have a reasonably solid industrial base, one which had blossomed during the war, and it was there that the experience of the box-wallahs was felt. Indian industry had experienced a period of rapid expansion between 1942 and 1946 – steel, chemicals, textiles and cement had all benefited from the wartime boom and Nehru hoped to build upon that foundation of success. The shift towards industrialisation also meant that 17 per cent of the population now lived in cities and although they only produced a meagre 6 per cent of the national income they did provide hope for the future: according to Nehru's economic theory India could not be truly free until she had gained her own means of industrial production. This had been largely encouraged by the British, who continued to have a substantial financial stake in the country after independence. Tea-planting was largely a British concern, as was jute, and a large number of manufacturing businesses remained in British financial control until well into the 1960s. Ever since the outbreak of the Second World War Britain had encouraged Indian industrialists to build up a strong local economy which was essential if India were to compete with the rest of the world.

The point is taken up by Dr Bharat Ram, who remains convinced that 'in a developing country, unless there is a very strong public sector, growth will just not take place'. His own concern, the Delhi Linen Mills, had branched out into sugar production in 1934 with the help of government subsidies but the war had been the real boom time. In 1942 they started manufacturing fertilisers and chemicals for the war effort.

> It was perhaps the only time when every businessman said, 'Business is good.' Because of the war the demand for various things was tremendous and people were making money. I used to find that we were making garments and tents for the government and the prices were high. Really, people were minting money during the whole of the world war period.

Naturally enough, Ram and his colleagues wanted to see the good times continuing. For that reason they supported Nehru's policy of insisting on a heavy investment in steel, coal, engineering and chemicals, all of which required a lengthy period to develop to their full potential. That strategy also meant that Ram's own textile industry would not be developed to the same extent – Nehru did not want to take work away from the handloom weavers – but it did mean that India would be provided with the broad industrial base which he felt was necessary for her survival. Ram was also enthusiastic about the reforms because he remembered the recent past when it seemed that Britain was actually working against the best interests of Indian industry.

> The colonial need was to sell, not to buy, and they would only buy those raw materials which they didn't have. And even then, I am sure, every step was taken to buy cheaper from colonial areas instead of from competitive areas. There is no doubt that they did not encourage the growth of industry in India but during the war the need was such that industry grew . . . By and large our relationship with the British businessmen was that we bought machinery from them. That was the main contact.

The other reason why Ram welcomed Nehru's economic strategy was that it had been evolved by an Indian government for the people of India. 'People now felt that they had the opportunity to do what they wanted to do. The government was helpful in assisting you to develop industry and there was a feeling that it would have to grow.'

Although Dr Ram is careful to point out that there was no immediate change, within a few years of independence he did notice one striking difference in the conduct of business matters. Whereas it had once been the done thing to cultivate the senior officers of the ICS, in the new India the businessman would bypass the official and go straight to the minister. 'In the old days, to meet a Deputy Secretary was something of an achievement, but now everyone thinks in terms of meeting the Minister because nothing will happen unless he says so.'

Nevertheless, India had been left with a strong administration and many Indians will claim that the tradition of service embodied in the ICS was Britain's greatest legacy to the new dominion. By 1947 Indians outnumbered the British in the service and they were ready and trained to take over senior administrative responsibility. Govind Narain had already stamped his authority in Aligarh where, as District Magistrate, he coped successfully with a potentially explosive refugee problem. That he was able to do so efficiently and calmly, he claims, had everything to do with his initial training.

> I learned most during the British administration: the rules of the game, the discipline, orderliness, punctuality and precision in one's thinking and in one's orders. I used to tour with British officers and I used to go with them to the villages. There were many good things I learned which I remember to this day and I think they were good lessons for me.

The big difference for Narain lay in the heady feeling that he was working for his own people in an independent India. Although he had always been loyal to the British he felt much happier that his political masters were now Indian politicians who were responsible for their country's destiny. It was a feeling that was common throughout the service and in the army, too, where the officers – many of them Sandhurst-trained – kept up the old traditions while working towards the creation of a new Indian identity. In messes and on parade grounds throughout the country the customs and the vocabulary were still English enough, but the pride and the spirit had to be Indian. One tradition that did remain was the long-standing convention that the armed forces kept themselves aloof from politics.

> Politics was a banned subject and we never discussed it in the army and we never talked about it in the mess. I think it was the best legacy, along with the discipline and the training.

General Das became the Indian Army's first Director of Military Intelligence and he speaks only for his own country. In Pakistan the army did involve itself in politics, bringing to power General Ayub Khan in 1958. Quite apart from the desire to retain the British tradition, another reason for the continuing political neutrality of the Indian Army was Nehru's institutionalisation of the Indian system of government in which each element was given an identifiable role. For General Candeth, at the time a senior army officer, this was the basis of all the pride he took in the new India – working hard in the early days of a better country.

> There was a tremendous sense of pride and we felt that it was now up to us to make the army as good, if not better than it was previously . . . there was tremendous enthusiasm that India had at last got its freedom and so it was the aim of everyone to see that we made a success of our jobs. We had all been promoted rather rapidly and we felt that we had to live up to the new responsibilities and not let the country down. So there was a feeling of joy and a resurgence of patriotism that we must make a success of it, whatever the hardships or trials we had to face.

In such an ambience the British official would always run the danger of feeling out of place. Alastair MacKeith had decided, for personal reasons, to stay on in Pakistan after the transfer of power but he knew that he would never be able to see out his career there. As a public servant he had promised to serve faithfully the government of the new dominion but he soon began to feel that his presence was not entirely welcome. 'Just possibly, as Indian officers may not always have been trusted by us when we were ruling, I had the feeling that we were not wholly trusted now.' MacKeith concedes that in neither case was the distrust justified but his colleagues' suspicions did influence his decision to leave Pakistan nine months later. Because he had been anxious to distance himself from Pakistani politics he had moved back to the paramilitary Frontier Constabulary and was District Officer in Bannu at the time of the Kashmir affair. With his own eyes he had seen the armed tribesmen from Waziristan passing his headquarters en route to invade Kashmir. Carrying unlicensed weapons was an offence, but when he consulted the local Political Officer he was told to do nothing. Being kept deliberately in the dark about Pakistan's move against India only reinforced his growing belief that, as a British officer, he was not completely trusted by his new colleagues.

John Christie also found that he had to keep his political

antennae tuned to the changing scene. After a lifetime serving as one of the heavenly ones of the ICS it was not always easy to adapt to his new role serving an independent India.

> This was a period when the non-official British in India were having to accustom themselves, not always easily, to the realities of a change of government; to understand that the British High Commissioner was in India to represent not their interests directly, but those of his Government; to recognise that the consular functions of the High Commissioner did not amount to a protective shield, and that it behove them to organise themselves to watch their own interests and to establish proper relations directly with the Government of India. Some adjustments along these lines were also having to take place among the officers of the High Commission.

It was also vital not to appear condescending in any way. This was the mistake made by the American Ambassador, Chester Bowles, who moved out of his palatial official residence into a humbler dwelling and exchanged his Cadillac for a bicycle. However well-intentioned his republican gesture might have appeared, it caused a good deal of offence amongst the Indian diplomats in New Delhi. By the same token, Christie was taken to task by Jagjivan Ram, the Labour Minister, when he removed his shoes and sat on the floor at a committee meeting to raise money for a memorial to Sardar Patel. 'You cannot do that,' remonstrated Ram. 'It is not your custom, though it is ours. Please sit in a chair.'

Fortunately, Christie's ICS training was equal to the moment. 'Look here, sir,' he protested. 'How would you like it if you went to London and they insisted that you should sit on the floor, while they sat in chairs, because it is your custom?' It seemed the British and the Indians still had to work hard to exorcise the ghosts of the recent imperial past: no easy matter, for Christie still felt that Britain's prestige in the world was as high as it had ever been.

Like many other observers of the Indian political scene after the transfer of power, John Christie was fascinated by the rivalry that existed between Nehru and Sardar Patel, both of whom he had come to know well during his ICS days. The difference between the two men could hardly have been more striking: Nehru, the Western-educated liberal, was the thinker and strategist; while Patel, a hard-boiled veteran nationalist, seemed to Christie to be 'a Congress Tory of the deepest blue'. Sardar Vallabhbai Patel was a Gujerati lawyer who had emerged as a major Congress leader after organising the *satyagraha* in the Bardoli district of Gujerat in 1928. Close to Gandhi, he was a hard-nosed political fighter who had built up a closely knit network of political support. By the 1940s he had emerged as the political boss of the Congress Party and a clear rival to Nehru. Patel was a Hindu traditionalist who regarded political power as a means to an end and could be quite unscrupulous in using it, whereas Nehru was a Brahmin intellectual who tended to view power as an abstract theory. There had been times in the past when their mutual antipathy was in danger of creating an open breach but, as Christie noted at the time, Gandhi was the guiding influence in keeping the two men together for India's sake.

Shortly before Patel's death in 1950 Christie attended the opening night of a visiting production of scenes from Shakespeare's plays. Nehru and Patel were also in the audience, whose members were 'thoroughly enjoying themselves, repeating aloud the familiar speeches in a continuous low murmur simultaneously with the actors, sometimes even ahead of them'. Their pleasurable anticipation was heightened when the programme included the quarrel scene between Brutus and Cassius from *Julius Caesar*. The audience could not fail to see the similarities or to hear in Shakespeare's words an echo of the rivalry between their two leaders. Anxiously, they craned their heads to see if the two protagonists had also noticed the analogy. 'Shakespeare would have been delighted by their intelligent appreciation of the political reference,' noted an equally delighted Christie.

Patel's death in 1950 allowed Nehru to proceed apace with his reforms for the creation of a new India, one whose government would be based on a solid democracy. By then Gandhi was dead, too, having been gunned down by a madman in an act that smacked more of ritual martyrdom than planned assassination. In his death he brought India to her senses, purging the country of much of the violence and communal hatred that had so disfigured it.

Christie was living in a street only a quarter of a mile away from the Birla House, in which Gandhi was murdered. He had had a premonition of disaster, 'like the rumble of an approaching earthquake', and had hurried home to be with his family. His wife and he heard the sound of shots from the garden of the Birla House.

For a few seconds after that there was dead silence, then a confused murmur of people and the noise of cars starting and moving away. It was difficult at first for those at the scene of the crime to believe what they had seen or heard, or to give a coherent account of it. For nearly an hour the truth was not generally known, and uneasy rumours were abroad. If the assassin had been a Muslim, as some were at first inclined to believe, the consequences in India, and between India and Pakistan, could have been appalling. The shock, however, had stunned the people. There was no violent reaction, and the outpouring of grief and devotion at the Mahatma's funeral next day was a sufficient purging of the emotions.

Gandhi's death also brought Nehru and Patel closer together – Mountbatten told each of them that it had been the Mahatma's fondest wish that the two men should be friends. It also allowed Patel to embark on the last act of creating a united and independent India – the necessary task of bringing all the princely states into the Indian body politic. Kashmir had fallen into India's lap by virtue of the Pathan invasion the previous year: the acquisition of Hyderabad also required the use of the mailed fist and Patel was the man to wield it.

The Nizam of Hyderabad was a Muslim who ruled over an independent state which was larger than many a European nation. He had survived the transfer of power intact and hoped to be able to continue that happy state of affairs for some time to come. Christie had witnessed the earlier negotiations with Mountbatten which had ended in stalemate and it was obvious to him that neither Patel nor his senior civil servant and right-hand man, V.P. Menon, would continue the discussions for much longer once they controlled political power in India. And so it proved. Following further fruitless negotiations the Indian Army moved into Hyderabad to annex the state in September 1948. Amongst their number was General Das who had also served in the Kashmiri campaign in the previous year.

We knew exactly what to do and also what the people in Hyderabad wanted us to do. It had to be a quick action to forestall any further interference from anyone else because there were people in India and Pakistan who would have been prepared to run guns or to go to Hyderabad to fight us.

Das and his fellow intelligence officers in the Indian Army had been taken by surprise when the tribesmen moved into Kashmir, and they had arrived in Srinagar without any clear idea of their enemy or his capabilities. Hyderabad was a different matter: the state had to be annexed quickly and cleanly to prevent casualties and, just as important for the Indian government, to forestall an international outcry. This time the problem had been simmering for several months, thus giving Das the opportunity to build up a clear intelligence picture from the Hindu citizens of Hyderabad who were clamouring for Indian intervention on their behalf. When the army did move, it acted quickly and efficiently, and Hyderabad, like Kashmir and Junagadh, the other princely states which had held out, became part of a united India. 'The best of the Princes and their states were preserved in the new territorial divisions,' noted Christie. 'The rest were compensated more or less, and merged with oblivion.'

For Christie and for the other members of the New Delhi community of British expatriates – as they had now become – life was good in 1948. Once the riots and communal problems of the previous year had been sorted out most people's lives settled down to a familiar and easy routine. Inevitably, there were some differences which could not be ignored. In the Gymkhana Club, long the bastion of Western manners, notices began to appear by the poolside asking gentlemen with long hair to wear bathing caps – in deference to the new Sikh members. Indian women began to appear at the club in greater numbers, 'contributing by their appearance, their wit and gaiety to the pleasure of life', and Christie also noted that the younger set were prepared to join in the dancing at the weekend. On the debit side, he found evidence that the club's committee, now predominantly Indian, exercised much stricter rules of admission than the British had ever done, and woe betide any parvenu counter-jumper who tried to become a member without first establishing his financial or social credentials!

As New Delhi was India's capital city a diplomatic community quickly came into being and to cater for its needs a modern enclave was constructed in the open country between the Delhi Ridge and Qutb Minar. This had been a favourite riding ground for the British and Christie regretted that the forgotten lanes and ruined tombs of a bygone age had to make way for the featureless face of modern architecture. The British had always prided themselves on maintaining a certain reserved sedateness in Delhi; it had, after all, been the centre of their imperial rule and even the official buildings seemed to reflect standards which would endure. The broad avenues spoke more of Rome than London and the government buildings were constructed from the same red sandstone that the Mogul emperors had used: most glorious of them was the Viceroy's House which had been designed by Lutyens and completed in 1931. These edifices still remained as symbols of an empire that would rule for ever – provided it had the support of the people it governed. Now they rang to more cosmopolitan sounds.

> A French military attaché, who used to wear a flower through a bullet hole in the lobe of his ear – acquired, he said, during the 'resistance' – carelessly backed his car into another standing in front of the Club. The owner of the injured car, an Indian lady, proceeded to give him a piece of her mind in English. He walked away remarking, rudely but distinctly, *'Va-t-en, vache!'* But the lady had lived in Paris, and could understand honest French; and although a Hindu, she was not mollified by the ingenious explanation that the Frenchman, believing Hindus held cows in reverence, was trying to pay her a compliment. The scandal caused the attaché's embassy hurriedly to discover that he was already under orders of transfer.

As the representative in Delhi of British industrial and trading links Christie had to keep closely in touch with government servants and ministers and was well placed, therefore, to observe the period of readjustment that took place after the transfer of power. Whether it was playing polo with the newly reconstituted Delhi Polo Club or parleying with committee members on All-India Councils, Christie eased himself, and helped to ease others, into the new daily round, reminding himself regularly that he was now a guest, so to speak, of an independent country. The task was made simpler for him by the spirit of the age, for Christie could not help noticing that independence had brought with it 'an exhilaration and a zest to all who breathed its air'.

Prem Bhatia was about to pick up again the traces of his career in journalism, transferring to work with *The Statesman* in 1946. For him, the first days of independence were like a dream from which he did not want to wake. Quite apart from the natural elation that came from the granting of independence, there was also a feeling that his country was now on its own and that its destiny lay in the capable hands of his fellow countrymen. There was the added bonus, too, that the break with Britain had been 'clean and nice'; had it been otherwise, he argues, then the euphoria would have evaporated very quickly.

> Also Nehru was a much loved man, so was Gandhi, and there was a whole galaxy of big people. We've never had the same group again – I don't think we ever will. It so happened unfortunately that most of them had grown up to that age fighting for independence and when it came they were very close to ending their lives . . . but Nehru was around and he had a very good team so we looked forward to their performance, to give us what they had promised. If this is the way we want to grow, let's do it.

Above all else, Bhatia prized the parliamentary form of democracy which had been bequeathed to India and which Nehru staunchly promoted. Although India opted for a strong central government to bind together its federal constitution, Nehru was adamant that there should be universal suffrage. This brought him into conflict with those who thought it a mistake to give the vote to the illiterate masses but Bhatia supported the view that democracy would be the 'most cohesive factor in the continuation of India as a free nation'. And so it proved. After a short phase as a dominion India became a republic in 1950, and as Bhatia pointed out, India's ability to sustain a democratic form of government in the forty years since independence is in direct contrast to the experience of Pakistan and most of the former British colonies in Africa.

The fact that it had all been accomplished without an armed struggle was also a plus mark. While he regretted the communal violence in the Punjab, which he had escaped in Kerala, A.K. Damodaran believed that the outrages were just a symptom of an age-old problem. He noticed that in the provinces in the south the transition was 'very smooth and almost dull': the feeling of elation was there but it was balanced by a certainty that India was going to take her place amongst the nations of the world and that there was now a job to be done.

> We're very proud of the fact that we didn't have to pay the price the Russians had to pay and which we were slowly beginning to realise the Chinese were paying. Even now, in retrospect, the

British, too, should be proud that they didn't leave behind such a mess as the Dutch left behind in Indonesia, and the French in Indo-China or the Americans, the crypto-imperialists, in China.

It has been claimed by some Indians, though, that although colonial violence had been largely avoided, the British did leave behind a poor and backward country who would have to surmount many economic problems before she could make her way in the world. Rationing had been introduced, prices were rising and there were shortages of food in both India and Pakistan. It was to take many years before famine was entirely banished and the British inability to evolve a workable agrarian policy left a legacy of neglect which would take time and energy to overcome. Some 26 per cent of the population were landless labourers and the unequal distribution of land meant that some parts of the country were relatively prosperous – Punjab and Gujerat, for example – while others, like Bihar, languished in the doldrums. In most rural areas life went on as it had done for centuries; it was almost as if the Moguls and the British had never been there with their drainage schemes and plans for the rotation of crops. In the early years of independence much progress was immediately nullified by the sudden population explosion: this had increased from 318.7 million in 1941 to 439.2 million in 1961.

With the benefit of hindsight, and after the inspection of economic statistics for the period, it is possible to argue that India was in dire financial straits when Britain pulled out in 1947, but that was not the way it was seen at the time. Corruption, poverty and violence had existed for many centuries and, as Inder Malhotra reminds us, in order to stamp them out Britain would have had to be far more draconian in her imperial policing than she had been. Yes, there was a grotesquely uneven balance of wealth, he argues, but the British could hardly be blamed entirely for its presence. More to the point, India had been left with a political structure which worked and in which Indians could take a great deal of pride. 'The fact that we were serving the government of an independent India: that created a very good impression.' Malhotra still believes that the hundred-odd years of British rule were cast off in as many minutes. Very soon, he says, the memory of the raj with its burra sahibs, memsahibs and orders of precedence became a thing of the past and Indians felt able to speak to Europeans on equal terms. Of course, that had been possible before but now it could be done unselfconsciously. It was not a sudden or blinding revelation, a throwing away of crutches, but a feeling which grew with each succeeding year.

In 1954, for *The Times of India*, Malhotra covered the courtesy visit to Malaya of a squadron of ships of the Indian Navy. The country was still in the grips of the 'Emergency' – the long-drawn-out fight against the Chinese Communist guerrillas – and it was still very much an imperial enclave. Nevertheless, the officers and men of the Indian Navy received the traditional courtesies wherever they went. At Port Swettenham there was an official reception and in Kuala Lumpur, the capital, the government threw a dinner party and dance for their guests. Malhotra was amongst the number and he was impressed not so much by the lavishness of the British hospitality as by the effect it was having on the other non-European guests.

> I noticed that there were some local Kuala Lumpur Indians and Chinese standing alongside the wall [of the reception room] while the Indian naval officers – and I – were dancing with the wives of the British rulers of Malaya. It was a shock to them: here were brown fellows with no kind of complex about slapping the High Commissioner on the back and asking him about what was going on in Malaya. It caused consternation.

Being free and independent, Malhotra noted drily, brought benefits at which others not in that happy position could only marvel.

Perhaps because it was small and relatively self-contained the Indian Navy had fared slightly better than the other services in settling down to life in post-independence India. The naval chief, Geoffrey Barnard, was British, but he quickly made it clear that his loyalties lay with the country which he now served. While on a cruise in the Indian Ocean which included an official visit to Dar es Salaam, A.K. Chatterjee and his colleagues had a somewhat different reception from the welcome accorded to Inder Malhotra in Malaya. At the time he commanded the cruiser *Delhi* and when the squadron arrived in the East African port an invitation arrived for Admiral Barnard requesting his presence at Government House in Nairobi. He accepted on condition that he could bring Chatterjee and two other Indian officers. As Chatterjee recalls, Barnard was not trying to be difficult – everyone knew that Kenya operated a colour bar at that time – but it was a matter of principle. When challenged by his hosts Barnard simply said that he was paid by the Government of India and would do whatever was in that country's best interest: if his fellow Indian Navy officers were not acceptable at Government House, then neither was he. 'He displayed a high sense of values. I learned an enormous amount from him and from the four other British admirals while I was captain of my ship. The relationship between us Indians and the British officers was absolutely perfect.'

Experiences like that helped to erase the memory of the Bombay naval mutiny which had threatened at one time to weaken the whole fabric of the Indian Navy. Chatterjee had always felt that it was a temporary aberration, but no service likes to have a stain on its record, especially when it impugns the men's loyalty. However, the Indian Navy, like the other armed forces, was now a new service, one based on old-established traditions perhaps, but nevertheless one which had to create its own *esprit de corps*. And as had happened in other sectors of public life independence had brought with it a sense of excitement and self-respect. Chatterjee remembers bursting with national pride when his squadron made the first official visits to other countries. Not only was he anxious to show the flag but he wanted desperately to underline India's importance as a new power in the world. While visiting Colombo he put down a local politician who was 'shooting a line' by reminding him that Ceylon was only the size of a district in the Punjab. 'It wasn't strictly true, of course, but the feeling stayed with me for a long time.'

This feeling was not just confined to the Indian and Pakistani communities. In Bombay Dr Taylor and his British colleagues had no thought of leaving India but were delighted to share with their students and Indian colleagues the new sense of freedom which independence had brought. That feeling of welcome made it easier for him to stay on in India; it was not as if he and his British colleagues were unpopular for they did make a substantial contribution to India's education system. 'I think our students would have been horrified if we had all packed up and trooped out.'

To begin with Taylor had noticed few changes at Wilson College, the daily round of lectures and tutorials went on as before and it was not until India became a republic in 1950 that he began to notice the first rapid acceleration in India's educational policies.

> The thing that has greatly interested me personally has been the development of science and education. When I came to India there were only sixteen universities and ten medical colleges and the rate of progress was very slow. Progress in a country like India has to be counted numerically in the first place. It has to grow quantitatively as well as qualitatively. When I left India there were about eighty universities and the number of medical colleges had grown too.

As a scientist Dr Taylor's first love had been the development of physics, and he played his part in the rapid growth of science and technology in the years following independence. He was on the staff of the Tata Institute of Fundamental Research and helped in its development under its brilliant director, Dr H.J. Bhabha. From this base Bhabha developed the prestigious Atomic Research Centre at Trombay and the rapid growth of nuclear technology in India was largely due to his vision and direction. India has extensive uranium deposits, chiefly in Bihar, and thorium resources in Kerala which are amongst the largest in the world, ensuring a supply of nuclear fuel for the foreseeable future. Bhabha and his colleagues, from the time of independence onwards, stressed the importance of nuclear power for India's future progress, and today many research and power reactors are in operation.

Taylor recalls the fact that many of his former students have played, and are still playing, a major role in these developments. Much of the credit, he claims, must go to Nehru's insistence on rapid technological development, but he adds the rejoinder that it took an independent India to make it all happen. 'It couldn't have occurred by itself because under British rule we wouldn't have had such rapid progress. The whole thing accelerated after independence.'

Dr Taylor is justly proud of the contribution which he and other like-minded colleagues made to push forward India's scientific frontiers. It is very much in keeping with the idea that an underdeveloped country will always remain in that condition unless it evolves its own scientific and technological know-how. The decision, therefore, to invest in applied science and technology did wonders for India's development. The country had produced many outstanding scientists before independence, some of whom, such as Meghnath Saha, Satyendra Bose and Sir C.V. Raman, won international recognition, but it was only afterwards that funds were made available to build up the necessary institutions and research centres on a large scale. This was to bring about a rapid expansion of the whole field of science and technology and a large increase in the number of highly trained and highly motivated young scientists and engineers.

There were critics, though, who felt that this kind of educational progress was taking India in the wrong direction. Nehru hoped that the development of technology would help abolish poverty, but it was not until scientific developments could be harnessed to meet the challenge of India's age-old farming problems that any appreciable changes were seen in the country's agriculture. It was not until the late 1950s that increases were noted in the production of foodstuffs through the use of fertilisers, the proper understanding of land usage and the introduction of co-operative farming. Another stumbling block in the forward progress was the decision whether or not to use English as a medium for teaching. The majority of scientific papers were written in English and for most people an education in English was a place on the conveyor belt to success. (In the face of pressure to introduce Hindi as the universal language Nehru had allowed each state to honour its own languages or dialects.) The need to maintain the traditional English-language schools was particularly acute for the Anglo-Indian community, most of whom would be throwing in their lot with the new India.

There had been a time in the past, well before the introduction of modern means of travel, when intermarriage with the Indian people had not been discouraged and the pages of India's history are thick with the names of empire-builders who had Indian blood. Lord Roberts, for example, the cynosure of the Indian Army and the symbol of British military pluck, was a descendant of a Rajput princess. The arrival of European wives and the strict rules of social conformity which they brought with them altered attitudes. British society in India first sedulously aped middle-class mores at home and then began to develop its own particular manners and social conventions. In such a world the Anglo-Indians became an embattled group, living largely in isolation in places like Calcutta, Madras and Bombay and working on the railways – almost entirely an Anglo-Indian preserve – and in the postal and customs and excise services. It was their lot to be shunned by Indians and British alike, and if people thought about them at all it was usually in condescending terms. During the war, however, there had been a general relaxation of these social taboos. Conscript servicemen who were in India for the duration of the war often paid no heed to the rules and preferred the congenial suroundings of the Anglo-Indian Railway Institutes to the staider clubs which did not always offer a warm welcome. It was also difficult to avoid Anglo-Indians in public life for they had taken the opportunity to prove their loyalty and had thrown themselves wholeheartedly into the British war effort. These changes of attitude, however rapid they might have appeared at the time, were slow to still the suspicions of the old India hands.

Wilfrid Russell had been undecided about his future once the war had come to an end. In 1945 he had thought of returning to Britain largely because the prospect of working in the 'emasculating and exasperating atmosphere of a Hindu republic' did not appeal to him. He also noticed that his Indian colleagues were not as friendly as they had been before but, after brushing his fears aside with the comforting thought that they were bound to regard the British in 1947 rather differently than they had in 1939, he decided to stay on. After a short spell of leave in Britain he returned to Bombay to become managing director of Killick Nixon's cement factories and buried himself in his work. '1948 was an odd sort of year for me, as it was for India. The keynote was nostalgia – homesickness for the England I had left so cheerfully only eighteen months before. The infernal pendulum that was forever swinging backwards and forwards inside had started off again.'

In that same year, 1948, he met the problem of the Anglo-Indians head-on when he was asked to become the chairman of the Bombay Education Society which ran two great Anglo-Indian schools – Barnes High School in Deolali and Christ Church in the downtown area of Bombay. Throughout India Anglo-Indians placed a high premium on education and their schools were grand affairs. Not only did they offer the means of bettering themselves by providing educational qualifications but they also reinforced the belief that the Anglo-Indians were integral members of a wider British culture. The schools tended to be carbon copies of the great English public shools with one obvious difference: whereas the British had been schooled in an easy and unaffected acceptance of privilege and *noblesse oblige*, the Anglo-Indians worked terribly hard to achieve those ends. They were very keen on developing the little snobberies which the British took for granted if they thought of them at all – cultivating a refined public-school accent, wearing the old school tie, playing rugger and not soccer and indulging in colloquialisms of a type that had long since disappeared from ordinary English usage. At first, Russell doubted whether he could be of much help, but before deciding he went to Barnes, the boarding school, to see what it was like.

> They played games in the English way. Rugby and Marlborough were so far away, their reflection in distant India was faint indeed, but when I saw the boys and girls doing much the same things as I had done so far away and with so much better equipment, my heart melted. I decided to try and help them.

The threat facing the Anglo-Indian community in Bombay was that the Indian government had decided to phase out grant-aid to Barnes and Christ Church. Without that support the schools would fold, and the only solution – suggested by the previous chairman of the society, Sir John Greaves – was to sell Barnes to provide funds for Christ Church. Having weighed the pros and cons, Russell was inclined to agree with his predecessor and when the Railway Board of the Central Government offered to buy the building for £150,000 this seemed to settle the matter. As chairman he recommended that the society accept the offer but, to his surprise, the proposal caused an uproar. Frank Anthony, the Anglo-Indian nominated member in the Constituent Assembly, requested a meeting with Russell and pleaded with him to think again. If their standards of education ever fell, then their cherished relationship with Britain would count for nothing. 'If you sell, we are done for,' Anthony told Russell. 'It is our standard, the only thing that can inspire us in the future, and you know how dark that future might be.'

Russell was greatly affected by Anthony's counsel but, feeling that he had done all he could, he resigned rather than push through an unpopular measure. At the time Russell felt overwhelmed by the situation. He also thought that a solution might never be found because it was generally believed that the Indian government would adopt a ruthless attitude towards the Anglo-Indians. After all, they had sided with the British to preserve their prestige and many had adopted patronising attitudes towards the Indians. They also lacked political power and existed in a social limbo. Those who had decided to stay on in India feared the worst, living in a country whose constitution only recognised them as one of the six minority castes. In such an uncertain new world it became imperative, therefore, to hold on to the vestiges of their former privileges and to keep open schools like Barnes.

In fact one of their worst fears, that they would be dominated by a Hindu raj, never materialised and in Bombay the education question was solved by that most British of political solutions – compromise. Barnes did not have to close because the Bombay Education Society decided to ease its regulations and to allow Indian pupils into the schools. Thus Indian money, by way of fees, helped to save the society from financial ruin and its immediate future was assured. Five years later, in 1953, Russell was forgiven by the Bombay Anglo-Indian community when he was invited to serve once more on the society's governing council. Later, in that same year, the episode was to have a curious sequel when it was immortalised in one of the best books to be written about the Anglo-Indian community at the time of the transfer of power, John Masters's *Bhowani Junction*.

Masters had been a career officer who had served in the Gurkhas before and during the war; after independence he had left India and had settled in the United States. The first part of his autobiography, *Bugles and a Tiger*, is one of the best accounts of life in the pre-war Indian Army but he had also started writing novels set in the history of British India. *Bhowani Junction* was his version of the fate awaiting the Anglo-Indians once the British had pulled out of the country. Its protagonists are instantly recognisable: Victoria Jones, the daughter of an Anglo-Indian engine driver, whose wartime service in the Women's Auxiliary Corps (India) has opened her eyes to the gulf that exists between her community and the British; Patrick Taylor, the stubborn and clumsy Anglo-Indian railwayman who struggles to maintain his sense of Britishness while the world he has known for so long is breaking up around him; Rodney Savage, a Masters alter ego, the

Indian Army colonel who acts as a catalyst to bring Victoria and
Patrick to their senses.

His picture of Anglo-Indian society in the railway town of
Bhowani is as vivid as certain passages from *A Passage to India*
and, like Forster, Masters allows the reader to become fully
involved in the true tragedy of those distracted times. Above all,
Masters was able to present a credible picture of life in India in
1946 and to get to the heart of the Anglo-Indian fears. The
swift-moving, yet controlled, narrative carries the story forward
at a cracking pace as Victoria tries first to find solace among the
Indians before dropping into the emotional safety net provided
by Colonel Savage. In its first draft the novel was to end on a
bleak note with a dreary future unfolding for Victoria and
Patrick. It was at that point that Russell became involved when
his experience with Barnes was to provide *Bhowani Junction* with
another and more optimistic ending. After deciding that his
future lay with India, Russell had written a short account of his
experiences in a book called *Indian Summer* which had been
published in Bombay. Somehow, Masters had read the book and
had liked it; he decided to write to the author to enlist his help.

> I am writing a novel about India in 1947 [*sic*]. It will be all tied up
> with Anglo-Indians, especially those who work for the railways. I
> came across a copy of your *Indian Summer* and would like to use
> the part about the Education Society and the school you wished to
> sell. May I do so?

Russell was intrigued and offered to read the manuscript. The
world described by Masters he pronounced to be real enough and
he felt that he knew all the main characters too. He had come
across Patrick many times and feared that he might have mocked
at his ways. Victoria could have been head girl of Barnes a dozen
times and Rodney was just like the regular Indian Army types he
had met during the war. 'Victoria is my heroine, the Anglo-
Indian girl who served in WAC(I) during the war,' admitted
Masters. 'We've all met her in the railway institutions up and
down the country. We all know her tragedy. Does she belong to
India or England?'

The question troubled Russell because he was aware that by
1953 the Anglo-Indians had managed to overcome their worst
problems. They could talk about themselves and their future, and

their leaders, like Frank Anthony, had persuaded them that their best hope for progress lay in India. Masters's novel seemed to be slightly out of tune with the new mood. One of the smaller tragedies facing Patrick is the prospect of his old school, St Thomas's, closing. In the original version Patrick loses everything, his job and his heritage: Russell's main suggestion was that the novel could have a brighter ending with Patrick coming to terms with the new circumstances offered by independent India.

> As regards Patrick and his prospects, could you not indicate very lightly a different future for him in some other sphere, which is not impossible? How about, for instance, introducing our big cement factory at Kymore near Katni, which can't be very far from Bhowani Junction? Could not the President of the Education Society be a director and offer him a job?

By then the two men had met in New York while Russell was visiting the United States on a business trip and Masters had come to value Russell's comments. When the novel was published in 1954 it ended on a note of unbridled optimism. Victoria has decided to throw in her lot with her own people and Patrick is allowed to face his future with a new sense of confidence. Despite the fact that he has disgraced himself by accidentally killing Savage's Gurkha orderly in a frightful incident at Bhowani railway station, benison arrives in the shape of a new job and the promise that his old school might survive if it accepts Indian scholars. The agent is a thinly disguised Wilfrid Russell who appears in the novel as Mr Stevenage, a businessman. Not only does he provide the key to the problem facing St Thomas's but he offers Patrick employment 'as manager of our cement-works railway over in Cholagat'. Just as Russell hoped, this provides Patrick with a lifeline.

> Of course I knew all about his firm's little railway. It was forty miles long, single line, with a few passing places, running from the cement works at Cholagat to the Bhanas branch at Sihor, which is ninety-four and a half miles from Bhowani Junction. They had a few little engines, and all the traffic was cement and machinery. It would be quite a come-down after the D.D.R., but I am a railwayman, and there is nothing else I can do. Being offered this job was so like a miracle, when it happened on that day of all days, that I couldn't believe it.

When *Bhowani Junction* first appeared it met with a hostile reception from many Anglo-Indians who felt that Masters was simply capitalising on their predicament. They also believed that the background he described and the characters he created were inaccurate and that he was making fun of the Anglo-Indian community in India. It is most unusual for a beleaguered or threatened community ever to be satisfied with any attempt to portray them and their problems and in this case the Anglo-Indians were no exception. Later, the novel was filmed, mainly on location in Lahore, and when it appeared attitudes had softened: today *Bhowani Junction* is recognised for what it is, a sensitive portrayal of a disturbed period of British history. In time, Masters, who died in 1987, came to be regarded rather differently too and the Anglo-Indians like to consider him 'as one of us'.

At the heart of Masters's novel is the real problem which faced the Anglo-Indians at the time of partition: were they Indian or were they British? To compound the dilemma there seemed to be few outstretched hands of welcome, for neither the new India nor the departing British took much interest in their predicament. Not only did they feel betrayed after having given so many years of service to the creation of a modern India, but they also felt that no one understood or even cared about their fate. 'Labour was in power and they knew nothing about us,' claims Frank Anthony, the doyen of the Anglo-Indian political leaders. When Cripps arrived with his second mission Anthony was perplexed to discover that he had no plans to deal with the constitutional rights of the Anglo-Indian community. 'How can I give you representation on the Constituent Assembly?' Cripps asked. 'The Assembly will be based on one seat for one million people. How can I give you 500 per cent weightage?' Anthony attempted to persuade Cripps that political percentages were not the solution. After all, he retorted, the Sikhs had 30 per cent of the places in the officer corps of the Indian Army yet they represented only 2 per cent of the population. Cripps, though, remained unpersuaded.

After visiting London and making representations to Clement Attlee Anthony was elected to the Constituent Assembly as the nominated Anglo-Indian representative in 1946. Previously he had been a nominated member of the old Central Legislative Assembly, but he was desperate to have the rights of the

Anglo-Indians written into the constitution. Eventually it was Gandhi who solved the problem when he suggested in 1947 that there should be three nominated Anglo-Indian members of the Constituent Assembly. Even so, it was a long struggle to have this accepted, as several leaders, including Desai, still believed that the Anglo-Indians were suspect because they had helped to shore up British rule. Earlier, however, Nehru and Patel had been won over to the Anglo-Indian cause with a speech made by Anthony in Bombay in 1946. This was seen by them as a major change of direction which aligned the Anglo-Indians with the new India.

> I said that we are Anglo-Indians by community and of that we have reason to be proud. We made a contribution to India out of all proportion to our size – in the military, aviation, engineering. Let us cling, and cling tenaciously, to everything we hold dear, our English language and our way of life, but let us always remember that we are Indians, that we have an inalienable Indian back-ground. The more we love and are loyal to India, the more India will love and be loyal to us.

It may have been a pious hope, but it was a beginning, an affirmation of Anglo-Indian loyalty to the land of their birth.

In the years following independence those Anglo-Indians who had decided to stay on in India added to their laurels by giving loyal service during the Kashmir border conflict and later in the 1965 war against Pakistan. The Indian Air Force was largely made up of Anglo-Indians and their abilities were recognised by the state – over 50 per cent of the gallantry awards in 1965 went to Anglo-Indian aircrew. Before that they had worked selflessly in the refugee camps in Delhi during the civil unrest in the Punjab: Lady Mountbatten told Anthony that the Anglo-Indian nursing auxiliaries were the finest she had ever met. At one point Patel even suggested that the Anglo-Indians should form a paramilitary peacekeeping force in the Punjab and although this was rejected by Anthony many Anglo-Indians served in the police force throughout that troubled period. Later, in thanking them, Nehru admitted that the Anglo-Indians had been completely impartial.

But for all these small triumphs there was a steady haemor-rhage of talent from the community which Anthony represented. Twenty-five thousand Anglo-Indians decided to emigrate in 1946 and 1947; some to start new lives in Australia and the United States, others to try their luck in the country they had always known as 'home'. In Britain they tended to camouflage the evidence of their previous existences and failed to form a recognisable group; understandably, considering the prevailing conservatism of British attitudes towards people of other races. In Australia it was rather different. When they created their new lives there they stuck together and kept in touch, with the result that they are still a flourishing community: for instance, the Australian men's hockey team has been dominated by Anglo-Indian players in recent years and they take a great pride in their racial origins. The one sadness facing the Australian Anglo-Indians is that India's strict immigration laws have prevented the older members from spending their last days in the country they left behind so many years ago.

As for the Anglo-Indian community in India today, many of the difficulties which faced them in 1947 are still present. Forty years have helped to integrate them into the community of peoples which make up India, but many still regard themselves as being separate – and different. Colour of skin is important for younger people – the lighter, the better – and the scions still attend expensive schools which provide a superior English education. Frank Anthony has given his name to a public-school system in which most of the teachers are Anglo-Indian and the standards are very high. Britain is still a model for the young, not the Britain represented by the burra sahib but the Britain of fashion and popular taste. And it is here, perhaps, that the greatest changes of outlook have occurred. Once upon a time, the British middle and upper classes were objects of admiration whose manners and style were the inspiration of the young Anglo-Indians of Anthony's youth. Now, when he comes across young British people in India, he finds it difficult to place them. 'The British, too, have changed,' he says. 'The kind of British chap you meet nowadays – even those from good families – you can't distinguish from a common-or-garden hippy.'

Of all the people who stayed on in India after independence the Anglo-Indians were the least fortunate, for they were bound to the country in a way the British could never be.

Chapter Ten

Forty Years On

Over forty years have passed since British rule in India came to an end and the concept of the British Raj passed into history. The events of Gandhi's *satyagraha*, the rise of Congress and Muslim League nationalism and the Quit India movement are as far away in time from a later generation as the Reform Bill and the emancipation of the slaves were from the late Victorians. Names as different as Dyer, Curzon, Cripps, Linlithgow and Wavell sound like bells in the far distance; even Mountbatten, shame-fully murdered by the IRA in 1979, looms larger than life, a pro-consul from the imperial past. The battle honours of Aliwal, Assaye, Carnatic, Chillianwallah, Lucknow and Seringapatam still adorn the colours of many fine British regiments but many of these poignant reminders of past campaigns have long since been laid up in the naves of churches in quiet British county towns. Other names, other places and other sounds still have the power to stir memories: the bungalows of Simla, so reminiscent of the Home Counties; the Taj in Bombay and the nearby Gateway of India, so often the first and last sights of returning or departing imperial servants; the lonesome whistle of a North British Company locomotive as it navigates the fearsome bends of India's mountain railways; morning service at St Andrew's Church in Madras, still called 'The Kirk' in deference to its Presbyterian origins; the Gothic extravaganza of Gilbert Scott's architecture in Bombay. All these images swim into focus to remind us that, however dead the idea of the British Empire might be, its memories and memorials still linger on.

The wonder is that British rule lasted as long as it did. What began as a commercial enterprise evolved into empire-building by war and treaty, a haphazard progress which few people thought would survive into modern times. Montstuart Elphinstone, the astute and benevolent governor of the Bombay Presidency, had written in 1827 that British suzerainty in India could never be 'contemplated as a permanent state of things', and as late as 1835 Macaulay introduced his famous minute on Indian education with the thought that, come what may, self-knowledge would lead to self-rule and that would be 'the proudest day in British history'. The Mutiny or Great Revolt helped to change all those fine feelings: whereas before 1857 it had been expected that the British stay in India would be short, thereafter most people believed that it would last for a very long time, perhaps as long as the Mogul rule, perhaps even for ever.

The Mutiny brought most of India under direct British rule and in most spheres of life the administration changed things for the better. Government, the legal system and education helped to improve the lot of many Indians and the British way of life became a mighty engine of progress and efficiency. Many material benefits ensued, largely because Britain controlled India's economy and subordinated it to her own needs. This was on the debit side of imperialism for greed was a driving force and the British genuinely believed that commercial supremacy was one of the rocks on which her empire should be based.

The Mutiny also introduced other subtle changes. Older *laissez-faire* attitudes inherited from the easy-going days of the eighteenth century disappeared and the British became more detached from the country and the people. India could no longer be regarded as home and this change of heart was to have a lasting effect on the last ninety years of British rule. When the soldiers and administrators retired, the thought of staying on in India rarely entered their heads; instead they dreamed of going back to the green meadows of the shires or to the hills and glens of the Highlands. They tended to retire early, too, with the result that not only were there few elderly Europeans in India, but when the time came they were not there to resist the growing tide of Indian nationalism. White settlers in the African colonies might have raised their voices – in vain as it proved – against the decision of the European governments to pull out of their African possessions in the 1950s and 1960s, but the same voices were not heard in India thirty years earlier.

People at home, long retired from Indian life, might have complained that Attlee was making a gross mistake or that Mountbatten was a traitor, but they were calling to the wind. There was never any substantial body of British opinion to oppose the independence movement; indeed, by the end of the Second World War most people welcomed it. There was a joke that India had been conquered by the Scots, ruled by the English and given away by the Labour Party, but, in truth, most people were pleased to see India being given her freedom with such style. The result was that there was a great deal of goodwill on all sides when Britain transferred power to India and Pakistan. With the passing of the years that feeling has been magnified so that India is now as much a romantic idea as an episode in British history.

You can't go back, you know, is the thought most widely held by those who lived the greater part of their lives in British India. This is not so much a regret for times past as a feeling that India was another and much more enjoyable kind of existence, a life that has gone for ever. Ron Fraser eased his return passage to Britain by working in a jute-mill in Thailand for Mackies of Belfast before finally settling in Scotland. By then his family had grown up and his time in India was receding into a period that he could look back upon with much pleasure. 'I liked India and the Indians very much and I felt just as much at home in India as I did in Britain. I never felt a stranger when I was there.' And like most people who have exchanged the heat of Bengal for Edinburgh's windy streets, he finds that he misses the sun.

Man would not be human, though, if he did not yearn to take one last look at a place which had given him so much pleasure and in which much of his young life had been so happily spent. General Das is always pleased to welcome back British officers when they make nostalgic return trips to visit the scenes of their former glory. When the Rajputana Rifles rededicated their memorial a number of former officers flew out from Britain with their wives and families to take part in the ceremony. 'We talked about the old days with the 4th Indian Division, so on that level there is still a close link between the British and the Indian officer.' Das also keeps in touch with the families of British officers who died during the war and in spite of a lingering belief that Britain left the Indian Army in a poor material condition in

1947, he remains a strong believer in the idea of the regiment as extended family. Those British officers who do go back notice that in some areas things remain much the same as they remember them – the mess silver, the uniforms, the traditions are all familiar, the crown and four-pointed star might have been replaced by the three-headed lion and the *chakra* as symbols of rank, but the military ethos is still recognisable. Other things have altered considerably – after forty years of progress it could hardly be otherwise – and it comes as a surprise to see sepoys carrying Russian weapons and operating under standards of discipline which might seem lax to the traditionalist.

For them, as for Dr Taylor, trips back to India are like 'going home', home being a state of mind. The cultural traditions which he came to admire as a young man and the many friendships which he made in the course of a long career call him back. The size of the country and its variety still impress him as well. Having lived in Bombay and Calcutta he finds them as different and as far apart in culture, language and society as Italy and Poland, but that is part of India's charm. 'It just gets into the blood: we still have friendships among many different kinds of people.' Among his many pleasures has been the progression to maturity – and often prominence in Indian life – made by his many students but the lasting emotion, like the flame of an old love affair, is with India itself.

Individual experiences still come back to me. I often recall great times in the Himalayan foothills; the adventures one had going about and being able to compare the tropical luxuriance of Kerala with the bare deserts of Rajistan; the marvellous Mogul India. All these things it has been my privilege to know. Or lying in bed at night I remember that it's fifty years ago today that I was on top of this hill or whatever. These are the kind of things that come back to me . . . but above all, it's the people. There are no people in the world so outgoing and when I go back it's absolutely overwhelming.

The last time I went back [1982] I met students whom I had not seen for fifty years and we were able to pick up again as if nothing had ever happened and there had been no interval. It was a little surprising to find that they were old and had beards and were producing grown-up grandchildren to be introduced but apart from those details there might have been no interval. This is the marvellous thing, the abiding friendships, for there are no people more capable of loving, outgoing friendships than the people of India and I found that everywhere – in Bombay, Calcutta and the hills of Assam.

Taylor's India is the India of schools, colleges and the Christian Church, an India that was largely ignored by the British administrators, soldiers and box-wallahs, but it has left an enduring legacy for the people of the two countries. His gift to India, in return for all the personal pleasure and fulfilment, was the privilege of working for the nation's future, training the young men and women as scientists and giving them a head start in life. Dr Winifred Bailey feels the same way about the India she knew as a medical missionary: it was peopled by the poor, the sick and the dispossessed and it was, therefore, a very different kind of India from the one known by the average memsahib. Like her colleague, Dr Taylor, she looks back to her time in India with 'great satisfaction' –

> that I had the skills and the knowledge to use in the service of people who so badly needed them; and the joy of the relationships which my profession enabled me to make with many Indians and other nationalities from many castes and creeds and all walks of life. In the many years I remained in India, I made deep and lasting friendships; I received in many ways much more than I was able to give: and I had many rich and rewarding experiences.

The tradition of care through the Christian Church continued long after independence and several of India's and Pakistan's leading schools and colleges still retain friendly links with one or other of the Western Churches. British missionaries, for example, still work in India, often as community doctors in the villages which still make up 80 per cent of the country. Small wonder that the ties are so strong, for the missionaries there, of all Churches, were great pioneers in education and medical work and they made perhaps the most lasting and valuable contribution to British India.

The greatest changes were noticed perforce by those who had occupied positions of authority. Whereas the missionaries worked in an India which had changed little in centuries – and which is still in existence today – the administrators were bound to see the difference between a country which had been ruled by the British but which now belonged to its own people. But when

Alastair MacKeith went back to Pakistan forty years after the transfer of power his initial impression was that he was not at all surprised to find that many of the British police details remained unchanged. 'The composition of the Frontier Constabulary platoons, for example – exactly the same number of men in a platoon and exactly the same tribal composition. You would know that number 15 platoon was Bangash and there seemed to be no change at all. It was rather amusing.' The biggest change was that the country seemed to be rather dull, that the modern state of Pakistan, ruled by Pakistanis, was just like any other country. What he was missing, and what every man in his position would miss when he looks back to a past spent on the North-West Frontier, was a sense of adventure, of being a young man in a position of authority in a huge and exotic country. As British officers of the ICS, the army and the police were obliged to make extensive personal tours of their own territory it is hardly surprising that their memories should be so vivid.

> Social life went on in little islands. You lived in little pockets, little European pockets where you would get a very pleasant social life. Going from one pocket to another you could always feel confident of hospitality and congenial company when you reached the other pocket. Going back to Pakistan forty years later I was conscious of the fact that the pockets were no longer there. When one arrived at the end of a long and dusty journey one would have to make do with what was in essence something foreign. We had these little islands of our own culture which you could rely on finding at the end of the journey – and which were no longer there.

One of the drawbacks of that kind of rule was that it was too deeply rooted in the Indian countryside and the administrators spent too much time amongst the rural people at the expense of the town-dwellers. When he casts his mind back to India Alastair MacKeith finds that he remembers best of all the smell of burning cow dung and woodsmoke, so very different from the kerosene and petrol fumes of the towns. It was in the urban areas, though, that the young middle-class Indians were turning to nationalist politics, much to the discomfort of those civil servants and soldiers who preferred the country types, plainsmen, hillmen and the like. Their preference was for Sikhs, Pathans or Punjabi Muslims, peoples who were loyal and trustworthy and who seemed to mirror British public-school values – in stark contrast to the argumentative lawyers and *babus* of Bengal who clamoured noisily for independence.

The relationship between the British and the Indians was one of the cornerstones of the empire. If it was good then conditions would be generally good, too; if it was tense then the very foundation stood in danger of toppling. By the time of the Second World War there was very little left of the unthinking racism which had undoubtedly existed during the late Victorian period. The process of Indianisation also helped matters and during the 1930s the two races had come much closer together than at any time since the eighteenth century.

Sheila Coldwell was in a good position to judge, for she stayed on in India until 1964 and the closeness between the two peoples never ceased to amaze her.

> There was a great feeling of affinity between British and Indians (and Pakistanis) and this I think is worth stressing. We were truly like brothers with a fondness for the same things and a deep understanding of one another, each having the same qualities and feelings. Above all, we had the same sense of humour which must have helped in many a tight corner.

Whatever else the British might have felt they always knew that they were safe in India. This was partly because of the British presence which was all-pervasive and strong, but it had something to do with the comradeship which existed, however superficially, between the British and the Indians. As a child Elizabeth Catto had come into contact with many Indian businessmen who were friends and associates of her father. 'Indians are lovely people to be with. They have such caring qualities – and that's what the British liked so much.' She feels that this is particularly true of her servants, whom she regarded as an extended family – as indeed did the servants themselves. When Elizabeth Catto came back to England in 1956 both her bearers came with her, not because she required servants in her new life but because a promise had been made years earlier to keep them in full-time employment. 'I think they wanted to expand their horizons. They knew that they would be able to save money in England and send it back to their families. When they finally went home they had been with us for twenty-five years.'

To modern eyes this might smack of a feudal relationship which has no place in twentieth-century domestic arrangements. That would be to miss the point for, as Martin Wynne explains, there were many reasons for maintaining large numbers of servants and then for looking after them as one's own.

> Why did they have to employ such a quantity of servants? Anyone who visits India immediately becomes aware that the demarcation lines drawn by the Trade Unions in this country as to who does what and when are as nothing compared to the restrictive practices enforced by the caste system. The syce who looks after the horse will not cut the grass to feed it, and the servant who waits at table will not wash up the dishes afterwards. If it is asked why employ servants anyway, the answers are several. Life in a spacious bungalow may be delightful, but it presents problems of cleaning in a very dusty country, if there is no electricity and therefore no vacuum cleaner. If it is two miles from the market, it presents problems in the hot weather if the only transport you can afford is a bicycle or hired tonga; and in the absence of a refrigerator it was necessary to buy food on a day-to-day basis. If there is no running water a bath must be drawn from a well and then heated in kerosene tins over charcoal. Besides, employment was being provided for a number of people who would otherwise have remained in India's large army of the unemployed. If another reason is desired, it should be remembered that India thrived on *izzat* or prestige. An official, be he Indian or European, had to maintain a certain standard of life-style, if he were to be respected by those lower in the hierarchy. This may be considered utterly reprehensible, but it was a fact of life.

In other words, it was the custom of the country and there was no shame whatsoever attached to the master-servant relationship. Lest it be thought that the British only knew Indians on that level, Wynne also points out that the Indian Police was a fully integrated service and that by the 1930s Indian officers were recruited on the same level, and lived in the same messes, as their British opposite numbers. One of his colleagues remembers with gratitude the kindness of an Indian officer who checked his uniform for him before his first mess night. 'If you even have one button upside-down,' he warned him, 'it will cost you a round of drinks.'

Of course, it would be ideal to pretend that there was no sense of white superiority. Most people took it for granted that an Indian would move out of the way for a European on a busy pavement; it was unusual for Indians to travel in the same compartment as a British occupant during a long railway journey, and there was a general dislike for the practices of the Hindu religion. There was also a tendency to despise the merchant classes, but many of those prejudices were based on the fairly rigid class system which the British applied to their own people. A newly arrived police officer, for example, would be invited to stay at Government House for a few days so that he could be vetted 'by H.E. and his lady'. Wynne recalls that future social contacts could depend on his being available to walk after breakfast with Her Excellency in her rose garden.

By the outbreak of war many of those shibboleths had been cleared away and with the process of rapid Indianisation there was a greater feeling of equality. In the Indian Army Indians commanded battalions and the old system of operating 'Indian-only' regiments came to an end. During the course of the war Indian and British officers served alongside each other in the line and shared the same messes when out of it. J.D.M. Watson had joined the 11th Sikhs shortly after the outbreak of war and had been struck by the differences that existed between the old India hands in civilian life and his own regiment.

> If I happened to be going to the bazaar and a sepoy was going in the same direction, I'd fall in step with him. He would, of course, salute me and say 'Good morning, sir.' And I would say good morning to him. Then we'd walk along the road together and blether about who had won the last hockey match or whatever.

Watson had come across what might be called old planter attitudes when he had shaken an Indian by the hand and been given 'a hell of a ticking off' by his hostess. In his regiment that would have been impossible: 'I expect that behaviour of that kind had been going on for donkey's years and, if it had, then it was a very good reason for Britain to quit India.'

Most people will admit that while a feeling of continuing white supremacy never completely disappeared it was still possible to get on well with Indian colleagues. One of the fondest beliefs held by the British in India was that there was never any racial intolerance of the kind practised by the Europeans in the African colonies or by the South Africans in their own country. They point to the comradeship of the officers and men of the Indian Army, to the British and Indian civil servants of the ICS working happily in tandem or to the up-and-coming Bengali engineers who worked alongside men like George Robertson and Ron Fraser. All that was true, and it is one of the triumphs of British India that there never was a legalised colour bar. But alter the focus to an Indian point of view and a rather different picture emerges.

The main problem was the club. Indeed, it has been said that the existence of the club with its rigid rules and regulations was one of the main reasons for the unpopularity of the British during the inter-war years of this century. If the British had shown a greater willingness to accept Indians as members, the argument continues, then there would have been a more relaxed dialogue and political mistakes might have been avoided. As long as the club remained a symbol of white power and exclusiveness then there was less chance of Indians and British existing happily together. Of course, there were a few notable clubs which did admit Indians, provided that they met the conditions of membership, but they were in a minority. By and large, the club was a secluded enclave, a bastion of Britishness in a foreign land: the British often preferred it that way and clung obstinately to a belief that Indians would not be happy as members, especially as *purdah* excluded their wives. Nevertheless, the feeling that they were not welcome in the club helped to erect many a barrier between those Indian and British colleagues who worked happily enough together in the office or in the field.

The same difficulties sometimes existed in the Indian Army. In spite of the convention that all officers are equal in the mess, and in spite of the many instances of close friendships between British and Indian soldiers, some Indian officers were bound to feel cut off from the ordinary social round. This was less true of the companionship of the younger officers who used the mess as a second home but it did infiltrate relationships with the older married men. D.K. Palit was commissioned into the Baluch Regiment in 1938, he had already spent five years in England and was a keen polo player. His family had served the Mogul emperors as soldiers, yet for all his military virtues he felt that he still belonged to a race apart when he joined his regiment.

There was almost no social contact between British and Indian officers in the army. In the civil there was – youngsters who went out as SDOs would be asked home by the Deputy Commissioners – but I don't know of a single case where a British and an Indian were friendly. I myself was aghast to see that there was no mixing of the races – the British didn't like us. At best we were called wogs or niggers and in the whole of my experience only one British officer was ever friendly with an Indian. I was never asked by my commanding officer, my second in command or my company commander for a meal or for a cup of tea in his house. There was just no contact even though the one army fought the same enemy and carried the same weapons. But we never mixed.

Palit points to the Indianisation in 1921 of the eight All-Indian regiments as one reason for the existence of this antipathy. Had the process been extended across the board to all the regiments of the Indian Army, he argues, then the process of assimilation might have had a chance of succeeding. During the war, he has already noted, the influx of wartime emergency commissioned officers proved that attitudes could change and throughout that period of rapid social change the races did move closer together. It remains his view that Indian officers lived in a social ghetto before the war, one that was not of their making. Yes, he says, the British did love their men – in a way they could not love British troops – and a close bond existed between them, but they did not always care for India or for the Indians in general.

> The British officer of the Indian Army loved the comforts of India; his womenfolk didn't have to work or cook or shop. They loved the life here and their nostalgia for it is based on that – not on any love of Indian society, because they had none. There was no cultural, social or racial relationship between the two peoples.

As a committed anglophile Palit denies that he is being cynical but he refuses to subscribe to the nostalgic view that all was for the best in the best of all possible worlds in the regiments of the Indian Army. Of course, he insists, there were exceptions – his brother officer General Das owns to a deep and lasting friendship with Major-General T.W. 'Pete' Rees who commanded the Punjab Boundary Force in 1947 – but, by and large, the close ties were not there at the time. On the one hand the social snubs Palit remembers could be excused by the fact that it would have been unusual for a junior officer to have received an invitation to dine privately with his commanding officer but that is purely cosmetic. What he is describing is a refusal to pay lip-service to a fondly held belief that there was a strong nostalgic, one might almost say mystical, link between the two races during the period of the British Raj.

Even outside the family ties of the regiment where breaking rank is considered bad form, the feeling persisted among many Indians that the British only enjoyed their time in India because life was good and privileged. After independence Kushwant Singh, another anglophile, became a journalist and novelist who also wrote a history of the Sikh people. He greatly admired the British for many of the virtues which they introduced to India – justice, fair play and, above all, incorruptibility – but he believed that their way of life was underpinned by a flagrant arrogance which was wholly unnecessary. 'They indulged in it in their exclusive clubs. They wouldn't relax with Indians and Indians never relaxed with them.' When there was a point of contact, he insists, it was marked by a type of benevolent paternalism which lay at the heart of the imperial system of government.

> The British in India were never close to the Indians. If they ever made any friends it was in a benign attitude towards their servants. It was very rare to see a close friendship between an Englishman and an Indian at the higher levels. There was a certain amount of entertaining and banter but there was no relaxed sentimental affection between the two. I really think that in this case the British were at fault because the Indians would have liked a relationship to be built. British nostalgia for India is really a figment of their imagination. Most of them hated this country when they were here and hardly had any Indian friends to call their own.

This is the voice of a dispassionate observer who is talking about British imperial government. In his personal life Kushwant Singh enjoyed many close friendships with British families who lived in India and he made many other friendships during his education in England. The lasting legacy of the English language gave him a window to the world and he is pleased that India has remained a member of the Commonwealth. All these benefits are greatly admired by many Indians who admit that their country would have been very different but for the presence of the British. What Singh and Palit refuse to accept is that there was ever a feeling of brotherhood between the people of India and their British rulers.

That kind of emotion is not always understood by the English themselves. They once enjoyed cultural and political pre-eminence over many countries and long after the empire had disappeared the memory of it lingered on. It may come as a surprise to them, therefore, to find that their presence was not always welcomed, that they were often considered to be arrogant and stand-offish and that many peoples regarded them as cold and unlovable types. Nearer to home, nationalists on the fringes, the Scots, Welsh and Irish, often harbour similar suspicions about their aloof neighbour but like other predominant races the English are usually blithely unaware of the feeling or choose to ignore it. The same situation existed in India during the period of British rule but intellectuals like Kushwant Singh could see that even his closest English friends were unaware of the drift. As he reminded them, the rulers are rarely aware of the real nature of their subjects' feelings, nor can they ever be.

The amazing thing is that there was never much animosity: however upset many Indians might have been about the lack of social ties their feelings rarely turned to anger. According to Govind Narain this was because the Indians admired the British style of leadership and were prepared to learn its finer points. 'At a personal level the relationships between the ICS officers of Indian origin and the ICS officers of British origin were good, and throughout the difficult period the service remained in control of the situation.' After independence Narain remained in the Indian Administrative Service, as the ICS became, and he retired in 1983 after serving six years as the Governor of Karnatica. To his surprise, he found that when the last Indian officers recruited by the British started retiring during the 1970s they could be as nostalgic as their British counterparts when they started talking about the past and preferred to see it through rose-coloured spectacles.

In particular, he finds that the fondest memories are for the pukka sahibs, the public schoolboys who had joined the ICS after leaving Oxford, Cambridge or one of the ancient Scottish universities and who had then given a lifetime's selfless service to India. These were the real guardians of a style of government which insisted on fair play, equality and total incorruptibility. Whenever there is a breakdown in India today or wherever social or political problems exist, Narain is not at all surprised to hear Indians saying to each other, 'You know, it was not like this under the British. In those days you were always given a fair deal.'

They are probably referring to a particular type of British

person, the officer of the ICS, and it is perhaps they who left the greatest mark on the Raj. Badr-ud-Din Tyabji, with an impeccable background of his own, admits to preferring the older kind of ICS officer who came out to India with a degree in classics or history and with a firm commitment to the country he was about to serve. 'So far as I was concerned, I didn't have any difficulty because as soon as an Englishman opened his mouth, I could place him.' After independence he joined the foreign service and served as Indian ambassador in several countries, including Germany and Japan. He still believes that when the ICS officers were good, they were very, very good.

> A lot of them were splendid people and there were many Englishmen whom I greatly admired. I'm afraid, though, that I can't help feeling that those who did best were those people with some background – you can't be a colonial governor without having a background, because it's too heavy.

If his colleagues had any faults, he concedes, it was a failing which led them to prefer the simple Indian peasantry and to fear the educated middle classes. 'They were also prone to be taken in by people who represented their conception of the oriental . . . independence of mind did not really go down well with them.'

Like his fellow ICS officer Govind Narain, Tyabji enjoyed many close friendships with his immediate superiors whom he knew he could trust and whom he knew to be committed to India. After all, he says, both were working for the good of the country and he never ceased to marvel at the professionalism of the British officers. Many knew that their ultimate goal was the transfer of imperial power to the Indians, yet they never shirked the task in hand and devoted themselves to the maxim that if a job were worth doing then it was worth doing well.

In time the divine right to precedence which is implicit in any imperial rule became a thing of the past. General Palit is amused and surprised when he sees young British people in Delhi riding in the buses and eating in Indian cafés, oblivious of the ghostly frowns of past generations with their solar topees, pig-sticking and warrants of precedence. 'There is a general desire to know India as such,' he claims. 'That would never have happened before. The British in my day lived their own lives in cantonments. Little Englanders all over. What they missed was that little England but that little England had gone for ever.'

General Palit feels that the young Indians have changed too. In the army that he served, British standards of excellence for its own sake no longer apply and many of the older and quainter customs have fallen into disuse. Young soldiers have only a sketchy knowledge of the British connection even though some of its elements are part of their daily routine. After they have beaten retreat they march off to 'Abide With Me', their pipes and drums still play the tunes from Lochaber and the Braes of Angus, in garrisons all over India there are memorials and silent statues to long-dead soldiers, but these are merely curiosities from the past.

Elsewhere, in the cities of India, similar statues of public figures still stand, in spite of the decisions, taken at various times, to dismantle them. The statue of King George V was removed from its commanding position in Delhi shortly after India became independent but his effigy remained in place in other cities for many years to come. Seeing one such statue for the first time as a very young girl Inder Malhotra's niece asked if the old gentleman was her grandfather. Only when she was a little older did Malhotra tell her that it was the King-Emperor and that it had been placed in a public position because the British had once ruled India. Her response was unexpected.

> She laughed at me and said, 'No, uncle, you are trying to pull my leg. It can't be. How could anybody come here and rule us? We are so many millions of people.' A child of four in 1961 was unaware that the British had ever ruled here and was making the assertion that it was inconceivable that anybody else could come to India and rule over the people.

Although many of the statues of British dignitaries still stand – often in sad groups in neglected parks – it upsets Malhotra that there is not one to the memory of the man who did so much for modern India: Clement Attlee. The only memorial to his name is a mass which is held each year in Bangalore and which was first organised by an Indian civil servant who worked with Attlee during the Simon Commission of 1927.

Curiously, Attlee's name is often kept in the background of any discussion about the transfer of power, yet he was the Prime Minister of the British government which speeded up the decision to quit India. The man whose name does quicken emotions is Mountbatten, the last Viceroy. Was he right to bring forward the date of the transfer of power? Did he err in agreeing too quickly to the partition of India? Was he responsible for the massacres in the Punjab and elsewhere? On these and on other questions Indian opinion is as sharply divided as British.

Attlee had appointed him to get Britain out of India and although Mountbatten treated the duty with his customary showmanship he was sincere in facing up to his responsibilities. Britain was not prepared to hold on to India while the politicians talked – as they were to do later and to such little effect in Northern Ireland, for example – and Mountbatten's role was to carry through a measure, which, although unpopular in some quarters, was entirely necessary at the time. That he brought to it an aura of drama was perhaps inevitable, for the granting of independence to India and Pakistan was a momentous event in Britain's history and Mountbatten clearly relished the part he had been asked to play. A year after Mountbatten had left India, in 1949, Kushwant Singh met him in the corridors of India House. The moment was not auspicious. Mountbatten had been kept waiting and Singh asked him to join him in the press office where he worked. It was obvious that Mountbatten was irritated and Singh could also see that the great man was uncomfortable in the company of one person. To make him feel more at ease he turned the conversation to the last days of British India and asked him what he felt about the aftermath of partition. 'I don't care what people say about me,' Mountbatten replied. 'I will be judged at the bar of history.'

Other leaders will be judged there, too, not least the two great Indian leaders, Nehru and Gandhi. For many Indians what illumined their lives during the build-up to independence, and afterwards, was the personal leadership displayed by Nehru. Gandhi might have been adored as the great spirit who had breathed life into the freedom movement and as the man who had offered the promise of unification, but Nehru was the solid pragmatic politician. His greatest appeal was to young people, students like A.K. Damodaran, who believed that Nehru was the one man capable of taking India forward into the modern world. The fact that he seemed to keep himself young at heart counted in his favour as did his espousal of Fabian socialism. Like many young Indians in the 1940s Damodaran was a fervent reader of the *New Statesman* and in the hothouse atmosphere of student politics it was the theory as much as the practice of socialism which appealed to him.

That sense of revolutionary fervour, of anything being possible provided one worked for it, finds an echo in Tyabji's memory of Nehru. As a servant of the government he was by inclination and habit loyal to the political leadership, but it was the man himself who sparked off the greatest devotion.

> He really was a most marvellous man. Whatever his failings were – and I'm not one who thinks that everything he did was perfect – he was a wonderful person. If you got to know him as a friend you really loved him. I can still see him on the bonnet of a car haranguing a crowd – all refugees, all Sikhs with bloodshot eyes and covered in blood, having killed I don't know how many Muslims – and calling them damned scoundrels. He could easily have been shot by anyone; it was just sheer personality and a kind of magnetic power over the crowd. He was one of the finest types of men I have ever served.

Nehru's most obvious fault, adds Tyabji, was a tendency to act precipitately without thinking through the problem. In this case he cites Nehru's decision to support the Quit India movement of 1942 as the most glaring example but then he is prepared to excuse it when he remembers the lifetime of service which Nehru gave to India. After independence, however, Tyabji noticed that events began to overtake the Indian leader and that Nehru had less time for himself and his friends. 'People just crowded in on him,' he says. 'We destroy our leaders by the excessive interest we take in them. Nowhere else in the world is the leader besieged like the Indian prime minister.'

In contrast, Gandhi evokes a variety of different responses. Today his calls for All-India unity are seen as so much wishful thinking, however much they might have been heeded or admired at the time he made them. His name still produces a sense of veneration, even though his statue in Calcutta was torn down by student rioters in 1970, and the museum in his memory is a forlorn place, but few of his principles have survived in modern India. General Palit regards him in the same light as he does Mao Tse-tung, a guerrilla fighter who believed in using all the weapons at his disposal. In that sense non-violence became a weapon which could be deployed against the British. 'He was never a Christlike "turn the other cheek" sort of person. That is to misunderstand him totally. He was a very sly and astute guerrilla fighter.'

The general's interpretation of Gandhi is a military one which might not be shared by many of his peers. (In support of his theory Palit argues that whereas Nehru had the down-to-earth human qualities which allowed mistakes to happen, Gandhi was a shrewd and calculating organiser of political resources.) Several Indians who knew Gandhi, like Tyabji and Damodaran, claim that Gandhi's biggest failing was a need to appear all things to all men. He wanted to show the British that he enjoyed all-party support but all too often he was forced to compromise with those who supported him. A story told by Nikhil Chakravartty illustrates that contention.

Before he quit the Congress to join the Communist (Marxist) Party Chakravartty attended the famous conference at Ramgarh which proposed the introduction of non-co-operation with the British war effort. At that time Congress conferences were still movable feasts and consisted of a large encampment beside an amenable town or village. On the second day of the proceedings, during his customary early-morning walk, Gandhi was dismayed to see a red flag flying in the part of the camp reserved for foreign delegates. It belonged to the Doboma Asiyayan party of Burma – a violently anti-British nationalistic league led by Aung San, later to lead a gang into Burma on the Japanese side and later still to become his country's first leader after independence. Even though the flag was a party flag Gandhi insisted that it be taken down. Nehru was summoned to deal with the problem and what happened next owed more to farce than to any high drama.

'This cannot be within the Congress compound,' Gandhi told Nehru, pointing to the red flag. 'You have to deal with it.' Nehru consulted the chairman of the reception committee, Rajendra Prasad, who was the chief minister of Bihar at that time. Prasad then immediately got hold of the local magistrate and arranged to use the *dak* bungalow which was lying empty at that time. With my own eyes I saw Nehru arrive in an old tourer and go up to Aung San. 'You are uncomfortable here,' he said, 'so I have fixed a place for you.' Nehru started packing up their belongings but Aung San said, 'No, no. We are used to being in forests and this is quite comfortable.' But Nehru insisted that they go to the *dak* bungalow which was a mile or so away from the Congress camp and there they were settled and there they were allowed to put up their party flag.

The action upset Chakravartty and other young Congress members who felt that Gandhi was acting imperiously towards fellow Congress delegates all because 'he did not like the red flag'. To him it seemed a gross piece of intolerance which was unworthy of Gandhi. Later that day, in the afternoon, Chakravartty was forced to revise his opinion.

A banned Communist member of Congress who was also wanted by the police had turned up at Ramgarh, and although it had been easy to conceal him at night time he was certain to be picked up by the plain-clothes policemen when he came to make a resolution at one of the open plenary sessions. Such an eventuality would doubtless have recommended itself to those Congress leaders who were antagonistic towards the Communists, but then Gandhi took a hand in the affair. Hearing about the member's predicament he said, 'He'll go in my car.' The ruse worked. Gandhi's car arrived at the back of the platform, the Communist member emerged to move his resolution – which was defeated – and then spoke to the other leaders before being spirited away from under the noses of the waiting policemen.

As had happened so many times before in Chakravartty's experience no one had known which way Gandhi would jump. In the morning he had shown a fair degree of prejudice towards the Burmese delegates because it did not suit his purpose to see a red flag flying at Ramgarh. In the afternoon it had suited him equally well to display magnanimity towards a political opponent in front of his own people – probably because he knew the member was not dangerous. In both cases he was displaying his will but as Chakravartty admits, if his own people could not always understand Gandhi, then how could the British?

That is one way of looking at Britain's relationship with India. However close the British may have felt themselves to be to the Indian experience, there was always going to be a gap of understanding. All those classicists, soldiers and businessmen might have had the best interests of the Indians at heart but they could not always get inside the Indian mind for all that they learned the languages and made a point of understanding the customs and culture. It was one thing to know a *charka* which made the *khadi* or to know that the orthodox Hindu would not eat meat but might be offered alcohol while that was not always true of the Muslim; it was quite another to know the reasons why an Indian might appear loyal or subservient one moment, truculent or argumentative the next. Allied to this feeling, there was also a certain amount of what might be called 'sucking up', a natural desire to please those in authority. 'As is well known in every society there were some sycophants, so when the British were rulers there were naturally a lot of sycophants,' says Govind Narain, who was in a good position to observe his fellow country-men in action. 'They wanted to keep the British flag high but they were not looked upon with favour by any sane-thinking Indian.' While admitting that the British usually saw through the actions of the lick-spittles Narain also believes that toadying was a corollary of imperial rule and another reason why it had eventually to come to an end.

Britain undoubtedly made many mistakes in her dealings with India – which ruling power has not? – but the overwhelming effect, surely, is that the relationship was not all bad. Britain gave much in return for a system of rule that had begun as a commercial venture – a settled judiciary, a parliamentary democracy and a sense of unity which had been absent since the heyday of Mogul rule. All these benefits are self-evident but the one virtue which is praised most highly by Indians and remembered with pride by the British was the utter incorruptibility of their rule.

Although some businessmen were forced to accept the custom of giving bribes, and sometimes receiving them, the government servant was beyond reproach. This was a source of wonder to the Indians, for it was not part of their tradition, but for the British it was a matter of principle. If they were occasionally hard on the Indians, they could be equally hard on themselves. Living thousands of miles away from home and often in isolated communities in India, they insisted on high standards of public and private behaviour, all of which helped to maintain the supremacy of their rule. It was in their integrity and total scrupulousness that the British surely made their greatest impact. They actually cared about the nature of their rule in India, for it was a trust that had been handed down to them.

Accordingly, there was a certain inevitability about the transfer of power to India and Pakistan in 1947. The laboured process of Indianisation from the 1920s onwards had been one factor; the long string of British promises to honour an obligation another. These were known and understood by the British guardians, even though they might have wished privately that the lives they led could have gone on for ever. But speaking for his own career in the ICS John Griffiths believes that what hastened the process was the realisation that power had drifted away from the British in India to the British in Britain.

> It was in England and in Europe where policy was made that ideals requiring change had taken root. The countries of Europe had fought each other to a standstill in two world wars; and in the second the people had been subject to such discipline that their prime object after the war was to enter a new world of freedom for themselves – where freedom would take the place of regimentation and rights take precedence over duties. These new ideas were disseminated rapidly by speed of modern communications and the direct appeal of 'leaders' purveying a simple message to 'the people'.

In such a world the administrator would always play second fiddle to the economist and the businessman. Gradually, as Britain shook off her former imperial holdings and became smaller and more self-contained, there was no longer any need for the type of man who had once ruled India. The evolution of Britain under Margaret Thatcher's tutelage appears to have proved Griffiths right and by way of further argument he cites Bob Geldof's efforts to raise money for the starving in Ethiopia. 'Bob Geldof had no difficulty in finding the money, and even less in finding the food, but what failed him, as he himself seems to admit, was the administration at the end of the line – on the ground.' What Geldof needed were men of the calibre of the ICS District Magistrate or the Indian Army field officer.

It is perhaps futile to look back into the past and mourn the mistakes that were made or to sigh over what might have been. A halo of romantic sentimentality will always surround the memories of those who lived through momentous, or simply pleasurable, times. It might be the memory of faithful servants whose faces are slowly blurring with the passing of the years or it might be a flashback to the animal pleasure of riding along a dusty road during the cool season. A sudden glimpse of a coloured sari in a crowded British street or a hint of the sounds and smells of the bazaar can stir the mind to reverie. Photographs in a leatherbound album can sometimes be more evocative than diaries or letters, yet a glimpse of a King-Emperor stamp on a faded envelope can still haunt the memory. Did it all happen such a long time ago?

In all those scenes, however faint they might appear now, the British are always present. They believed that they would always be part of that memory – picnicking in the hills, marching the plains, ruling the people. It is one of their enduring strengths that when the time came to go they departed from the stage with exemplary grace and dignity.

Further Reading

The books which have been written about the British in India are legion. As this study is concerned primarily with the end of British rule the following selection of twenty-five titles provides useful background reading for this fascinating period of British history.

Allen, Charles (ed.), *Plain Tales from the Raj*, London: André Deutsch, 1975; *Lives of the Indian Princes*, London: Century Hutchinson, 1984

Bolitho, H., *Jinnah: Creator of Modern Pakistan*, London: John Murray, 1954

Bonarjee, N.B., *Under Two Masters*, London: OUP, 1970

Brown, Judith M., *Modern India: The Origins of an Asian Democracy*, London: OUP, 1985

Campbell-Johnson, Alan, *Mission with Mountbatten*, London: Hale, 1951

Collins, Larry, and Lapière, Dominique, *Freedom at Midnight*, London: Collins, 1975

Desai, Morarji, *The Story of My Life*, Oxford: Pergamon, 1979

Gopal, S., *Jawaharlal Nehru*, London: Cape, 1975–9

Hunt, Roland, and Harrison, John, *The District Officer in India*, London: Scolar Press, 1980

Mansergh, Nicholas, and Moon, Penderel, *The Transfer of Power*, 1–12, London: OUP, 1970

Mason, Philip, *The Men Who Ruled India*, 2 vols. London: Cape, 1953; *A Matter of Honour: An Account of the Indian Army, its Officers and Men*, London: Cape, 1974

Mehta, Ved, *The Ledge Between the Streams*, London: Harvill, 1984

Menon, V.P., *The Transfer of Power*, London: Longmans, 1953

Moon, Penderel, *Divide and Quit*, London: Chatto and Windus, 1961; (ed.), *Wavell: The Viceroy's Journal*, London: OUP, 1973

Moorhouse, Geoffrey, *India Britannica*, London: Harvill, 1983

Moraes, Frank, *Witness to an Era*, London: Weidenfeld and Nicolson, 1973

Mosley, Leonard, *The Last Days of the British Raj*, London: Weidenfeld and Nicolson, 1961

Nanda, B.P., *Mahatma Gandhi*, London: Allen and Unwin, 1957

Trevelyan, Humphrey, *The India We Left*, London: Macmillan, 1972

Tuker, Francis, *While Memory Serves*, London: Cassell, 1950

Ziegler, Philip, *Mountbatten*, London: Collins, 1985

Index